Dreams
and
Shadows

Dreams and Shadows

Radka Yakimov

iUniverse, Inc.
New York Lincoln Shanghai

Dreams and Shadows

Copyright © 2006 by Radka Yakimov

All rights reserved. No part of this book may be used or reproduced by any means, graphic, electronic, or mechanical, including photocopying, recording, taping or by any information storage retrieval system without the written permission of the publisher except in the case of brief quotations embodied in critical articles and reviews.

iUniverse books may be ordered through booksellers or by contacting:

iUniverse
2021 Pine Lake Road, Suite 100
Lincoln, NE 68512
www.iuniverse.com
1-800-Authors (1-800-288-4677)

ISBN-13: 978-0-595-39071-7 (pbk)
ISBN-13: 978-0-595-83460-0 (ebk)
ISBN-10: 0-595-39071-4 (pbk)
ISBN-10: 0-595-83460-4 (ebk)

Printed in the United States of America

CONTENTS

INTRODUCTION vii
Chapter 1	THE RAIDS 1
Chapter 2	FATHER 8
Chapter 3	GRANDFATHER MIRKO. THE WILL 10
Chapter 4	THE DEATH OF THE TSAR. VLADAYA 14
Chapter 5	THE DESCENT OF THE IRON CURTAIN . . 26
Chapter 6	THE PARTISANS 39
Chapter 7	STARTING GRADE SCHOOL 44
Chapter 8	MOVING TO A NEW PLACE, NEW SCHOOL 49
Chapter 9	GRANDFATHER VASSIL. THE ESTABLISHMENT OF THE NEW REGIME . 55
Chapter 10	CAMP. LAST TRIPS 61
Chapter 11	MARA 71
Chapter 12	THE TURNING POINT 78
Chapter 13	HEARTBREAKS AND HARDSHIPS. MOTHER. END OF STALIN 90
Chapter 14	HIGH SCHOOL 105
Chapter 15	END OF HIGH SCHOOL 119
Chapter 16	THE SECRET 128

Chapter 17	UNIVERSITY. MATURING............142
Chapter 18	THE LOW POINT....................155
Chapter 19	LIVING UNDER DICTATORSHIP OF THE PROLETARIAT......................160
Chapter 20	STARTING WORK. FINAL DISILLUSIONMENT..................174
Chapter 21	USSR, EAST GERMANY, CZECHOSLOVAKIA, HUNGARY, YUGOSLAVIA......................178
Chapter 22	DESPAIR. "GOOD-BYE" FOREVER.......199
EPILOGUE.................................209	

INTRODUCTION

At the end of the eighties, a world that was supposed to last forever came crashing down, leaving people stunned by its sudden and complete disintegration. Its rotten foundations had finally faltered.

I knew part of that world. I was born and raised there.

Before that monumental event occurred, at times a thought to write about life behind the Iron Curtain used to cross my mind, only to be cast aside instantly—for a sense of futility took the wind out of my will. Then, in 1989, hope was reborn, and, for a while, it seemed that the world had become a much safer place. The pain of remembering the past did not go away; indeed, the regrets grew even stronger. Yet millions of people, tired from lives spent in drudgery and hopelessness, captivated by the word *change,* rejoiced, ready to declare, "It is time for new beginnings. Let's forget the past." And for a while this seemed to be the right thing to do. We all deserved a rest. However, as the euphoria of those early times subsided, reality settled in—the newfound hope started to loose some of its brightness, the certainty of the future became overshadowed by anxieties. What was lost, destroyed by decades of ruthless injustice, could not be resurrected fast enough for the weary.

Finally, once again, a short-lived illusion—that humanity had turned a corner along its journey into time, leaving fear and destruction behind—was dispelled. And with that came the realization that the time to tell a story about pain, struggles, and lost futures had never gone away indeed.

The world is changing so fast now, faster than before. Some people are beginning to forget, and most were not even born when this story began. Others still remember, but they remember it differently—many of their old memories have been superimposed by new ones. Mine are fresher and clearer. Perhaps it is because when I left, everything stopped and remained frozen in time. During the few years after leaving the country, when I was neither here nor there, I often dwelled on my past. There was no hope of ever returning, of ever seeing my parents; only their letters and my memories kept me close to them.

I still reminisce and tell stories, but since the world shook and the once unimaginable trip back home became a reality, an urgent need to free myself from the despair of a disconnected existence, to make my life whole again, gradually possessed me.

But first I had to write about the way it was.

For everything had changed there, everything. Not only the streets and buildings, but the people. They treated me as a stranger, and some even with suspicion. The darkness that hung over their heads for forty-five years had cast a permanent shadow over their lives, over their minds. Skies were clearing now, but the darkness had penetrated some so deeply that it could not be reached by the light.

So I have to write about the past the way I remember it—for future's sake.

I belong to a generation that grew up with vague memories of the pre-war, pre-Communist past, constantly reminded of it by the lamentations of our parents about the present and the happy stories about the past. Sometimes it was hard to sort out where the truth ended and the myths began. I have never been told that it was a perfect time, only that it was an optimistic one, when people were gaining confidence in the direction the country was moving.

Pictures and smells of these times, etched in our minds, were also hard to ignore. The Sunday promenades in the shadows of chestnut trees, the aroma of chocolate and orange juice, totally absent in the post-war reality—all contributed to the nostalgia for the "good old days." It was hard (at least) and incomprehensible (at most) to reconcile the memories with the present. Everything that could have been was teasing us from the pictures on the glossy pages of smuggled Western magazines. And while we kept sighing after our lost future, the new cadre, the backbone of the Dictatorship of the Proletariat, was being brought from the villages to be educated hastily in the newly created Workers' Faculties, so they could assume their leadership roles with at least some degree of legitimacy. Still uncomfortable with the urban environment and caught up in their own nostalgia, they hung around the bus terminals, hoping to see a familiar face or to hear some news from home.

Things looked out-of-whack, and, except for the tyrant with the benevolent smile living in the Kremlin and his Politburo, nobody knew for sure where it was all leading us. But the arm of Moscow was long, and its grip was like iron.

The system was very efficient; it worked like a clock. In no time, we had our own homegrown "leaders" to keep us marching in step to the drum of the Soviets.

Life after September 1944 was not a string of nightmarish experiences. We were happy at times. We laughed and sang and danced. We had hopes. And, once in our lives, we had sunny dreams full of promises. Alas, for those of us who came to the conclusion that the only way to survive was to leave, there came a moment when all hopes faded and we could not continue to laugh, sing, and dance as before. It was a moment when we realized that something was very wrong. We went our different ways—to all corners of the world—trying to find our lost hopes, to find and fulfill the promises. Many of us succeeded. All of us paid a price.

So I wrote this book for my daughter, Audrey, and my husband, Andrei, who, as a child and young adult, went through experiences that no child should ever go through but never let bitterness cloud his consciousness or mar his love for the country of his birth.

However, I dedicate this book to my parents:

To my mother, who, from a beautiful young woman with a radiant smile, grew into an embittered but defiant older woman, who never stood silently by, afraid to show her anger at the ever-present petty injustices that made life so oppressive and hard to bear;

To my father, who, from a sensitive, idealistic dandy grew into a stoic and prophetic old man, an inspiration to many who would come to him, if only to hear him say, "It is going to end soon! There is no doubt! Next month, when…" and there would be a reference to some international political event, which, in his belief, was bound to make a difference. And on a high note of hope and in a categorical voice full of unshakable confidence, he would end his pronouncements, "This time it is going to happen!"

Nothing of what he promised to everybody happened in his lifetime, but this did not diminish the admiration of those who knew and trusted him.

On November 10, 1989, it happened, but neither of them lived to see the end of their nightmare.

They died oppressed and cheated. Their lives were destroyed when they were still in their prime, when all choices were taken away from them, when they failed to adapt to a new society morally unacceptable to them. Now, many, too many, confronted by the revelations of the cruelties and lawlessness of this profoundly unjust, corrupt, and spiritually impoverished system say, "We did not know," and as I listen to them, I remember my parents and think, "Well, some did."

1

THE RAIDS

A short story:

I am still half-asleep when Father grabs me wrapped in a green-and-red tartan blanket and starts hurriedly descending the seven flights of stairs leading to the underground. A few moments later, the monotonous droll of approaching aircraft becomes audible, getting louder and more menacing.

At every landing, we are joined by more men, women, and children—all rushing, pushing forward, clogging the narrow way. Some are carrying briefcases, some are dressed in their pajamas, and others are still in their daytime outfits. The noise of their running feet on the cement steps reverberates off the walls, covered by yellow glossy paint.

Underground are the cellars: a row of small rooms, like catacombs, along the basement walls of the apartment building. They serve as a storing place for the heating coal and the barrels of pickled cabbage to be consumed during wintertime. There is no old furniture, clothes, or toys—those are stored in the attic, under the roof of the apartment building. It is a bright and fascinating place up there, next to the sun; but it is dark, dingy, and smells of anthracite down, in the belly of the building. Now, many have piled the coal in a corner, as high as they can, to free some space for cots—for the children and the old people.

At the bottom of the staircase, the steady stream of people breaks into small groups, each family heading toward its cellar.

Then the explosions begin. Some are clear and loud; some are muffled and distant. Every time a loud one shakes the air, my mother's face acquires a grayish hue. She is not sitting on the cot. She is crouching in the corner, her ears stuffed with cotton, her eyes closed, her face twitching at every sound. My mother is the most doting mom. I am her little sparrow, but during the air raids she is not my mother. She is only a terrified, almost-crazed woman.

I am not scared. For that matter, most of the children are not either; or, more precisely, our fears are eclipsed by our curiosity. Filled with trepidation, we would try to sneak out from the protective eyes and hands of our parents and run up the stairs into the courtyard. There we would huddle by the building, raise our eyes to the sky—searching for the airplanes, listening and fidgeting excitedly—ready to dash back inside at the sound of an explosion. The tension and anxiety that overwhelm the grown-ups do not affect us. We are more afraid of being punished for our recklessness.

Sometimes the air attacks last for hours and sometimes for such a short time that we will hardly have reached the underground when the signal is given that it is over. For its duration, people usually remain huddled in their cellars, mostly quiet or speaking in hushed voices—their attention directed toward the sounds from the outside.

I don't remember anybody crying—even Mother. She endures the unbearable agony and terror that assaults her sensitive and fragile nervous system as bravely as she can.

At the end of the raid the "off" signal is given. The sound is hardly audible. It takes a while for the people to respond. Finally, faces relax and voices rise. The ascent to the apartments begins.

This is the end of the short story, a quilt of memories assembled from patches of fleeting recollections of different raids.

Here I skip the descriptions of the blackouts, the sheaves of light shooting from the ground straight to the sky above—incessantly moving, circling, crisscrossing each other in search of aircraft hidden by the darkness. I don't talk about the foreboding deadly silence—the precursor of each air raid either. I don't mention the faint, wailing sound of the manual siren drifting into the apartment and abruptly dispelling the calm inside, or try to emphasize the overwhelming sense of urgency emanating from Father as he grabs me, wrapped in the memorable blanket…All those are components of familiar pictures depicted in so many war movies in far more effective ways than I could ever be able to summon forth.

This short story is my own, unique one. It is the picture I have carried in my mind for so many years—a tale I have been relating to anyone willing to listen.

And there are the rest of the stories—the ones I remember for a particular reason: a glimpse of understanding, an insight of a perceived truth revealed to me for the first time on the dramatic background of the raids and later reinforced, at one time or another, by consequent events defining my life.

Finally, there is that one, single moment that does not belong to either category. As a matter of fact, this was the first time bombs fell on Sofia. It happened on a spring day, right before Easter. It was also the first time we heard the wail of a siren—and the last time we treated it as nothing more than a persistent, pulsating noise, best left ignored.

The door to the kitchen balcony was wide open, letting the fresh spring air carry in the unfamiliar sound. For a moment Mother looked intrigued, but not enough to interrupt her work—kneading the dough for the Easter bread. By then we must have already painted, decorated, and rubbed to a brilliant shine at least a dozen eggs. The apartment must have been thoroughly cleaned in preparation for the upcoming feast, and we must have been well set into the festive spirit. Eventually, a distant blunt rumble compelled Mother to move away from her unfinished chore and to quickly step out on the balcony. As usual, I followed her.

I saw Mother standing there, perfectly still like a statue—her arms bent at the elbows, hands raised, crossed in front of her breasts—the Easter bread dough sticking to her fingers and palms all the way up above the wrists. Her eyes were fixed, gazing into the space above the red roofs of houses and the low buildings scattered all over the area in front of us, as far as one could see.

Later we were told that we had been bombed. The news, though, had a puzzling aspect to it: the damage was limited to the cemetery!

This was the beginning of the carpet-bombings the inhabitants of Sofia endured for a few years. Shortly after this first attack, the black opaque blinds would be installed, the cellars would be readied for their new use as hiding places, and people would stop wondering why the bombs had hit this or that…

Looking back at these times of extraordinary, unforgettable experiences, one might wonder why a pair of old, dirty drapes would stick into the memory of a young child. And not only that, but, as stories go, this is the one that always makes me smile…

The "off" signal had sounded already, yet we were not allowed to go back upstairs. Instead, we were sent outside, to the sidewalk across the street. Guards stood in front of the building, barring anybody from entering it.

Before long a rumor started about an unexploded bomb that had been spotted in the courtyard of the adjacent building—a movie house with a restaurant on the street level and a movie salon upstairs. However, no person of authority came around to tell us what the situation was, nobody with the least bit of information to soothe frayed nerves, to relieve tension.

Time was passing.

It was getting cold.

Fatigue and anxiety were swelling; patience was wearing thin. People began asking, then demanding to be allowed to go up to their apartments to pick up some clothes or food.

The guards did not budge.

After a while, a new rumor started to circulate among the crowd: except for some type of metal container, probably an empty fuel barrel discarded by a plane, there was no bomb, mine, or anything dangerous at all lying in the courtyard behind the building.

Still the alert was not lifted; still we were kept out on the street where, thirsty and hungry, dressed in light housecoats over light nightgowns or pajamas, we were shivering from the cold.

Finally, an official-looking man came and announced that someone in charge had relented: a decision had been reached to let one person per family go into the apartments to fetch some necessities. A few points were made clear: the investigation was still going on, there were no assurances that it would conclude any time soon, and the outcome was uncertain—one way or another. Suddenly, there were more than our immediate needs to think about—this could be the only opportunity to save something valuable from all the possessions we had, including all documents left behind, forgotten in the confusion and haste to flee to safety.

Excitement, almost panic, set in. Men rushed toward the building, admitted inside in small groups, forewarned that they had only a limited time to spend in there. Father joined them while Mother and I remained standing on the sidewalk, our eyes fixed on his back, watching him quickly disappear into the dimly lit stairway, swallowed by a cavernous hole.

A long time passed before Father emerged from the doorway looking tired and frustrated, carrying a large bundle under his arm. As he neared us, Mother ran toward him, pulled the folded material, and shook it open.

A pair of old, dirty drapes fell out.

Anger, hopelessness, and finally tears filled her eyes.

Sometime later, without much explanation, the guards moved away and the all clear was declared. A mob of exhausted people started moving toward the apartment building across the street in a silent march, accompanied only by the rustle of shuffling feet. A long time had elapsed since the air attack had been called off by the sirens. The usual commotion and noises that followed the raids—the sharp, piercing sound of an ambulance, the bustle of people emerging from shelters and rushing home—all had died out. The city had fallen into an eerie slumber.

My most vivid and, in one respect, poignant memory of the air raids comes from the district of Nadejda. That was where my grandfather Mirko's house was. It still stands there in dilapidated grandeur, bursting at the seams—overcrowded with generations of descendants, born and raised there. At one time, this area north of the city was nothing more than empty fields. Grandfather selected it as the place for his young family's new home, so that his children could grow up riding ponies and running freely in the open spaces.

It was early January. There had been a lull in the frequency of the air raids: one hadn't occurred for more than two weeks. After the last raid, we had gone to Lialintsi, determined to stay away from the city. But as Mother grew restless, as usual, while away from home, and the news kept coming that no bombs were falling on Sofia, her urge to return home overcame her fears. We were back before the tenth of the month. The apartment was cold, there was no food there, so my parents decided that it would be more convenient to go to Nadejda and stay with Grandmother. By then Grandfather had gone. Even though a house located in a suburb seemed to be a safer place, nobody considered the fact that close by was the Central Train Station, that the district was almost surrounded by railway tracks along which freight cars carrying supplies were running, and that this probably made this site the only legitimate military target in Sofia.

It was dark when the bombs started falling. Our hiding place was a cellar deep in the ground under the couple of stores located on street level. Uncle Sanyo and his family occupied the second floor of the house, and Grandmother Raina lived on the first floor with her two younger, unmarried daughters, Aunt Rada and Aunt Tina. The oldest daughter, Aunt Julia, who lived with her family in another house in the same courtyard, had left the city with her children and lived somewhere in the provinces—joining the hordes of evacuees that had already fled the capital. I do not remember exactly which of the relatives were in the cellar on that particular evening, apart from Grandmother and Uncle Angel, Aunt Julia's husband. I remember just shadows, moving around, emerging from the darkness into the flickering light of a burning candle.

The raid went on for a long time. The noise from flying airplanes and explosions mixed with the sound of moving vehicles along the street in front of the house. The street was actually the main road that led north out of the city. The loudness of the explosions suggested that the bombs were falling in close proximity. An atmosphere of anxiety continued building inside the cellar until someone went out to investigate. The news he brought back was frightful: the bombs shaking the ground were incendiary. Looming fires surrounded Nadejda, the wall of flames tightening. Convoys of military vehicles were leaving for the north.

It was dark and tense down there. Father had seated me on top of a wooden barrel full of pickled cabbage heads. Perched on its round edge, I was continuously trying to balance my weight, to remain as still as possible, for even the slightest movement would cause the loose cover on top of the barrel to start wobbling ominously. While Father was supporting me with his hand, his attention was directed elsewhere, a fact contributing to my overriding worry: the possibility of falling into the barrel and drowning in the stinking brine.

Meanwhile, Mother was crouching somewhere by the cement walls, her ears stuffed with cotton. Grandmother was walking around, crossing herself at the sound of each blast or heightening of the noise coming from outside.

Suddenly, Uncle Angel, looking pale and shaky, darted toward the door and disappeared, the sound of his running feet dying away. The dark shadows of people in the cellar started moving, bunching together. There were excited whispers and brief expressions of surprise and bewilderment that lasted for a short while. Then the pantomime was restored, everybody assuming his or her previous position.

The time continued to drag on. The noises from outside did not abate at all.

Finally, it was all over. Instead of going upstairs straight away, we went outside to take a look. In front of the house, the commotion was great. The convoy of vehicles kept on moving, accompanied by the monotonous sound of running engines. In the distance, brightly burning fires were lighting the night skies.

Sometime before the end of the raid, Uncle Angel had returned to the cellar. He looked worn out, dirty and distraught. He had tried to climb onto the back of many trucks, chasing one after another, following each failure to make it. He must have been pushed and dragged, persisting for quite a while, determined to get away from the danger of approaching inferno, hoping to eventually get to his wife and young children.

In the end, he had to abandon the fruitless effort and come back to the shelter. Nobody said anything.

Later, I heard about what he was doing that night outside while the bombs were falling on Nadejda. Not that anybody had made a big deal out of it, but I remembered it. The thought that popped in my mind then, and kept coming back on different occasions, was based on the observation that Mother and Uncle Angel were acting differently than the rest—aunts and uncles, the direct descendants of Grandfather Mirko. On their part, "The Mirkovs," as they preferred to identify themselves collectively, hardly ever displayed any emotions, even in extraordinary circumstances when fear and sorrow challenged the toughness of the most obstinate. At moments like these, they seemed to be made of different stuff from the rest, and they always made a point of showing it.

Now, many, many years later, I still dream of the raids, but it is never the way I remember them. In my dream I am chased by a low-flying plane. I am running. My heart is pounding. I can't run fast enough. I turn my head, looking backward and up, and I can see the man in the cockpit. He is flying so low that I can see him looking at me with cold, hard eyes. He does not hate me, but he is going to kill me.

I think the dream came from a painting I saw after the war. It was by a Russian painter—a very large, almost empty canvas, depicting a boy running away from a German plane. It was clearly German. The one in my dream has no insignia; it is painted just a solid dark gray. The country I grew up in was on the wrong side in the war, so it could not have been German. Come to think of it, it must have been British or American.

In my dream, though, it could be anybody's.

2
FATHER

There was general mobilization, and Father was summoned to join the army. Only he was not trained as a soldier; he did not know how to shoot.

As soon as he reached draft age, his father bought him off. It was a common practice in well-to-do families—it allowed the sons to continue their education without any interruption caused by compulsory service after graduating from high school.

It was just as well that Grandfather did that for more than that one reason—Father hated the military.

In his youth he wrote poetry and even published a few personal, probably sentimental, poems with names like "Sad Accords" and "Tears of the Day." He wrote under pseudonyms, and I never read any of them because by the time I was old enough to want to, he had become quite a different person. Then he told me that he did not remember any, or when and who published them. Once, though, he mentioned that he used to publish in a very popular newspaper to the left of the political ideological spectrum of the time with the poignant name of *Red Laughter*.

When mobilization was announced, instead of being enlisted in the army as an officer, which was the rank all university graduates were given automatically, he was sent to a training camp to undergo the training he did not get when he skipped the draft.

He was to get ready for GI service.

All his life Father lived by strict principles, reflecting the values and morality of the people who inspired him. The philosophers of ancient Greece, Voltaire, and Rousseau filled him with admiration. He found greatness in the incorruptible Robespierre, the iron-willed Cromwell, and the tenacious Churchill. At school he excelled in math and physics, but once he discovered the law, he embraced his profession with an abiding zeal that never left him. There was nothing he would rather be but a lawyer.

He believed in self-discipline and fierce individualism—leading a life strictly defined by his unyielding convictions. He possessed a mind that questioned everything and everybody.

Somewhere, on a bleak afternoon, clad in heavy brown uniforms, complete with heavy backpacks, boots, and metal helmets, a detachment of sweating new recruits marched hour after hour under the unrelenting barrage of curt, repetitive commands barked out by a sergeant obsessed with self-importance.

Dusty and exhausted, totally unconvinced that what he was ordered to do served any other purpose but to inflict punishment, Father stopped marching, threw his rifle on the ground, and walked away. The rest of the day, it seems, he spent in the barracks sprawled on his bed.

Night fell. Nobody had come to arrest him or take him away for questioning. Soldiers drifted in. He dozed off. Presently, he was startled by a tap on the shoulder and a whisper in his ear, "Comrade, well done! You are invited to the meeting of our cell tonight. Are you bringing us directives? We are ready!"

Father was surprised and annoyed. His answer, "You are mistaken. I am not a comrade," did not seem to be taken at face value. In the morning, a bright red flag brushed against his face as he was getting up. The banner was stuck in the frame of his bed. Incensed, he broke it in two.

Eventually he was sent back to Sofia where he expected to be court-martialed.

Father never mentioned the incident in front of me. But Mother, probably in an effort to alleviate her anxiety and reluctant to share her fears with anyone else, told me the story. I don't know what happened with the case; in a way it had a happy ending: Father did not go to prison. He spent the rest of the war in uniform, observing the sky over Sofia, carrying binoculars instead of a rifle. His job was to spot aircraft bound for the city and to phone in the alert.

In 1942 he spent short periods of time in Berovo, Bitolia, and Yakoruda from where he wrote long, beautiful letters. In some he included small poems, which he composed for me, sprinkled with distorted "baby" words that I had used as a toddler. He kept inventing funny, endearing names to call me, and he signed my letters with "Your daddy K."

His letters to Mother were full of tenderness and counsel.

3

GRANDFATHER MIRKO. THE WILL

My paternal grandfather's name was Mirko Grigorov. He died a wealthy man at the age of fifty-nine. His star rose fast and burned out early.

He wanted to build a dynasty and for a while seemed unstoppable. He even named his first three children Alexander, Konstantin, and Julia, after tsars, kings, and emperors. But he was doomed. Even if he had not died at this early age, he would not have survived the events of September 1944. Too many people envied him, and many were killed for less.

Mirko Grigorov was a self-made man. At one time, his most prized possession was a shirt, lavishly embroidered by his sister. He was a handsome man with fair hair and blue eyes; his goatee was always trimmed and neat. He dressed impeccably in dark three-piece suits, sparkling white shirts with stiff collars, and a waistcoat sporting a gold pocket watch dangling on a thick golden fob. He was fond of jewelry and wore handsome rings on his fingers.

None of his children inherited his drive. They grew up in affluence, and sometimes that can take the edge off great ambitions.

I liked him. I liked him very much and had the feeling that he liked me too. This is what makes it so hard for me to understand why he left that will.

His wife, my grandmother, was a short, dark woman with a broad face and very tight, curly hair, which she passed on to her children. As she grew older, she became heavy and started using a cane to support herself. Her hands were fine, with elegant fingers.

She was cold to me, and her presence oppressed me. When I went to visit her, I felt uncomfortable and tried to cut the visits short. I did not dislike her; I just could not understand her. She was a conservative, inflexible woman whose greatest virtue was her loyalty and obedience to her husband. After he died, she withdrew from life completely.

She lived to be eighty-five. She spent the last thirty years or so of her life inside the domain Grandfather had built for his children. There were three houses that occupied a block on the corner of a wide major street and a narrow side one. The big house faced the main street, and the others were protected from the outside world by a fence and a wall. All shared a common courtyard, covered in flagstones.

When Grandmother passed away, many people must have been surprised. They probably thought that she had been dead for years.

We have a picture that was taken at Grandfather's funeral. Five priests and a crowd of people are standing on the steps of the big house, some spilling into the courtyard. In the forefront is Grandfather's body, lying in an open coffin. Behind it, standing or kneeling in two rows, are all the aunts and uncles with their spouses, and Grandmother. There are no children, and nobody is crying. Only one of the aunts seems to be wiping her eyes, hiding her face behind a large white handkerchief.

Grandfather died after a stroke. For a few days he lingered unconscious, comatose. My parents took me to say good-bye to him. This was the last time I saw him—lying in the middle of a large bed, an ice pack on his forehead, eyes closed, oblivious, distant.

The children were not allowed to go to the funeral, and, if it were not for the photograph from the courtyard to jog my memory, I would probably have forgotten the last time I saw him. Likewise, I did not witness what happened after the funeral, but it was so big and overwhelming that for years I was constantly reminded of its consequences.

Grandpa Mirko was not only smart and shrewd, he was also driven. As a boy he did very well at school, and since the church was on the lookout for bright young students to be educated for service in the cloth, he almost ended up in the seminary. The problem was that he was not timid enough, and for this reason alone he was dropped from the list of otherwise suitable boys selected for consideration.

However, poor as he was, he fell in love with the right girl: the mayor's daughter. And to impress upon his future father-in-law that it was love and nothing else that he was after, he issued a challenge for himself:

"I don't want any of your money," he told his father-in-law-to-be, "but mark my words, someday you will come to me for help!" And he went on in life, amassing wealth and acquiring power. He also loved politics. He loved to influence, even manipulate, political events but always inconspicuously, from the "back rooms." He was plotting the political futures of his sons.

Grandfather became successful. One of my aunts told me that his prophecy had also been fulfilled. His father-in-law had fallen on hard times and came to him for help. It must have given Grandfather great satisfaction.

I knew him when he was a notary, and Father and his older brother were working as lawyers with him. They had an office in a building opposite the courthouse, known as the Palace of Commerce. The office was located on the second floor. There was a large sign under the window that said: "Mirko Grigorov & Sons." The way to the office from street level led into a dark concrete stairway, then turned into a long, dingy corridor. The air was permeated with a pungent odor coming from the washrooms located along the hallway. A couple of turns to the left, and there it was, the office filled with heavy cigarette smoke that hung like a blanket over the entire room. The window that ran across the width of the wall overlooked a covered arcade, preventing the sunrays of ever shining in. The precious little light that came through filled the room with dusk at all hours of the day.

The furniture was massive. Two huge desks arranged at right angles to the window faced each other. A low round table stood between two large leather chairs. Surrounded by paintings, an octagonal clock that chimed every half hour hung on one of the side walls. The paintings were presents from clients or were bought from artists who made the rounds with their portfolios.

Grandfather was usually sitting on a Viennese wicker rocking chair that stood away from the rest of the furniture, giving the impression that he was just a spectator observing a scene. When I visited him with Mother, he would pick me up and sit me on his knee.

He exuded patience and good-naturedness.

Leaning comfortably against his shoulder, I would play with his pocket watch and chain. Sometimes he would take me to Father's desk and teach me to type on the Remington, pressing my fingers one by one on the keys.

I remember the busboys passing at intervals, carrying trays in bell-shaped cages with glass tops, and the fascinating small porcelain "filjans" (small coffee cups) placed inside them, covered with colorful designs and filled with thick, aromatic Turkish coffee. The covers had small doors, big enough to squeeze the full cups out and put the empty ones back in.

In that office Father worked every day with his father. There they must have had the argument that led to the disastrous consequences that came to haunt even me. It happened not long before Grandfather had the stroke that killed him.

It was deemed that they had political differences. Father was a compassionate and sensitive person; Grandfather was a pragmatic and ambitious person. He accused Father of being too much to the left. In his anger and agitation, he must have felt that Father's independence and refusal to conform were nothing less than ungratefulness. It was proof that he was bad for himself and everybody else.

In such a frame of mind, Grandfather must have written the will. With it he disinherited Father completely. He went even further, proclaiming him the black sheep of his flock. He piled insults and accusations upon him. He wrote that Father owed everything to him and even to his siblings. The document was placed in a safe in the house.

After the funeral the safe was opened and its contents examined. Some were surprised to see the bulky sealed envelope with the inscription, "To be Opened in Case of my Death" and expressed their misgivings about the wisdom of doing just that, while others knew about its existence and insisted on the inviolability of grandfather's wishes. In the end the latter prevailed.

It was late in the evening when Mother and Father came back home from the reading of the will. Mother had no makeup on, and her smooth, fair complexion seemed to glow in its paleness. Father's face was drawn and his jaw tight.

That evening was the only time I had ever seen them so completely in unison, sharing the same pain and shock, and the same tenderness toward each other. It was unbearably sad. Mother sat on the couch; Father knelt in front of her and buried his face in her lap.

It was 1941.

4

THE DEATH OF THE TSAR. VLADAYA

On August 28, 1943, Tsar Boris the Third died. Every time that statement is made, it is accompanied by another statement: "He died under suspicious circumstances."

I was too young to remember the commentaries of that time. In my memories all circumstances of that historical event are imprinted like faded photographs.

Boris the Third was a popular tsar. He had captured the affection of the common people, especially the peasants, with his unpretentious manners and kindness whenever he came in contact with them. And that used to happen quite often. On his hunting outings, he liked to stop unexpectedly at villages and drop in peasants' huts to share a meal and conversation with them. The tsar's family was perceived as leading modest and simple lives. It was not unusual to see him riding on horseback along the streets of Sofia without the visible protection of bodyguards.

The tsar's residence was also a modest affair, still nice enough for the quiet and somewhat provincial capital of a small nation reemerging from five hundred years of oblivion. There was a large, protruding balcony over the entrance of the main building where the tsar's family showed themselves frequently. The complex included a number of structures surrounded by a handsome wrought-iron fence that circled the east side of the palace. That was where the tall gates were, flanked by good-looking, smartly dressed guards, and that was where people gathered and waited patiently to get a glimpse of the tsar, Tsaritsa Joanna, Princess Maria-Luisa, or the heir to the crown, Simeon, affectionately referred to as "the little tsar."

The death of the tsar came as an enormous shock. The news of his demise was met with incredulity, followed by a torrent of spontaneous and genuine grief. His body was laid in state in the cathedral of Alexander Nevsky. A long line of people waited patiently for hours to pass by the casket. When we went with Mother to join the queue, the end of it almost reached the palace. It ran along Boulevard Tsaria, curved by the National Assembly, and ended at the south entrance to the church.

The procession of people never stopped moving, slowly and silently. Coming in from the bright light, the inside of the church was cold and dark. When we reached the coffin, Mother lifted me up so I could take a better look. I saw the tsar's face, the flowers, his uniformed body. Behind him, in the darkness, I could see only shadows. We exited through the north entrance. Close by, large tents were pitched. There, tired and emotionally spent people were being helped.

The funeral itself was another picture. The slow-moving cortege winded along the boulevard leading to the Central Train Station. Thousands of people a few rows deep lined the sidewalks, and more leaned from the windows and balconies of buildings that were draped in black banners and flags. Many were weeping.

The tsar's body was taken to the funeral train to be transported to Rila Monastery for burial. It was befitting that his last journey should be on a train. He loved driving them, and many times passengers were surprised to find out, at the end of their voyage, that the person behind the locomotive's window had been none other than the tsar himself.

The airwaves emitted by Radio Sofia filled the ether all day long with the coverage of the funeral. And as soon as the cortege reached the Central Station, the masses of people lining the route of the funeral procession hurried away from the streets of Sofia, rushing inside their homes to stand by the radios and listen to the solemn male voice describing the happenings along the tsar's farewell journey.

It was a slow, long ride. At every town, at every village, and all the way up the railway line, winding higher and higher up the mountain where the monastery lay almost hidden in the majestic landscape, city people and peasants alike, emotional and bewildered, came to meet the funeral train, to bid farewell to the tsar they loved.

The voice on the radio belonged to Uncle Pecko. He was the newscaster at Radio Sofia who delivered the daily news in a pleasant voice with distinct timbre and clear diction. His was also the voice on the preview news films shown in the cinemas before the main feature.

Uncle Pecko was Father's cousin. They grew up together, played soccer on the same team, wrote poetry—which Uncle Pecko continued to do for a living, writing lyrics for popular songs, the so-called schlagers. Good-looking, he was sort of a ham. He had played small parts in a few movies made by the budding movie industry. He also had a hobby: photography. With his Leika hanging about his neck, he was always on the lookout for willing subjects. Judging by the number of pictures he took of my parents and myself, along with his wife and sons, we must have been among his favorite ones. But because he never let anybody touch his camera, among the piles of photographs he took, there is not a single one of him.

His wife's name was Blaga. She was also good-looking, fashionable, and flirtatious. Their two sons, Milcho and Bojidar, were younger than I was. Milcho was fair and delicate; Bojidar, called by his diminutive name Darcho, was a cute, overactive boy with long, curly blond hair.

It was late afternoon on a day of a year that I can't recall with certainty. Darcho was just a toddler, and Father was at home, two facts that stand vividly in my memory, but which, in terms of reference to time, generate more questions than answers.

In front of the doorway of our apartment, right in the middle of the landing, still clad in their nightclothes, stood all of them: Uncle Pecko, Aunt Blaga, Milcho, and Darcho. All were dirty, disheveled, and tired. A small briefcase hung from Uncle Pecko's right arm. From their sorry appearance it was quite obvious that they had been through an extraordinary experience: they had just survived a most horrifying ordeal.

Early that morning there had been an air raid. The children had still been in bed when the sirens came on, and the descent to the cellar must have been a hasty one.

The apartment building they lived in had taken a direct hit; fortunately, the bomb did not penetrate all the way to the underground. The explosion, though, had been strong enough to bring down six or seven stories of concrete, burying men, women, and children hiding underneath.

It had taken a long time to dig them out of the rubble. Finally, emerging from the debris, they felt lucky, though barely alive. Now they needed a shelter and rest.

Late that evening, as we were settling for the night, the sirens started wailing again—a persistent call to start moving to the cellars. But for Aunt Blaga and Uncle Pecko, it was too much—nothing could make them drag themselves back underground. All their strength and fears were spent.

We all went to bed.

In the morning Father and Uncle Pecko went somewhere. For the rest of us, the day went like a mad scene from a play. Mother was hysterical. The situation was becoming impossible in the city. Mother kept saying, "We have to get away to save the children." We all got dressed in whatever she threw our way, grabbed small hand luggage, and dashed to a street behind the apartment building to get a bus out of the city.

An excited crowd of crazed and determined people had already gathered on the street—all bent on leaving Sofia. They were running around, asking, screaming, demanding that there be buses. Rumors flew around all day, hopes were raised and dashed, the crowd kept moving in waves from one corner to another. Two buses came and went overloaded, swaying dangerously from side to side. We did not make it.

Late in the evening, exhausted, resigned, we returned home.

Soon afterward, Uncle Pecko, Aunt Blaga, Milcho, and Darcho moved to a new place.

Besides the wail of sirens, the airplanes' drone, and the bomb explosions, accompanied by the roar of anti-aircraft artillery, there were other unforgettable noises. Throughout the war we lived on the top floor of an apartment building situated on a busy boulevard. The street was paved with cobblestones. In the middle of it ran a streetcar. About a hundred feet away to the north of us, the tracks curved from a side street to the boulevard. At every turn of the tram, the wheels made a sharp, screeching noise of steel rubbing against steel. The runners above the cars, sliding along the electric wire, used to jerk and disconnect frequently. That produced showers of sparks that flew all over and sounded like firecrackers. Those were the daytime sounds that died away at nightfall when the streetcars stopped running for a few hours.

And then, I remember a distant thud breaking the silence, slowly growing in intensity, turning into continuous thunder—the sound of tanks slowly, deliberately making their way through the street. The steel chains running over the cobblestones made a rhythmic, frightful noise. Where did they come from, and where were they going?

I lay between my parents, awake, listening, waiting for the noise to die out. And I could feel that they too were listening and waiting for calm to be restored.

1943 was slowly coming to an end.

We were strapped financially. Being mobilized throughout the war, Father's earnings turned into a trickle. Every leave he had, he would run to the office, attempting to work and make some money to provide for us.

The raids went on. Mother was exhausted from the tension. She hated leaving Sofia; it seemed she could not live anywhere else. A few times we went to Lialintsi, but, after only a couple days, she would grow restless. Pointing out at my ruddy cheeks and sudden burst of energy—unmistakable proof of the benefits of the fresh air, emphasizing how much I enjoyed spending time in the village, playing with the peasant's kids, and eating Grandmother's homemade bread—none of this made a difference. In another day or two, she would be dragging me back in spite of my protestations, as well as Grandmother's.

Finally, life in the city became so difficult that we had to move away. The closest place that was considered safe was the mountain village of Vladaya—a vacationing spot located only fifteen kilometers from Sofia.

But before we moved there, an important event in my life took place.

Winter was approaching; it was cold and miserable. We had been walking for a very long time with a crowd of people streaming out of the city. All had different destinations: ours was a small village in the outskirts of Sofia. This was just one of the short trips, usually not planned in advance but taken on impulse, to alleviate Mother's anxieties. They were like emotional valves that opened only when the pressure reached its breaking point. On these trips, Mother never took much luggage.

On that day, many of the people must have been leaving the city for good or planning to spend a long time away from home. Men, women, and children were hauling, pushing, and rolling all kinds of improvised carts. Spring cots, piled up with mattresses and bags, even with stoves, were being pulled through dirt and mud. At one point we had to cross a narrow suspension bridge. The flimsy structure was swaying violently sideways and undulating ominously with every step we took, as if it was going to break or turn over at any moment.

Eventually we reached a village called Philipovtsi and arrived at a small, nice house. Aunt Nina, Mother's sister, was there. I don't know if what followed had been prearranged or was an accident. In normal times such event would have been planned, but those were not normal times.

For one reason or another, I had not been christened on time, that is to say, as the Orthodox Christian faith required it. For some time, that had been bothering Mother for, I thought, a strange reason: I couldn't have been buried in consecrated ground if we were killed in an air raid. And this weighed on her heavily.

It was quiet and peaceful in the small, bright house. The priest, who came from another christening of a baby, arranged the small party around a font filled with holy water. Dressed only in my undershirt, with Aunt Nina—my godmother-to-be—by my side and my mother's soft eyes set upon me, I felt special.

It was a solemn ceremony. Instead of my godmother speaking on my behalf, I pronounced all the statements and took all the pledges. It made me feel as though I had entered directly into a covenant with God.

It happened on the twenty-first of November, my name day.

Nestled in the foothills of Vitosha, southwest of Sofia, was a picturesque village called Vladaya. The road to the village was wavering, steep, and dangerous in places. For a few kilometers it ran through a narrow mountain pass called Vladaya's defile. It separated Vitosha from the hills of the much smaller mountain, Liulin. The banks of the defile were covered by thickets, and tall forest trees threw dark shadows over the road. There was something mysterious, eerie in this confined, dusky crevice. Below the road, on the north side, a river rushed down the slope, snaking through a rocky bed. Above it ran the railway tracks. It was exciting to ride the train through the gorge. The fresh, pristine beauty of the place, the rhythmic clutter of the wheels, amplified by the mountainous echo, affected all of the senses. Passengers rushed to open the windows, sticking their hands and arms out, waving and smiling.

Half way up the road to Vladaya, just before the mountains squeezed the road into a narrow ribbon, there was a restaurant, the Black Merle. Before the war, we used to go there on our Sunday outings with Uncle Otto, Aunt Desha, Bobby, and Chris. Aunt Desha was Father's cousin. Mother felt great closeness and affection for her, and they remained friends for life. Uncle Otto worked for the Central Bank, sported bow ties, and enjoyed sharing a drink with Father. They were our partners on our mountain-hiking excursions. For these occasions, Uncle Otto put on his Tyrolean leather shorts and spiked mountain shoes. He looked quite smart. The restaurant was a pleasant and cheerful place before the war. Only now, every recollection of it evokes in my mind not the images of laughter and happiness but the memory of a terrible event that took place during the war, not far away from the spot the restaurant stood on, a memory that echoes both joy and fear.

Further down from the the Black Merle, the road leaving the defile used to make a sharp turn toward Vitosha, pass over a bridge, and, after another sharp turn east, continued toward Sofia, hugging the mountain. Once, on our way from Lialintsi, we had to find transportation for the second half of our trip. Somehow we had made it to Pernik, but we had to find a way to continue the journey to Sofia. There were a number of rickety-rackety trucks that came and went, full of people crammed in their open trailers like sardines. Every time one of them would stop and drop the rear wooden guardrails, a mob would rush off, pushing and shoving, climbing on top of each other. At one time we almost made it on when a couple of strong hands grabbed and pulled us down, almost throwing us aside. The truck pulled forward, and another took its place. This time we were the first in line and somehow managed to squeeze in.

The road to Sofia passed through Vladaya. After an hour or so, the truck reached the defile. It was rolling down the narrow road. The bumpy ride, shaking and rocking the standing passengers, made everybody clutch and grasp at anything each time the truck made a turn. Suddenly, just as we came to the end of the gorge where the road curved toward the mountain, a terrible scene emerged. An overturned truck lay at the bottom of the gully below the bridge. Around it, bloody people were trying to climb up the steep banks while others lay motionless, sprawled on the bottom of the ravine.

Our truck did not stop. It only slowed down a bit and continued on its way. My heart skipped a beat; this was the truck that we had almost boarded. Mother's arms enveloped me, squeezing me in a tight hug.

We spent the last year of the bombardment in Vladaya until the Germans left and the Russians came, that is, till the Red Army rolled in. The Soviet Army. It took quite a long time to make people use the term *Soviet*. Some never got used to it.

Throughout this period, we lived in three different places: first in a pleasant two-story house, next in a stable, and finally in a barn. The village was overridden with evacuees like us. In the beginning, the peasants moved out of their houses and rented them to the city folk. When the demand increased, they started clearing old stables and barns and began renting them to the ones that could not afford the ever-growing rent for the better accommodations.

The first place we lived was one of the houses near the entrance to the village at the end of the road from Sofia. It had two stories, and we had a room on the second floor, a nice, bright room. The owners were a young couple with two small girls. One morning, in early spring, Mother called to me from the backyard. She beckoned me to leave the room and run to the barn as fast as I could—there was a surprise waiting for me. A goat was giving birth to a kid. Everybody was there, and everybody was excited. I had never seen anything like that; it was like a miracle. Our landlord helped with the birth, competently and gently. But the most extraordinary thing for me was how fast the small kid got up, wobbling on its spindly legs, and, after a few nudges from his mother, unsteadily took its first steps. The goat mother was so touchingly tender, the kid so helpless, that all were moved to tears.

The second place we lived in was in the remote corner of a yard surrounded by a few houses and other nondescript structures hastily converted into residences. We moved into one of those—a low-ceilinged old stable turned into a dingy bedroom. For a couple of months, this was our abode. I don't remember how many families dwelled on the property, but it was a busy, noisy place. A row of outhouses stretched between our living quarters and the rest of the buildings, and, for some reason, a large, vicious dog was tied up near them. One had to be mindful of the lurking danger while venturing outside and wandering around the outhouses during the hours of darkness. It was a point well proved on the occasion when, in the middle of night, Father had returned from the outside with his pants in tatters. After the initial shock, when it became clear that he had escaped unharmed but for the pants, we had a big laugh and kept making jokes about his nightly adventures.

The last place we lived in was probably where we stayed the longest. This time it was in an old barn, again at the border of the property. Along the rear of the structure, far below, ran one of the village's dirt roads. The window overlooking it was so high that it felt as if we were living at the edge of a precipice. It was an airy, bright place with a cathedral ceiling. Here, as everywhere else, the property included a number of different buildings, and all of them were occupied. In a small shed lived a girl in her late teens. She was friendly and helpful, also slightly retarded. She was a girl from the village, probably related to the landlords.

And while our lives were not easy, suspended in the state of uncertainty and want for almost all material necessities of life, there was something that in better circumstances would be considered a luxury—we had all the time in the world. To pass it, the families organized hiking excursions in the mountains. The children played games in the yard and took care of a bunch of rabbits raised by the owner. We visited each other for talk and tea.

Vladaya was never bombarded, though all the planes going to raid Sofia passed over the village. They circled in the air high above it or flew in the number eight formation. Sometimes they passed quite low, and it was easy to observe them. We were not afraid. There were no targets of strategic value in the village, and nobody thought that the people themselves could be considered such. That complacency, though, had its limitations. We felt safe as long as we remained in the village and did not wander around the hills where there was a danger of being hit by empty fuel barrels that some of the pilots discarded on their way back, or, as it was rumored, some were even dropping their deadly cargo in the mountains rather than on the population. It was a romantic notion and probably utterly false, but it made us feel good. It let us believe that there was still some compassion left in the world.

Father used to visit us on his furloughs, usually after he had been to the office and done some work. On one of those occasions, he had come dressed in civilian clothes, somber and disturbed. He had just survived a particularly intense air raid, hiding in the underground of the Palace of Justice. The impressive, handsome building had been hit several times. A bomb had pierced the top concrete floor; another had entered the basement at a steep angle, killing a man standing next to Father. However the solid structure withstood, and the damage was limited.

Compassion and goodness did exist. And, luckily for me, we found them.
We lived on food rations. There was no milk, cheese, or butter; we survived on beans and sardines. After sharing one of those meals with Mother and Father, I fell sick, became feverish and very weak, and could not get out of bed. The diagnosis was jaundice. Soon I started spitting blood, and the whites of my eyes turned yellow. Mother was out of her mind with worry. There was no medicine, and the doctor said that, unless an injection of calcium could be found to stop the bleeding of the liver, there was nothing she could do. It was up to Mother to do something about it. So she ran out the door, not quite sure where she was going. A neighbor came to watch over me.

Six or seven hours went by before she came back, appearing on the verge of collapse, clutching a box in her hands. The doctor came right away. Without wasting any time, she opened the little package, took out the syringe and needle, assembled them carefully and quickly, and approached the bed, pulling the covers off me. At the sight of the needle, weak as I was, I started screaming and trying to fight off the doctor. Startled, she drew herself up and turned to look at Mother, probably hoping to get some help. With chagrin, she saw her lying limp and listless on the floor: my mother had quietly dropped into a dead faint. Her face was bloodless, and her eyes were closed. The doctor uttered a cry:

"What am I to do now? Whom am I supposed to revive?"

Without so much as a peep, I let her stick the needle in my rump. Slowly, Mother regained consciousness.

Later she told the doctor how she had gotten ahold of the medication.

When she had left the house this morning, Mother had headed straight to the bus station and somehow found transportation for part of the way to the outskirts of Sofia. She had made the rest of the way on foot. There she had spent a few hours running from one pharmacy to another, all to no avail. Remembering a relative who was working at an agency for distributing medical supplies, she had sought him out. However, he could not help either. With no more places left to go and time passing, she had made it back to Vladaya. Then, it had dawned on her that the military hospital had been evacuated to the village, and, with renewed hope, she had run there.

Inside, she had scurried up and down the corridors, accosting anybody who appeared to be a doctor or a nurse. Nobody had paid attention; nobody had wanted to hear her story. Finally, a young man had approached her, inquired what the problem was, and without any hesitation told her to wait, disappearing behind a closed door. Shortly he had returned holding a small box in his hand. He had handed it to Mother. At a loss for words and overwhelmed by this sudden good fortune at the end of a day filled with disappointment and desperation, she had asked him his name. The young man had touched her hand:

"I am just a medical student in my last year, and I am in training here. Please, don't mention what I have done, or I will get into trouble. I hope your girl will be all right."

It took a while for me to get better, spending my time lying in bed and taking a medication that tasted like charcoal.

I had recovered sufficiently to be walking about when we heard a rumor that Tsaritsa Joanna was coming to visit the military hospital. Mother decided that we should go to the village and see her. It had been less than a year since Tsar Boris's death; there was still a great amount of sympathy for the tsar's family, and many came to show it. So did we. We saw her standing in front of the building, surrounded by a large crowd of people.

But we hoped for more.

Mother never went back to the hospital for fear that somehow she might bring harm to the student whom she credited with saving my life. We talked about him often, and I wanted at least to have a look at him. This occasion provided an opportune moment to fulfill my wish. So we searched through the crowd; we lingered until the last man left, but Mother couldn't spot him anywhere.

We remained in Vladaya till the Russians came in September 1944.

The road from Sofia ran into the main street of the village, crossing it from one end to the other. In the center there was a restaurant with a verandah called Tsarevets. At a spot close to it, where the view of the road was unobstructed, we stood and waited to see the Russians. It was curiosity that brought Mother down to join a small crowd of onlookers. There was not much information. Most people did not know what to expect: when they were coming or whether there would be foot soldiers.

A muted thunder announced their approach. A column of tanks was advancing up the road. Disheveled, tired-looking troops, sticking out of the apertures behind the turrets or sitting on top of the tanks, looked down at us. Their uniforms were wrinkled.

A sense of uneasiness came over Mother. She pulled on my hand, and, without waiting to see the end of the filing tanks, started climbing toward our barn-house, scurrying through steep side streets.

By then Father must have been demobilized. He was commuting between Sofia, where he worked, and Vladaya, where he spent the nights with us. The day we saw the Russians, when he arrived from Sofia, he had learned that the soldiers did not move on; they were stationed in the village.

As darkness descended, unusual sounds drifted through the air. There was music, singing, and laughter. With the passing of time, those sounds became louder, clearer, and closer. At one point while this was going on, Father bolted the door, and Mother took a stand by the open window, overlooking the road deep below it.

Laughter and male voices penetrated our barn-house walls. A series of loud bangs shook the door. Father jumped on his feet; Mother grabbed the windowsill as though to go over it. Somebody was shouting persistently in Russian: "Open the door!"

Father threw himself against the wall and started shouting like a mad man: "Woman, give me the gun! Where is my gun? Give it to me, woman!"

Suddenly all went quiet outside. A short conversation in subdued voices followed, and shortly the only sound heard outside was of shuffling feet. Mother moved away from the window. Father relaxed.

We spent the rest of the night sitting on the bed.

In the morning, all was quiet in the yard. The neighbors were moving about their business, as usual, though women kept throwing surreptitious glances toward the shack where the retarded girl lived. She had been heard screaming throughout the night. Finally, someone went to check on her. The door was ajar; the place was empty. She was nowhere to be seen.

The evacuees started packing. The bombing had stopped, and, as far as we were concerned, the war was over. Everybody was ready to go home. So were we.

5

THE DESCENT OF THE IRON CURTAIN

On the first page of our family album was pasted a picture of Clark Gable. He was dressed in a safari outfit, standing between two water buffaloes with huge horns. There were also pictures of Shirley Temple, a few Hollywood actresses who looked to me very much like Mother, and few that did not. In our home, Nelson Eddy and Jeannette MacDonald were household names. The songs from their movie *Maytime* were my parents' favorites. They used to hum them: Father, while shaving, and Mother, whenever she was in a good mood. She sang sensitively and in key; Father sang boisterously and off-key.

Mother loved going to the movies.

After the war, before the Iron Curtain cut us off from the rest of the world, in some respects things went on as before. The movie houses were full; the films were mostly made in Hollywood. I probably saw all of them, or rather I was there, while Mother, mesmerized, was laughing, crying, or suffering quietly. I spent the couple of hours stuck in a seat next to her, too short to see anything; my view obstructed by tall people's heads and all kinds of hats. Films were not dubbed, and only the music made sense to me.

Things really had not changed at all as far as our almost daily trips to the cinemas were concerned. It still used to bother me sometimes when, in the summertime around three o'clock, Mother would show up on the balcony and shout my name. This was the signal to leave all games and get myself upstairs at once, where I was washed up and dressed up, my taffeta bow straightened. Than Mother, also all dressed up, her hair curled and arranged according to the latest fashion, would take firm hold of my hand, and brusquely, sometimes pulling me absentmindedly, would head to the movies.

Nothing could stand in her way of getting into the movie house. Not even the restrictions on some films. A movie with a title roughly translated (from the translation I remember it by) as *The Temptations and Punishments of Sins* was one that fell into that category. Children were not allowed. The day we went to see it, Mother put on a long, loose-fitting coat. A huge crowd was waiting for the next projection. Everybody was cramped into the theater's foyer, and, as soon as the doors to the salon opened, the tightly packed bodies started pushing toward the ushers standing by the gate checking tickets and letting people in. I could hardly breathe, squeezed as I was into skirts, pants, and coats. As we approached the ushers and there was only a short distance left to the door, Mother grabbed me by the shoulders, told me in a whisper to keep quiet, and shoved me under her coat. We passed through the gate, nobody stopped us, and Mother saw the movie.

This was a film I really tried to see—leaning forward, peeking to the left and right of the person in front of me. I even got some glimpses of girls living in dormitories, getting in and out through windows, climbing up and down fire escapes. Sometimes they wore white coats, like nurses' uniforms, and at other times they wore fur coats and very high heels. At the end of the movie, a few of the girls ended up in a hospital where they were given injections. It was scary and depressing.

After the movies we went to Father's office or to Aunt Nina's atelier.

Grandfather Mirko was gone. Now Father shared the office only with his brother Alexander, whom he called Sanyo. Uncle Sanyo was a couple of years older than Father. He was the oldest of the siblings. As children, they were buddies. They played soccer, even founded a local soccer club, which later was absorbed by one of the major clubs, Locomotive. They both went to the same university, both graduating in law. For a while Uncle Sanyo became involved in politics. He achieved certain prominence for which he paid a price; he was imprisoned after September 1944. Once out of prison he went back to practicing law full-time.

He was a very heavy smoker, never taking the cigarette from his mouth. It remained stuck to his lower lip even after it had been reduced to a stub. While talking, he manipulated it dexterously, pressing it against one side of his mouth and talking through the other side. The youngest brother, Liubomir, was away studying medicine in Zagreb. The three of them looked very much alike, except for the hair. Uncle Sanyo's hair wasn't as curly as Father's, and had a forelock hanging over one of his eyebrows. He was quite attractive.

I don't think that the two got along well. Uncle Sanyo was gregarious, danced elegantly, had a good voice, and for a while contemplated a career as an opera singer. He died in his seventies from a heart attack attributed to his heavy smoking.

At the time I am describing, he was just over forty, just out of prison, and apparently unconcerned with his health. Now the office was even darker and the smoke thicker. Father and Uncle seemed to float in a sea of fog. Both were doing their own typing, hunched over the typewriters, banging away on the keys with three fingers.

Most of the time, the office was filled with clients. Their clients were mainly peasants from the surrounding villages. Looking back at these years, it seems odd that this had only been a couple of years away from the time when collectivization of the land was enforced. Great changes had already taken place; unforgettable events had foretold the future. The People's Court had done its dirty work, showing no mercy or any sense of fairness. Still, most refused to see the handwriting on the wall. They were busy buying more property; they were fighting in the courts over disputed strips of land as passionately as ever. It was almost like a frenzy born out of desperate denial.

I did not like going to the office anymore; neither did Mother. We just went out of habit.

Soon, there was a change in Father's professional life. The past was being dismantled. Lawyers could not practice privately any more. The so-called collective firms were created, and all had to join. Father joined Collective 17. Grandfather's office was closed.

I don't know what happened to the furniture from the office, except for a few items. The rocking chair, the clock, and two small paintings ended up with us. A few months later, Father took back the rocking chair and gave it to Uncle Sanyo. That was in keeping with the will: Father was not entitled to any of Grandfather's property. The clock remained and was hanging on the wall of the last apartment we lived in before I left.

Twenty years later when I went back for a visit with my husband and daughter, my parents lived in a different place. The clock was not there, but the pictures were. They were dirty and damaged by the soot from the coal-burning stoves used to heat the apartment for so many years. We took them with us back home to Toronto, got them professionally cleaned, and framed them in gold leaf.

My favorite place to go after the movies was Aunt Nina's atelier.

Aunt Nina was Mother's older sister. She got married late, and, while I was growing up, she always treated me with great affection.

She had a fashion atelier. There were no ready-made clothes available at the time; the alternative was to have them custom-made. Aunt Nina designed ladies' outfits. She cut the material and did the fittings, but the sewing was done by a number of girls working for her. It was a business, and it was thriving. Auntie had a reputation as a good designer. It probably helped that she had graduated from the renowned school Maria Luisa.

The atelier was on Graf Ignatiev Street. It was also close to Slaveikov Square, where one of the most frequented movie houses was situated. The street was narrow, with a tram running so close to the sidewalk that every time the streetcar passed by, people jumped aside, startled.

Aunt Nina lived and worked in her atelier. It was in a house inside a courtyard—access from the street was through an arched passageway. On two sides, the yard was bordered by houses and on the third, by a high brick wall. All day long the trams rattled through the street, running at short intervals in both directions—the noise never stopped. It just varied in intensity. It was probably amplified by a tunnel effect created by the uninterrupted wall of apartment buildings flanking the narrow street on both sides. The courtyard was cut off from the noise and the crowd in the street, and, upon entering it, the sudden transition made me feel I was stepping into a sanctuary. But it turned into quite a different place on one of our regular afternoon visits to Aunt Nina.

I was hanging about, alone in the courtyard, when a boy from one of the houses appeared with a large dog. The dog was a German shepherd, and the boy had him on a leash. People did not keep dogs in the city, and I was not used to being around them. Sensing my fear, the boy started teasing and setting the dog on me. For a while, the agitated animal just kept barking and pulling in my direction, but the leash kept him restrained. It just seemed like a game the boy was in control of. Suddenly, he let the dog off the leash and, frightened out of my wits, I ran, almost flew, out of the courtyard, under the archway, across the street, straight through an open door where I fainted. It was a small confectionery. As I woke up, I saw people hovering over me, whispering, "How lucky! How lucky!" The tram had barely missed me. I hadn't heard it coming.

My aunt's clientele was fascinating. It included the best-known jazz singer, Laya Ivanova, and a few beautiful, elegant women who had an air of ease and confidence about them. Most of them smoked with abandon mannerisms. Among the drab crowds after the war, they sparkled, and it was hard to ignore them. Soon, they were branded as "zozas," and their male counterparts as "swings." Then they began to disappear from the streets, from the concert stages and restaurants where they used to sing or play their instruments. Most of them ended up in Belyane, a concentration camp on an island in the middle of the Danube River. Laya Ivanova, and violin player Sasho Sladura, were the most famous and beloved of all.

Some never came back.

I suppose the category of "swings" was a label for all the young men enamored with the rhythms and energy of the most popular dance music of the time: swing, a direct import from America, via Hollywood.

Uncle Manol was the right age to get caught up in it. Shortly before the end of the war, he had failed in his attempt to enroll in the Military Academy; he had not met one of the physical requirements. Instead, he enrolled in law school, and for a couple of years after the war he was a carefree, happy-go-lucky student, very much taken by jazz and the new fashionable dances. On many occasions, while visiting Aunt Nina's atelier, we would find him there or he would appear later, usually unexpected. And often, without any request or encouragement, he would jump from his chair and start dancing in a small clearing in the room crowded by a large table, screens, and chairs arranged around small round tables covered with piles of French fashion journals. He would be swinging and swirling, gripping the wooden floor with his feet, and moving his arms energetically about, all in sync with the music flowing from the radio. And throughout all that, a happy smile illuminated his handsome face. I remember him acting that way only at the atelier and never when he visited our apartment.

There was something exhilarating at Aunt Nina's—the eternal allure of the mix of fashion, music, and elegant women.

The last time I saw him and we parted forever, he was well into his seventies, a shadow of his former self. I left him sitting on the front seat of his old Mosckvitch, parked in front of the house—his part of the inheritance in Lialintsi—listening to Gershwin's *Rhapsody in Blue*.

A couple of years earlier…

The war was still on. We were in Lialintsi, a village hidden among the hills of a mountain range called Straja, in the shadow of Liubash—a mountain peak that rises high above all the others and hides the world from the village and the village from the world.

It was a rocky and bare place then.

It was also the place of my maternal roots. Her parents kept a house there, and, in the early spring at Aunt Nina's wedding, it was full of people.

The air was fresh, crisp. Spring comes late there.

Aunt Nina was getting married in the small, old church next to the graveyard. The church was only about two hundred meters away from my grandparents' home. "Home" consisted of a couple of houses at the top of a steep yard along the main street, better known as the high road. The new house was a picturesque, whitewashed two-story structure covered with red clay tiles, referred to as Turkish. Its roof extended over a narrow wooden verandah that ran into the wooden staircase, descending along the sidewall of the house and leading into the yard. On the ground floor, a large room called "odaya" that was dominated by a big, open hearth at the far end served as a kitchen. This is where Grandma prepared food during the summer. Next to it, another large, dark room was used for storing a variety of items: iron tools, wooden barrels, copper caldrons, saddles, and other riding paraphernalia. The air was stale and overpowering with the pungent smells of leather, wood, and metal.

Just below the house, under the shade of an old pear tree, were the water well and the large, oval oven. Further down, there was the barn.

All the doors and windows of the house, as well as the balcony, overlooked Liubash.

The other house was a combination of a tavern and a store. There was a third room, off the tavern, for overnight guests. Underneath was the stable. Here Grandfather kept his horses. The entrance to the tavern from the street level was protected by an extension of the roof; wooden posts at both ends, for support and looks, completed the facade. The patio under the protrusion was covered partially by a large, smooth boulder. Mother had vague memories of her grandfather, Toma, spending hours relaxing on its warm, smooth surface during the sunny days of summer. This was also where people from the village, in the grip of painful toothaches, sat waiting for Grandpa Vassil to bring a pair of ordinary pliers to pull their bad teeth.

A stone wall between the two houses, complete with a high wooden gate, hid the interior of the homestead from the street. In summertime, a patch of flowers in splendid colors thrived under its protection, scenting the air with sweetness. And among all this beauty, the most luxurious were the roses.

The yard, a corner, pie-shaped lot, sloped steeply downward, away from the houses. The street, the low road as it was called, that ran on the southwest side, dropped so far below the main street running along the north side that the property had to be fortified by a massive supporting stone wall. There was no protective fence on top of it.

It was quite a thrill to test my courage by going to the edge of the wall and taking a peek down at the low road.

It is impossible to talk about Lialintsi without thinking of Sredoreck, a piece of land that all of Grandfather's descendants identified with.

It lay at the end of the low road. By local standards, it was quite big, almost a recognizable landmark. It brought pride and joy to Grandfather Vassil when he was a young and vigorous man, and solace when he grew older and tired. Then, he built a hut in the heart of it, under the old walnut tree, and retreated among the new apple saplings he had planted to replace the old, diseased plum trees—with their twisted, aged trunks, callous bark, and barren branches. He knew that he would never see the new ones bear fruit, but he nursed them and protected them while the solitude and the tranquility of the place helped his body and soul heal.

Long before that, sometime during the period I am describing, when the plum trees were still healthy and fruitful, we used to go to Sredoreck for a ride or a picnic. The distance from Grandmother's house to the orchard was a couple of kilometers along a rough country road. By foot, the trip was tiresome and long, but riding in Grandfather's cabriolet, wrapped in blankets during the early spring or fall, it was great fun. Sometimes, though, the excitement was more than Mother could take. Uncle Manol—the enthusiastic driver, always willing to hop on the front seat, take hold of the reins, and whip the horse into gallop—was the cause of her anxiety. He was young, a bit wild, and even wicked at times.

As soon as the carriage would leave the yard and turn the corner, he would jump up from his seat, stretch to his full height, and energetically start waving the whip, landing sharp, fast strokes on the horse's back, yelling, and laughing with exhilaration. Meanwhile, Uncle Liubcho, always on the lookout, would appear behind, leaping straight from the yard, and start running as hard as he could after the disappearing cabriolet—his long legs moving ever so fast, his long arms flapping in all directions, and his booming voice beseeching, pleading: "Dadeee, Dadeee! Get off! You will flip over! This crazy man is going to kill you! Dadeee, you will kill the child!" *Dada* was the appellation for older sister in this region, and both uncles addressed Mother and Aunt Nina with it.

The pleas of Uncle Liubcho had no effect. After a while, exhausted and frustrated, he would abandon the chase, stop in the middle of the road, and keep on staring after us, while we continued on our wild ride. Mother's meek attempts to bring an end to it had no effect on Uncle Manol either.

Once, the warnings came true, partially. As we were coming out of a small curve, the cabriolet must have hit a bump or a rock; it shook violently, and Mother and I found ourselves in a shallow ditch by the road. Fortunately, the blankets we were wrapped in softened the impact of the fall. We were shaken, but not hurt.

In the orchard in the summertime, Mother would choose a place where the grass was soft and the ground even. She would throw a blanket there and then tie a hammock between two of the closest trees. Next, she would settle herself comfortably on the blanket, open her book, and become completely absorbed in it—from time to time pulling on a string attached to the hammock to keep it rocking leisurely from side to side. And I would lie in it, quietly and silently, never tiring of the sounds of rustling leaves and humming insects or of observing the patterns of slow-moving clouds passing across the patches of blue sky, showing through the tree branches.

Aunt Nina was getting married to a dashing, tall officer, much younger than herself. He was from the nearby town of Trun. Lots of relatives from both sides had come for the wedding.

Grandfather Vassil looked happy. After all, Auntie was getting on in years, but also, he was pleased with her choice. It was obvious that he was because of his generosity. At the time he had a number of dairies producing Kashkaval. He was going to give each family attending the wedding a cake of it, which was a most sensible, though expensive, way of showing appreciation at a time of food scarcity.

Meanwhile the cheese was stored in a room somewhere in the house, and its sharp smell permeated the air all over.

Father was there also. His thoroughly urbane personality made him seem out of place in the rural setting. Going to a picnic or even on a hiking trip, he never dressed other than the way he dressed every day going to work: in a business suit, shirt, and tie. The most casual I had ever seen him was, when feeling particularly relaxed, he would loosen the knot of his tie and unbutton the collar of his shirt. Then he would run his finger along the edge of his collar, and after few movements of his neck he would grin, indicating how comfortable he felt. It took a game of soccer to make him take off his jacket, throw the tie away, and dash after the football—the ball rolling between his fast-moving feet and his dress pants flapping around his ankles.

In Lialintsi he looked even more out of his element, uneasy and uncomfortable, looking for a way to get away from the hubbub that did not cease for a moment. So, when the opportunity presented itself, he was ready to take it.

Life in the village must not have changed much since the previous century. There was no electricity, and the only light indoors came from oil lamps. Oil was in short supply but much needed during the long evenings spent in the general excitement and merriment preceding such a happy occasion.

Somebody had to go and buy some from a village that lay on the main road, about five kilometers away, across a steep, bare, snow-covered expanse. There was no road to speak of, connecting Lialintsi with the rest of the world. People traveling on foot followed steep paths cut through the meadows or around the fields. For a stranger, at this time of the year, under the white blanket of snow, they might as well not have existed at all.

But Father was adamant, insisting that he could negotiate his way.

He left early in the morning, carrying an empty demijohn in each hand: one for the oil and one for the plum brandy, also in short supply.

The day passed, and he was not back. Twilight turned into a deep darkness, and he was still missing. Outside, all the noises of everyday life had died away; calm descended over the village, and the crispness of the air sharpened. Occasionally, the silence was broken by a dog's bark.

The tension in the house was growing. Mother and Grandmother kept stepping outside, listening for sounds, and looking at shadows. There was nothing for a very long time.

Finally, cracking sounds of tentative, insecure steps over the frozen ground drifted in. Someone rushed to open the door, and there was Father, the two demijohns in his hands, eyes glazed over, a deadly pallor covering his face. Somebody else took the jugs from his hands, helped him take off his coat, and cleared a place for him to sit down.

Father reeked of oil and brandy.

The story he related was nothing short of a fairy tale to me, which I listened to with fear and fascination. However, most of the other people's reactions were quite different. The grins that appeared on their faces throughout the narrative turned into suppressed giggles, and Mother's anxiety at the beginning of the story transformed itself first into relief and finally into vexation.

There was nothing remarkable in the first half of Father's trip. He had had no problem getting to his destination or finding and buying the oil and brandy. But all had started to go wrong on his way back; he had lost his way in the unfamiliar, vast, empty field. Lialintsi lay in a hollow on the northern mountain skirt, completely hidden from his view—the barren landscape devoid of any signs pointing to the location of the village. Disoriented and confused, he had walked for hours. Darkness had descended. Long-drawn howls had started coming from all sides. Fast-moving silhouettes had appeared, darting in all directions across the snow.

It was not unusual for wolves to roam the area.

To fortify himself against his fear and to alleviate his fatigue, Father had begun sipping from the brandy. It seemed that at one point he had drunk from the wrong jug.

Toward the end of the narrative, he became his normal self. He was exhausted, but relaxed. As soon as we went to bed, he fell into a sound sleep that lasted all night, while Mother kept checking on him, worried that he had poisoned himself.

The next morning, Aunt Nina and Uncle Hristo got married.

It was a bright, fresh morning. Auntie was dressed in a long white dress with a dark brown mink coat on top. She looked radiant and beautiful. My uncle-to-be was wearing his military uniform, tall, young, and strapping. In the bright sunshine, the whole wedding party, relatives and guests, walked to the small white church with the red roof.

A few months later, in the summer, I spent a couple of weeks with the newlyweds in Trun. Uncle Hristo was stationed there.

The town of Trun is situated in a small, deep valley, surrounded by mountains. The border with Serbia is only a short distance away. There had always been a military presence there, and, at times, access to Trun and the area around it had been restricted.

The Erma River passes through the city, and, a few kilometers downstream, it had sheared off the mountain, creating a breathtaking gorge. At its most spectacular point, the river at the bottom of the narrow, deep canyon can be heard. Only the sound of the fast-running water, bouncing off the cliffs on both sides, reaches up the open space. The almost-vertical walls are devoid of any vegetation. The area above the canyon is no more than a wider gorge, defined by steep mountains, receding just far enough to allow for a road to run along the banks of the Erma. Wild goats roam the steep mountain skirts; the scent of wild flowers and bushes hangs in the still air—confounded, trapped.

In one of the corners of the town square in Trun stands a monument erected in memory of the dead soldiers from the Serbo-Bulgarian War of 1885. The streets leading to and from the square run up and down the hillsides, lined by houses that from a distance seem to be standing on top of each other.

In one of these houses lived Aunt Nina and Uncle Hristo. He was the commanding officer of a military detachment in Trun. Auntie was playing the role of a housewife, making jams and cooking. She organized picnics and hiking excursions for the neighborhood kids and me. We went picking small, dark red roses (trendafil) that grew along the rocky paths, exuded a sweet musty aroma, and from whose petals Aunt Nina made jam.

Some days we went out late in the evening to hunt fireflies. We carried jars and matchboxes to keep the ones we captured.

On our visits to Aunt Nina's atelier, we never saw Uncle Hristo. For a while he just vanished.

After September 1944, Bulgaria joined the Allies and went on with the war fighting the Germans. Uncle Hristo enlisted with the Second Army, which distinguished itself in the Battle at Stratzin. It was a fierce one, with numerous casualties. Uncle Hristo fought there. But there was more—a story that stuck in my mind.

Uncle Hristo had fought at Stratzin next to his brother. At one point during the battle, he had spotted his brother sprawled on the ground, bleeding. In a mad dash, abandoning the fight, he had rushed to his aid. He had grabbed his wounded, listless body, thrown it on his back, and started running across the battlefield, searching for help, only to discover when he found it that his brother had been beyond help: he had been dead for quite a while.

On his return from the front, his bravery and sacrifice at Stratzin saved him from death—the fate that befell all officers from the Tsar's Army. It was not enough, though, to save him from the concentration camp or from a lifetime of heavy manual work in a cement factory.

Before becoming an officer, Uncle Hristo was a math teacher.

Under the Communist regime, when censorship ruled supreme, many things that happened during that time were better left forgotten, pushed away from people's memories. And when bits and pieces of events, not supposed to be discussed, were whispered, the stories perpetuating them came out distorted or ridden with falsehoods. The story of Uncle Hristo and his brother could well have been one of them.

I can't find anybody to corroborate the story about what happened at Stratzin now. All witnesses are gone. His sons, both born after the war, seem utterly ignorant about their parents' past. Aunt Nina had succeeded remarkably well in her zealous desire to protect them—what they did not know could not hurt them—or, in fairness to her, it simply could have been their lack of interest.

Still, I have believed it for so many years, and I like it so much that I had to tell it. It is the story of a hero, of Uncle Hristo as I prefer to remember him—before he was punished as a villain—as a sensitive and kind man and not as the man he became after, the brooding loner, irritable and hard to get along with, who liked to spend his free time in solitude, roaming the familiar mountains accompanied only by a dog and a hunting rifle.

Before the American movies disappeared from the movie screens, before all windows and doors looking toward the West closed, small cracks were opened and people, finally sensing that irrevocable change was about to occur, flocked like birds ready to fly away, frantically applying for immigration visas to the United States. The location where the applications were distributed was beseeched by mobs. It was not at the American embassy, though. That embassy, located opposite the National Assembly behind the monument of the Tsar Liberator, had been completely destroyed by bombs during the raids. Only its curved facade had survived. Rows of windows had been blown away, and, through the gaping holes, the piles of rubble almost two stories high, clearly visible from the street, remained there for years to come.

In an effort to bring some order to the situation, officials started distributing numbers to the crowd of would-be applicants. Without even consulting with Father, Mother went and picked up one.

It was a high number, and our turn never came.

The last movie Mother took me to was *The Swineherd and the Shepherd*. It was also the first Soviet movie we saw. It was about the romance between a female swineherd and a shepherd boy working on a cooperative farm somewhere in the Soviet Union.

The main characters were wholesome, politically enlightened peasants, who overcame all difficulties in their relationship and went on to become overachievers in fulfilling the Five-Year Economic plan toward building the socialist order.

The negative characters were reactionary, greedy kulaks, without any social consciousness.

The movie production and the artistic performances conformed to socialist realism.

6

THE PARTISANS

First came the Red Army, then came the partisans. They marched in fatigues, backpacks, and submachine guns called "shmizers" hanging over their shoulders, cartridge belts around their waists, and cartridge bands crisscrossing their chests. Some had adorned themselves with foliage and flowers, symbolizing the name they were called by: "shumkar"—a derivative from the word shuma (greenery, leaves) They were smiling and looking victorious, as well as better clothed and fed than most of the people cheering them.

Their ranks had swelled in the past couple of months before the events of September 9, 1944. Many, anticipating the coming developments, took the opportunity to achieve a fast and easy glory.

The partisans.

From time to time, I think about what I had seen and heard and the little I had witnessed during the time they were roaming the countryside of the western region. On September 9, 1944, they seemed to have been the only force with a legitimate claim to the title of fighters and winners for the Communist cause. They seemed to be the power that would succeed the ousted regime. After all, they had already fought, and some had given their lives for the cause. Slavcho Trunski was for Bulgaria what Tito was for Yugoslavia.

As it turned out, the partisans became totally irrelevant in the political life of the country. Their struggles and sacrifices were used for propaganda, for creating heroes, and, most of the time, preferably, dead ones. They were especially useful in the business of brainwashing the young generations.

Slavcho Trunski did not get very far or very high. He was pushed almost into oblivion, and, when he was imprisoned for a while, it hardly made a ripple outside the internal political circles.

There was one beneficial result of the Partisan Movement in the lives of the people living in the beautiful but poor western region—many of them received and lived on high government pensions and countless privileges as collaborators to the partisans. And it was not hard to prove that either. There were only two categories of people there: the collaborators and the noncollaborators, and of the latter, hardly anybody survived the arrival of the new order.

Another legacy of this brief, shining moment for the Communist movement was that all subsequent leaders of the Party had to have a few months of obligatory participation in partisan action somewhere. Thus, after several years, a picture began to emerge—there was not a single mountain, hill, or a forest where dedicated, politically ambitious apparatchiks had not claimed to have spilled some blood.

About forty-five kilometers west of Sofia, on the road to Trun, lies the town of Breznik. From this point on, the western horizon fills up with a never-ending chain of rising ground, hills, and mountains, growing in height and loftiness. Fifteen kilometers farther, to the left of the main road, Liubash towers over the landscape. From there, the view ahead is rather imposing—the mountains grow rugged; their peaks are bare, rocky, and inhospitable.

And somewhere, a few kilometers farther west, lies the border. For the outsider there is no natural divider to suggest where it is, but, from afar, the local people can identify every hill and valley and on which side of the border it lies. Here, in these mountains shared by two countries, the most sustained partisan activities in Bulgaria took place for a couple of years.

The big struggle was on the Yugoslavian side where the partisans were fighting the Germans tooth and nail. On the Bulgarian side, the numbers were much smaller; the activity was limited mainly to the killing of political adversaries or suspected informers. Few sabotage actions were carried out. The partisans moved freely across the difficult and in some places inaccessible terrain, crisscrossing the border. There was not a massive effort by the government to eliminate them completely but rather to contain their activities. From time to time, there were punitive strikes against them carried out by special army units. Atrocities were committed against some collaborators.

The most famous personality that emerged from this movement was Slavcho Trunski. He was from the town of Trun. In this sparsely populated place, it was no wonder that everybody knew him and that he knew everybody who had a claim on being somebody. He was something of a warlord in the region, and people treated him as such. For an outsider, the relationship between the partisans and the peasants was enigmatic.

As a girl of six or seven, I saw live and dead partisans; I heard whispered rumors of senseless cruelties; I heard stories about Slavcho Trunski's personal life; and I could never see a clear line of loyalties that explained or made any sense of the things that were going on.

One of these puzzles was an account of something that had happened to my grandfather Vassil. Late one night, a neighbor had snuck inside my grandparent's house in Lialintsi. She had whispered to my grandmother that she was bringing a message from Slavcho Trunski: "Tell Vassil Tomov from Lialintsi that tomorrow night I am coming to get him." There had been no questions asked or explanations offered. News and messages traveled mysteriously.

Grandfather had gotten dressed, picked up his pistol, and disappeared in the darkness. The next night, Slavcho had come accompanied by a couple of partisans. Grandmother was alone. "Vassil is not at home, and I don't know where he is." She had been telling the truth.

"Tell him that I will be back." It must have sounded quite ominous.

Upon hearing this, Grandfather had taken some money and clothes, had mounted his horse, and had ridden off again. This time he had stayed away for a long time, probably hundreds of kilometers east of the area.

Mother mentioned, on occasion, that he had gone as far as Varna by the Black Sea, running from the lawlessness in the region. It could have been at this instance that he traveled there, or later, during the uncertain, troubled times in the fall of 1944.

Over thirty years later, I heard an almost identical story that had happened at about the same time in a place a few kilometers northeast of Lialintsi. A similar message had been delivered to Simo Yakimov, my future father-in law. He had spent the night of the expected visit hidden in the hay in the barn, clutching a pistol in his hand. His wife and seven children had been in the house, only a few meters away from the barn. When the partisans had come inquiring as to the whereabouts of Simo from Zavala, all except his wife kept stubbornly silent. His wife had kept insisting, "I don't know. I have no idea."

On one of our brief visits to Lialintsi, quite unexpectedly, I saw a partisan. He was standing almost in the middle of the village, by a water fountain, in broad daylight. The village stood at the dead end of the road, and nobody passed through it, except on the way up or down the mountain. Strangers were easy to spot: this one was a tall man, wearing glasses and dressed in fatigues with a backpack slung over his shoulder. He looked like a schoolteacher.

The streets were empty. We had gone for a walk to the fountain, and, by the time we noticed him, it was too late to turn around. Mother squeezed my hand, and that alerted me to take a good look at him. In a casual way, he asked for directions, then produced a canteen, filled it with water, and unhurriedly, with even strides, went on his way.

Back in the house, still a bit shaken, Mother said, "There was a partisan by the watering fountain."

Nobody looked surprised or alarmed.

Cruelty shocks—only most people are spared the horror of witnessing it directly, for usually it is executed in dark places behind high walls or barbed wires. But when it is displayed in the sunlight, in a green place where birds are singing and wild flowers are growing, it makes one scream.

We were traveling in a horse-driven cabriolet along a country road, heading for the town of Breznik. All around us were green fields. Just past a curve, a row of tall willow trees with wide, pale green crowns dominated the view. On the other side of the road, opposite them, stood a small brick building, the canton of Bukova Glava. The canton was on a major intersection of roads that fanned out in different directions, each leading to a cluster of villages. And the traffic from all these places passed through Bukova Glava.

As we turned the curve, a large wooden sign, stuck by the side of the road, attracted our attention. The driver pulled the reins, bringing the horse almost to a stop. In bold letters and in thick black strokes was written: "Warning! This is the fate waiting those who collaborate with the Americans!"

Behind the sign, a meadow covered in high grass gradually sloped downward from the road. At the bottom were the willow trees seen from afar, branches spread wide and high. Up among the branches hung three bodies upside down, ropes wound around their ankles, hands tied behind their backs. All were in their underwear. Two of them had their undershirts on; one was bare-chested. They were young men, probably in their twenties. Their bodies looked small, shriveled. Large red spots marked the places where the bullets had hit them.

Under the trees, among the grass, to the left of the thicket, lay the fully-clad body of another man. He had a cap on his head; he looked large and heavy, his arms and legs spread-eagle in the rich, marshy verdure.

It took only seconds to take the picture in. Then we glanced back to the sign and the armed policeman standing by it, glaring back at us. Mother let out a heavy moan, at the sound of which the driver pulled hard on the reins and the horse leapt forward, fleeing from the gruesome tableau displayed in the beautiful meadow.

After a long silence, without looking at us, the driver said: "The policemen are there to make sure that nobody removes the bodies. They have been hanging there for a while. The guy in the grass was shot this morning."

7
STARTING GRADE SCHOOL

In the fall of 1944, a new, regular school year started.

During the last couple of years of the war, life in Sofia had become chaotic and unpredictable. Most of the activities characterizing our daily lives before were disrupted, suspended. The school system was affected also. It did not cease to function completely—only, it continued to exist in a rather symbolic way. There was very little teaching or learning going on. Ultimately, all instructional activities were suspended, and the schools were put to a different use—determined by the needs of the military.

For a while, education lost its priority in people's lives.

In the last school year prior to the end of the war, my parents enrolled me in the kindergarten class at the Catholic school Santa Maria. On my first visit there, Mother and I were given a tour of the premises by one of the nuns running the establishment. Then I was taken to a classroom full of toys and children and left there for a while to get acquainted with my future classmates. However, before I could start attending regularly, the school was closed—presumably because of the raids.

Next, I was enrolled in the public school close by, which I attended for a short while. On a couple of occasions, though, my daily walk to the school was interrupted by the frightful sound of the anti-aircraft sirens that sent me running straight back home. That really put a damper on my enthusiasm for education and brought an end to any further attempts at regular schooling.

Mother tried to keep me occupied by making me draw apples and pears. I went further than that by drawing colorful butterflies on the underside of the seats of all of our kitchen chairs.

So, in the fall of 1944, I started school as a member of the first generation to be educated under the new system.

And the system was changing fast.

Right away, instructions in religion were eliminated. That pleased some people. Soon, profound changes in the official literary language were introduced: harder sounds rooted in western dialects were replaced by softer ones from the eastern regions. Letters were dropped from the alphabet.

The border between Macedonia and Bulgaria was drawn into the language.

The new, softer speech sounded affected. For fun, we exaggerated the new pronunciations, accompanying them by gestures and grimaces of mock refinement and pretentiousness. In time, we were told to drop Mrs., Miss, and Mr. and address our teachers with the new egalitarian "comrade" that made everybody feel uncomfortable, students as well as teachers. It blurred the line of distinction, even though the roles remained the same.

Old holidays were scrapped; new ones were introduced. Old heroes were renounced; new martyrs were created. Old songs were forbidden; new ones were written.

Teachers, parents, and students were confused.

Yet the war was over, and we were taking everything in stride.

We lived on rations for food and clothing. For the children, the worst-felt shortage was for shoes. Our feet kept growing; and the soles of the old shoes got ever so thin. Layers and layers of folded newspapers helped get one through a block or two, but, once soaked with moisture, they started to fall apart and formed uncomfortable lumps of sodden paper inside our shoes.

A couple of times inspectors came to the school. In the classrooms, lessons were interrupted, and we were told by the teachers to stretch our legs and lift our feet. Everybody's soles were carefully examined by the governmental officials, and authorized notes were given to the worst cases. With them we could go and pick up a new pair of shoes from designated stores at a price set by the government. In the spring, we could buy sandals with wooden soles made of slats, each about two centimeters wide, the uppers made of canvas. The way the slats were arranged and attached to each other gave them a flexibility that made them quite comfortable. But they were noisy. Throughout the summer, the streets resounded with the loud clatter of wood beating against the flagstone-covered sidewalks; the noise grew to a crescendo in the parks and schoolyards where children congregated to play run and catch.

Back in school, we were learning more than reading and writing. Our teacher decided to organize a drama group and stage a play *Tatuncho and Dorotea*. I was cast as a pumpkin. Dressed in a round, bright, orange-yellow costume made of cardboard with two spindly legs sticking from the bottom and my head sticking from the top, in a thin and shaky voice, I had to recite, "I am the pumpkin…" The rest I have completely forgotten. I never liked my lines and had a hard time remembering them even then. In fact, I never liked the role of the pumpkin. I wanted to play Dorotea.

It was not long after the beginning of the school year that I started scratching my head incessantly. It took a while for Mother to notice, but when she did, it seemed she knew right away what was the matter. After a brief check of my scalp, the panic set in; the delousing started—scrubbing, cleaning, washing. I was not the only one to have lice. (The school was infested with vermin, brought in by the soldiers who had lodged there earlier.)

Eventually a team of fumigators was brought in, and they got rid of them.

On my graduation from grade two, Father took me to a small arcade called St. Nicola, right in the center of the city. The devastation caused by the bombardments was obvious all around. The heart of the city had been heavily damaged, and the ruins had not yet been cleared away. In contrast, the small, open arcade was bright and full of life. Flower shops displaying their colorful merchandise outside on wooden shelves or in pails cluttering the sidewalk encircled the grounds.

Father selected a bouquet of tall, delicately pink gladiolas and presented them to me. Then he hired a horse-driven phaeton and took Mother and me to a small place outside the city, famous for its grill. There we met Aunt Desha and Uncle Otto with cousins Bobby and Chris.

For me, the treat was the ride rather than the food. I kept clutching the bouquet in my arms, feeling the sunshine and the breeze on my face, listening to the rhythmic beat of the horse's hooves on the surface of the road. My parents were beside me. They looked content—I felt how proud of me they were. And I loved them even more for that.

Our meeting with Aunt Deshas at the inn must have been prearranged.

And that reminds me of the unique way in which we used to communicate. At those times, telephones were not a part of the lifestyle of the majority of people. They were considered a luxury. Only a very few lucky families had private lines.

We lived in the same neighborhood as Aunt Deshas. Both our families lived on the top floors of our respective buildings, and had balconies facing each other at an angle. The distance was considerable, and it was impossible to hear each other, no matter how loud one might shout. But the view between the balconies was unobstructed; only courtyards and low buildings stood between them. Our balcony faced west and theirs south. On a sunny day, it was easy to send a signal by catching the sunrays and beaming their reflection in the right direction. This simple lesson in applied physics became the inspiration for devising a system of exchanging messages. Unfortunately, it had its drawbacks—patience and skill were required for manipulating the mirrors, and, of course, it did not work at all times. On gloomy, rainy days, one might say our lines of communication were cut.

Maybe on that day we had used the mirror to signal a meeting at the inn; I am not sure. I remember that day as brilliantly bright and sunny, but then, it was also such a happy day. And the sunshine that we associate with times like that has much less to do with the weather conditions than with the way we felt.

The apartment building we lived in at the time was inhabited by Bulgarian, Jewish, Armenian and a young Turkish family that lived on the mezzanine floor. The husband was an attaché at the Turkish embassy, and his wife, Lehman, was a kind but sad woman. They had a small boy.

A couple of blocks east of our street was the district with the highest concentration of Jews. The synagogue was also there, close to the mosque and the church Sveta Nedelia. They spoke Yiddish. Many were well educated, and most of them were worldly. I never saw an Orthodox Jew or heard the word *kosher,* and I would not have recognized a menorah if I had seen one. Religion was taboo, and that made us all the same on the surface. Our spiritual needs and moral indoctrination had been taken care of by the new ideology and its high priests.

In our apartment building and in the one next to it, on the south side, lived Percy, Nicky, Rosy, and Meddy. Percy was a thin, dark boy whose looks fit my notion of a romantic hero. He played the accordion, so, on my only birthday celebration during this time, he provided the music, while, under Mother's and Aunt Nina's watchful eyes, half a dozen boys and girls tried to master the waltz. Nicky was short and fat; we called him "fatso." And even though we were not starving, there could have been more envy than cruelty toward the only overweight child in the neighborhood. Rosy and Meddy were sisters. Rosy was the older one, darker and taller; Meddy was delicate and petite, with reddish, curly hair and a freckled face. She used to wear pretty handmade tops with the front sides crossing over and buttoned to the back under the arm. Her grandmother knitted them.

In our building also lived a childless couple. The wife's name was Sonya. All the children called her Aunt Sonya. She spent her days mainly inside the apartment and now and then used to invite us to keep her company. Her place was sparkling clean and frightfully orderly. Along one of the kitchen walls stood a buffet with a hutch on top that had many drawers. Each drawer had a key sticking out of the keyhole, and each key had a pink ribbon tied to it. The large bed in the bedroom was covered with a perfectly smooth bedspread in the middle of which was seated a beautiful doll made of celluloid and clad in a resplendent dress, arranged carefully about it. On the wall over the bed was displayed a colorful skirt in a circle, undoubtedly part of the national costume of a northern district.

On the twenty-fourth of May, the day of the Cyrillic alphabet, she used to take the skirt off the wall and lend it to one of the girls to wear at the parade. Each marching unit started with the students dressed in national costumes, followed by the athletes dressed in shorts and sleeveless tops. Intermittently, the columns came to a stop, and the students dressed in national costumes performed a short folk dance while the athletes did a few exercises.

The year before we went our different ways, Aunt Sonya gave the pleated, embroidered skirt to Rosy. She told me that the following year, when I'd be grown up and could fit in it, she would lend the skirt to me. This is what I remember about Rosy.

In the spring of 1948, the neighborhood turned into a flea market for a while. The front doors of all the apartment buildings were wide open during the day, and streams of people wandered up and down the stairways leading to the homes of the Jewish families selling their furniture. They were getting ready to immigrate to Israel.

At the time I did not understand why they were leaving. As for the children from our buildings, we never said good-bye, and I have no recollection of any particular moment when they went away. Later, I remembered them like any other children that came in and out of my life, with the difference that I thought they were lucky. I kept thinking for quite a while about Percy and Meddy.

8

MOVING TO A NEW PLACE, NEW SCHOOL

At the end of the summer of 1948, we moved to a different place in one of the best areas of the city, sometimes referred to as the Diplomatic District. Along its tree-lined, quiet streets, large foreign banners designating the many embassies located in the area hung from protruding flag polls attached to the window frames or the balconies of old elegant mansions surrounded by high wrought-iron fences.

At the heart of the neighborhood was a small park—the Doctor's Garden—and, at the heart of it, was a monument dedicated to the memory of the medical doctors killed in battles during the Liberation War of the nineteenth century. Their names were inscribed on the faces of the rough-edged rectangular stones that covered the four sides of the monument—one name per stone.

The park was a peaceful place: benches lined curved paths running under a canopy of greenery; two wooden pavilions provided a shelter on a rainy day—or simply a place of privacy—a reminder of a more genteel way of life in days gone by.

The streets around it were straight and short, with rows of trees on both sides. Their wide crowns reached toward each other, forming leafy archways that threw deep shadows over the roads, keeping them cool all summer long. It was a tranquil and secluded neighborhood.

We lived on the boundary of the district, on the boulevard that ran along one of the two rivers crossing Sofia—though it was only on rare occasions after a big rainstorm that the narrow, murky stream of water lived up to its repute. Then the water became a torrent, filling the wide space between the high stone-covered banks, spilling through the evergreen hedges, over the green strips of grass on both sides, and, finally, flooding the street and the sidewalks. At times like that, it was a powerful, almost-uncontrollable force of nature, but most of the time it was nothing more than a canal with rats scurrying under the bridges.

Opposite our apartment, across the river, was the Military Academy. All that was visible from the street was woodland covered with trees and dark green creeping undergrowth. The fence along the street was made of old rifles aligned vertically and joined together by horizontal iron bars.

But the most remarkable feature of our street was the rows of very tall trees towering above the grassy strips and narrow paved paths on both sides of the river. They were called Canadian poplars. The dark green, shiny leaves never stood still. They shimmered and rustled with the slightest breeze. In the calm and quiet, their whispers were mysterious and enchanting.

I used to listen to them for hours.

In the summer, when the heat was at its peak, when everybody was hiding inside and the street seemed deserted, this same relentless sound, intensified by the loneliness, became depressing and filled me with anxiety. But that feeling never stopped me from loving them. Their unsettling hiss was the background music that highlighted the drama of the most memorable moments of our lives there.

The new school I was going to attend was located at the intersection of two streets: Aprilov and Shipka. The latter, a fairly long one that started right at the portal doors of the Military Academy, crossed the river, climbed westward to the south side of the Doctor's Garden, and ended by the University of St. Clement of Ochrid.

The school building was old and big on the outside, and old and dark on the inside. On the second floor was the salon—a big room with a high ceiling, a raised stage, and a heavy curtain. The main staircase connecting all the floors was also old and made of wood. The stairs and the wooden floors in the hallways emitted loud, squeaky noises under our running feet.

The schoolyard was quite large. A very tall iron fence ran along the two sides bordering the streets. And in the corner of the yard was a large wooden pavilion, a bench built around the inside. By the main gate stood a small house for the caretaker, and, not far from it, a modest monument to the patron of the school, Aprilov.

On the first day of school, I made a happy discovery: one of my classmates, a pleasant girl called Annie, lived in the same building as me. I thought I had found a friend. We started walking back and forth to school together. This lasted for a week or so, until one day Annie disappeared. She lived on the floor above us, but, being new to the neighborhood, we did not know much about anybody. Besides, people kept their distance. When I started asking about her at school, the answer was silence or quick, surreptitious glances that seemed to say, "Are you stupid! Don't you know?" There was a sense of conspiracy in the air, and everybody was part of it but me. Finally, somebody told me that Annie's family had been interned. They had been sent to a small place, far away from Sofia. She never came back.

Music occupied a special place in our school life. Many played instruments, and any who could carry a tune sang in the choir. The school wind band marched ahead of the columns of students during parades. Almost everybody appreciated music, and anybody who excelled in playing a musical instrument or singing was considered special.

Our room teacher, Miss Kostova, was soft-spoken, sensitive, and sentimental. She doted on a boy, Yavor, who was the best violin player at the school. One of my most pleasant memories was listening to Yavor playing in the wooden pavilion on a lovely spring day. Miss Kostova had asked him to bring his violin to school and announced that on that day, instead of our regular class inside, we would have a concert outside. Yavor stood for a long time playing piece after piece while we listened intently. Our teacher seemed most affected by the music, transported to another place or time, which we were too young to know or understand.

Fourteen years later, I heard Yavor play again. It was in a noisy, smoke-filled restaurant. He was playing with a small orchestra, the music drowned out by the clatter of cutlery and the chatter of people involved in endless discussions that sounded more like arguments. It was hard to hear the music.

But it was his choice. At the end of his university education, after graduating with a degree in engineering, instead of going for the compulsory three-year placement to a remote, provincial town, Yavor made his choice—he formed an orchestra, probably forsaking the degree that would have taken six years to earn. This was the price he had to pay.

No wonder. We all considered the three years as banishment, and any alternative that allowed us to remain in Sofia was deemed worthy of sacrifices.

The war had been over for more than four years, but the scars were still there: piles of rubble or craters created by bombs and shortages of food and clothing. We still lived on rations for some of the necessities. At school, during the long break, we were given a breakfast of powdered milk and buttered bread. Some of the food was unfamiliar to us. I still can't figure out what kind of spreads we were given: peanut butter, coconut butter? We got used to them and even got to like them. The food was donated by one international organization or another.

There was a general goods store on the next street that ran parallel to ours. It looked enormous with its empty shelves and counter. Older people, ever-ready with shopping bags in their hands, used to peek in or take a step inside several times a day in the hope of catching the moment of delivery of sugar or oil. Telephones were a rarity, but news traveled remarkably fast. It took merely a few minutes for a queue to form after the delivery truck was spotted. Usually, it was old people and children who had to endure hours of an exhausting wait in line. Sometimes, another member of the family would come and take a turn for a while. It was not unusual to see people fainting or starting to cry from frustration.

There was no choice but to line up and wait for the essentials; however, there were times when people simply joined a line as soon as they saw one, and only after that started inquiring what there was to be bought. Finding and buying food, preserving it, and cooking it imaginatively, would occupy a lot of time. Food was constantly on people's minds.

Mother used to tell me that before the war I used to eat bananas, oranges, and chocolates, and loved them. She asked me if I remembered, but I did not. As I grew more and more tired of the monotony of our meager diet and as Mother grew more and more frustrated with my leanness, I started thinking, "If only there were bananas, oranges, and chocolates…" So, when the first bananas were imported and the rumor spread that some were coming to the store, we were there. I don't remember how long we had to wait, but I remember that they were rationed. We took home only three or four. They looked very small, and Mother looked a bit surprised and confused. On testing them, the disappointment was great—they were dry, bread-like, tasteless. I think that, in romanticizing the past, Mother had been too lavish in her praise and not specific or accurate in the details. I was left with the impression that bananas were succulent and juicy.

The first time I remember having a chocolate, the experience was quite different.

We lived on the parterre of the apartment building. There were two apartments per floor. When we first moved, the one next to us was officially unoccupied, or rather, the occupants were not officially there. People went in and out late at night or very early in the morning. They were brought in and driven away in cars, another very unusual sight. There was something forbidding about all the goings-on, and people avoided looking at the place as though it did not exist—or if they bumped into someone going in or coming out of the place, they passed them as though they were invisible.

The backyard of our apartment building was partially covered with flagstones and fenced off by a brick wall—the plaster covering it crumbling. Spots of sickly grass, unattended by anybody, persisted, pushing through the hard soil all over the rest of the yard. An elevated platform, also covered with flagstones, stood at the farthest corner—a crossbar mounted between two iron posts. Early in the mornings, usually on Sundays, women took out a variety of kilims and covers, threw them over the crossbar, and started beating them with sticks, which they manipulated by taking wide swings backward onto the stiff surface of the heavy rugs, expelling gray balls of dust.

The courtyard was also the center of activities for the children from the immediate neighborhood. We played hide-and-seek, tug of war, hopscotch, and ball before and after school and all day long on holidays.

One quiet afternoon, when nobody was hanging laundry or gathering it, nobody was washing or tidying the kitchen balconies and the backyard looked deserted—except for me, hanging around, hoping that someone would show up—a woman stepped out on the balcony of the next-door apartment. She motioned for me to approach her. It took me a while to move, but eventually, curiosity won over apprehension, and I walked the distance separating me from her. She bent over the balcony and handed me a bar wrapped in fancy paper, then turned around and went in without giving me a chance to thank her or making an attempt to start a conversation. When I showed the bar to Mother, she took it in her hand, turned it around a few times, tried to read the foreign label, and gave it back to me, saying, "It is a chocolate. Eat it."

I peeled the wrapper at one corner, pulled back the shiny paper, took a small bite, carefully rewrapped it, and put it my pocket. It took me a long time to finish the chocolate. Every sweet little bite was as satisfying as a promise fulfilled.

Not long after, the people from next door disappeared altogether, as surreptitiously as they had appeared. A family moved in. It was rumored that the mysterious people were Greek Communist partisans, fighting in the ongoing civil unrest in their country. The sick and wounded were smuggled out of the country and taken to safe countries and places, like the apartment next door. Here they were nursed and cared for till they recuperated.

The woman who gave me the chocolate must have been one of the nurses.

At home, things were looking good; we were optimistic. The winds of war had died down, and everything appeared to be getting back to normal. In the villages people were buying and selling land. Father was working harder than ever: he was one of the tops.

At some time during the years he had been mobilized, he had sold his inheritance—an apartment in the fourplex in Grandfather's domain. In spite of the will, he was not completely disinherited—that would have been against the law. The apartment on top belonged to his sister, my oldest aunt. Pressed for money, he sold it to Aunt Julia without even telling Mother about it. The resentment that he probably felt about the way he came to own it must have made it easier for him to sell it. But Mother never accepted the fact—she thought it was not fair that Father had been taken advantage of instead of being given a helping hand in difficult situation.

Now he had collected the sum of money he had been paid for the property and, with the cash in hand, approached Aunt Julia, asking her to sell it back to him. Her answer was that the decision to accept or reject the offer should be made by a family council.

I was told much later that Grandmother and all Father's siblings had been present, and it had been decided that his sister had bought it fair and square. Furthermore, the argument had been presented that since she had two children, she needed two apartments. I was out of the picture.

In the long run, it turned out all right for me, but, after that event, Father never set foot in his father's house again, and Mother never forgot or forgave.

9

GRANDFATHER VASSIL. THE ESTABLISHMENT OF THE NEW REGIME

Grandfather Vassil Tomov was the oldest of seven children. He was the apple of his mother Trena's eye. Her full name was probably Trendafila. She was a woman born much before her time: enterprising, tireless, and restless. She came to live in Lialintsi when she married Toma, a timid and placid man who let her run his as well as everybody else's life. There, she opened a halfway house, a tavern, and a store, all under the same roof. Later, she moved to Sofia, where for a while she became a proprietor of a boarding house. Next she seems to have gone to a town south of Sofia, where she opened and operated a restaurant. I never knew her; she had died before I was born, but I saw her in an old, yellow photograph, probably taken when she was older. Her face clearly bore the effects of a stroke. I don't think that she could have ever been called pretty, even as a young woman.

Grandfather Vassil was very much like her, except that he was good-looking. He had a long mustache, straight and pointed, and he looked at the world with bold, confident eyes. He had a sprightly walk and, at the age I knew him, used to carry a cane, which he swung energetically forward at each step he took, the skirts of his long coat wide open.

He was a businessman and a merchant. As such, he made a few decent fortunes, each one after losing the previous one. He was a risk taker. On one occasion, as a supplier for the Turkish Army, he put all his fortune in a large, single load of meat, transported in railroad freight cars. At the border, all was declared contaminated and than confiscated—this was deemed as an act of revenge from a political foe. After filing for bankruptcy, Grandfather almost blew out his brains.

Politics was his passion.

He loved local politics and cherished his position as champion for his district. He was instrumental in building schools, public utilities, and roads in the western region around Trun. He was tireless and dedicated, but partisanship was a dangerous and dirty business sometimes. However, like a phoenix, he always rose from the ashes of his burnt fortunes—material and political.

He was also softhearted and was not too bashful to shed tears. Mother loved him.

From her stories, another image emerges: that of a reckless, almost-wild younger man. Most of his journeys were on horseback from one end of the country to the other, from the Yugoslavian border to Istanbul. He always traveled armed and was fond of his pistol and horse, on both of which he depended. Once, he had brought a beautiful, spirited horse that had been his pride and joy. Nobody but he could ride it. Mother was allowed to mount it, but somebody had to hold the bridle and walk along, while she was riding. When the horse had died, all in the family were heartbroken. They had given him a proper burial, and he had been laid to rest close by the house.

After a prolonged absence, coming back from a trip, Grandfather would gather his friends and have a noisy party in the tavern, at the end of which each guy would jump on his horse, and the whole gang would storm toward the mountains in a mad dash.

I can't identify one single house as my maternal grandparents' home. Ever since Great Grandmother Trena had moved from Lialintsi, there was always a house in Sofia, but Lialintsi was where the family gathered during the summers, where Grandma Lia loved to spend her time. All her children were born there and spent their early childhood there, attending the primary school in the village. The school building was quite attractive—the best of all in the neighboring villages and one of Grandfather's most cherished accomplishments. On graduating from it, the children were sent to Grandma Trena in Sofia, where they were enrolled in high school.

Of my mother's brothers, my favorite was Uncle Liubcho. He was the youngest of all the siblings. Uncle Liubcho was a kind and generous human being. My other uncle, Manol, on the other hand, was selfish and turned greedy in his old age. As a young man, though, he was handsome and very attractive. Physically, both uncles resembled their mother, Grandma Angelia. When I tried to pronounce her name for the first time, I could not say it; instead, I called her Grandma Lia. It stuck.

A long time ago, Grandfather Vassil, had accompanied his father, Toma, to a fair in a neighboring village called Stanyovtsi. Here he had seen Grandmother Lia. Theirs had been a love at first sight. At the end of the day, the fair ended and

Vassil had left the village with his father. But late that night, he had ridden back from Lialintsi, for he and Lia had decided to elope.

So, she had turned her back on her village forever.

Both were in their late teens. She was passionate and proud. Her features were strong and well-proportioned: dark hair parted in the middle, eyes steady and intelligent. She remained slim and kept her bearing straight, even in old age.

The death of her firstborn, followed by another couple of baby boys, must have taken away the joy of her marriage. More children were born and lost in childhood or early adolescence. At some moment during this time, her love for Grandfather turned into a bitter disappointment. She probably felt abandoned by her exuberant and frequently absent husband, but bore her growing bitterness without complaint. She took to cigarette-smoking ferociously, never admitting to her children that she was addicted to it, hiding from them wherever she could to have a few draws of the strong Turkish cigarettes she favored. Out of their sight, though, she would sit on a park bench and smoke, indifferent to the reactions of the people around her.

Grandma never stopped grieving over her lost children, especially her gentle Liubcho.

She loved to read and read everything, from *The Arc of Triumph* by Erich Maria Remarque to the detective stories by Edgar Wallace, and everything she read assumed a strange relevance to her limited world.

The village women did not like her. Her aloofness was branded as excessive pride; her independence and strength of character were interpreted as mean-spirited. She ignored them or darted sharp, cold glances in their direction, never getting into disputes.

Grandma Lia was cut from a different cloth than all the others. They could not understand her and resented her for that. She did not care.

In the summer of 1949, Georgy Dimitrov died.

Though he was born Bulgarian, when he was brought from the Soviet Union to head the new regime, he was a little-known personality in Bulgaria. He had no loyalty to his native country—for that matter, to any country—except perhaps to the USSR as the testing arena for the experiment of the Communist dogma. Deeply committed and dedicated to the fulfillment of the objectives of the International Comintern, as its president, his claim of renown and glory resulted from the trial in 1933 in which he defended himself against the charges brought against him: that he had set the fire on the German Reichstag. The accuser was Franz Goering, and his acquittal was hailed as a victory over the Fascists.

Georgy Dimitrov spent most of his life in the Soviet Union, became its citizen, and worked closely with Stalin, playing a role in some of the purges. He was steeped in the secretive, clandestine politics and activities of the international Communist movement. In his native country, he was virtually unknown.

When he came to Bulgaria in 1944, people saw a large man with wavy, grayish unruly hair, looking prematurely old. At an outdoor meeting, on the square in front of the St. Sofia Church, he delivered a speech from the balcony of a two-story house. He had great difficulty speaking, a whizzing sound accompanying every laboriously drawn breath. It was obvious that he was a very sick man.

More obscure expatriates started to appear from the mysterious world of the Soviet Union. The one closest to Georgy Dimitrov was Vassil Kolarov.

The first thing that bewildered the people of Sofia was the way in which Georgy Dimitrov took up residence. The selected location for his living quarters were immediately surrounded with an impenetrable high fence made of heavy, tightly arranged boards. The security and secrecy established around him were unprecedented. The memories of Tsar Boris riding on horseback along the streets were still fresh; indeed, the visibility of the tsar's family and all prominent politicians, the casual living arrangements of previous political leaders, were the accepted norms for the lifestyles of public figures. Not accustomed to the paranoia of a tyrant, people were rather bemused. They nicknamed him "Gosho Tarabata"(Gosho the Board)—a reference to the fence, the first of many yet to be built.

Meanwhile, the monarchy was abolished. At the time of Tsar Boris's death, Simeon, the heir to the throne, was only six years old. Regency was established. One of the regents was Prince Kiril, brother of the dead tsar.

Prince Kiril was one of the first victims of the People's Court created by the new regime. He was tried and condemned, not for what he had done but simply for who he was. He was executed along with the remaining of the hundred democratically elected members of the National Assembly, including the cabinet ministers of the fallen government. After a hasty referendum, the nine-year-old Simeon, his sister Maria Luisa, and Tsaritsa Joanna were expelled from the country. The palace was no longer a home to anybody. The tall wrought-iron fence was taken down; the structures in front of the main building were demolished; and the new open space was converted into a huge square, bordering the park called the City Garden.

On that spot, at the edge of the Garden, was erected the Mausoleum of Georgy Dimitrov. It was a two-story, white, rectangular building. A massive double door on the north side of the first floor broke the monotony of the marble-covered walls, and on the second floor, overlooking the square, a narrow terrace served as a reviewing tribune. The structure was erected in frantic haste (a week or so) after Dimitrov's death. One laborer perished on the site, and much later we heard that he had been our landlord in Vladaya, where I had seen the birth of the goat kid. Long walls extended from both sides of the mausoleum, the designated burial place for future leaders deemed worthy of sharing the spotlight with G. Dimitrov. Solemn honor guards, dressed in colorful uniforms, perfectly motionless, and stone-faced, flanked the double doors day and night. The change of the guards was an elaborate spectacle, repeated at regular intervals; it was nothing short of the pageantry of the rituals performed in front of palaces all over the world.

As students, we were all taken on a trip to the mausoleum. First, we were brought into a storage room where all our bags or hand luggage had to be left; then we were led outside to file into a two-man deep, slowly advancing line that led straight into the dark, cold chamber where, under a glass cover, illuminated by a dim light, lay the suit-clad body of Georgy Dimitrov. The oppressive austerity of the place, devoid of the comforts of faith and spirituality, inspired a feeling of dread, which could be dispelled only by the bright daylight and the fresh air outside.

It was a strange and macabre show that was hard to put out of my mind for a long time.

The other role of the mausoleum was to serve as a tribune, whence members of the Politburo lined up on the second floor and reviewed the numerous parades and marches. The square in front of it was the final destination for the columns of people who, upon exiting from it, scattered in all directions.

On the twenty-fourth of May, students waved flowers at the dignitaries; on the first of May, workers waved red flags and sang "The International" for them; on the ninth of September, the tanks, rockets, and planes thundered in front and above them, as soldiers marched stiffly, heads turned to the right, facing the tribune, hands raised in salute.

Upon entering the square, the activists would start running among the rows of marchers, reminding them of the slogans that had to be chanted in front of the tribune. Like cheerleaders, they gesticulated, jumped, gave encouraging taps on the shoulders and backs, threw radiant smiles at everybody, trying to pass their own enthusiasm on to the rest of us. The slogans were always the same: "Long live the Bulgarian-Soviet friendship," "Friendship forever," "Long live the Bulgarian Communist Party," "Long live the Soviet Communist Party," "Down with American imperialism," "Down with American capitalism." Slogans were very important, but they were somewhat limited by the obligatory words like *forever, never, long live, death to, down with*.

Chants were just as important: "Stalin, Stalin, Stalin," "Peace, Peace, Peace," "BKP" (Bulgarian Communist Party), "KPSS" (The Communist Party of the Soviet Union), and so forth.

The preoccupation with slogans in general brought a reaction of ridicule, which was best expressed in a graffiti that appeared on walls and fences all over the city. Much of it read, "Death to Fascism and its enemies."

Another phenomenon that emerged was the creation of the cults of the Party leaders.

They were never allowed to die.

Their words and deeds continued to inspire and lead the nation. In order to keep them alive in our memories, streets, towns, plants, and organizations were renamed after them. If there were not enough existing, new ones were created through the process of amalgamating smaller towns into big cities worthy of their big names. After Dimitrov's death, the ancient town of Pernik was renamed Dimitrovo, and three smaller towns were consolidated into the new Dimitrivgrad. Songs, plays, and movies were written and created to their glory.

For the first few years after the war, the relationship between Bulgaria and Yugoslavia was at its best: there was even talk of forming a federation of the two countries. Tito visited, and we saw him being driven from the train station in an open car; his splendid marshal's uniform covered with row after row of medals. A song was written that said, "Three suns are shining in the sky; three souls live as one: Stalin, Tito, Dimitrov."

Suddenly, the mood toward Yugoslavia started changing. The song, symbolizing the unity and friendship with our neighbors under the protection of Big Brother, was forbidden, though its popularity soared in a modified version: "Three suns are shining in the sky; three souls live as one: Stalin, hole, Dimitrov."

Tito had gone his way, moving away from total dependence on the Soviet Union, leaving a black, gaping hole in the Stalinist firmament.

10
CAMP. LAST TRIPS

The central prison in Sofia was located on the northwestern outskirts of the city. In order to get there, we had to take Streetcar 4 that ran along Pirotska, renamed Tito for a while, and by the end of the forties, after Yugoslavia's break away, renamed again—this time to Zhdanov. It was a narrow street, lined with ash trees. I am not sure of the exact location of the prison or the appearance of the building itself. Sometimes I think that it was made of red bricks with rows of small windows barred on the outside, and sometimes I think that what I see in my mind is a composite picture of all prisons I have seen in the movies, on the pages of books, or even as a backdrop on a stage. However, there are some things that I remember well—the cold, the semidarkness, the uneasiness bordering on fear that made me shiver.

We met Grandfather Vassil in a room, which seemed to me quite large. In contrast, Grandfather looked small. Over his prison clothes he wore a sleeveless sheepskin vest. At the time he must have been over sixty and already suffering from a heart condition. Mother and I took him small packages of food while he was in prison, incarcerated for antigovernment activity.

Some time before he ended up in Sofia's Central Prison, Grandfather had been arrested in Lialintsi and taken to Trun. Uncle Liubcho was taken along with him. There, they had been brought to the militia's headquarters and interrogated. Eventually, Uncle had been released, but the treatment he had been subjected to, ill as he was, never let anyone forget the episode. Grandfather, though, had been sent to prison on charges that stemmed from a discovery made during a search of the barn, a search carried out following an anonymous tip. A gun had been found, shelved on a ceiling beam. In his sentimental attachment, Grandfather had failed to submit to the authorities his old, rusty pistol. Now, this act of disobedience had been construed as proof that he was arming himself in preparation for an uprising.

Summer camp at the end of grade six in the heart of Vitosha—warm, sunny days and cool nights. The air was lucid and fresh. On the way to camp, from a spot at the edge of the mountain, one could see Sofia—its streets outlined by trees, the low buildings half hidden by their foliage, parks and gardens as dark green spots, and in the center of it all, its golden domes sparkling like jewels, stood Alexander Nevsky. Farther back, to the north, one could discern the bluish silhouettes of distant mountains.

At the end of a winding road was a place called the Golden Bridges. From there, the road turned into a steep trail up the hillside. The name Golden Bridges was inspired by the huge moraine that had been carried down and deposited like a petrified river, all the way from the top of the mountain. A wooden bridge connected the road on one side with the trail on the other. The boulders were all of different sizes and shapes. Some were round, some flat on top—wedged against each other, seldom leaving small openings through which the everlasting rumble of the fast-running water underneath could be heard. Some rose high above the rest, creating a number of small stone islands where one could find solitude to reflect or dream.

The camp was on a site a couple of hundred meters away from the moraine, on the side of the road. It ran throughout the summer holidays, in shifts, each lasting a couple of weeks. It consisted of a number of large tents, a long barrack, a cabin for the director of the camp, and an open mess hall with a wooden roof. Next to it was the assembly ground with the flagpole in the center, a large banner flapping from its peak during the day. Close by, there was a hazelnut grove.

As soon as the bus arrived at the campsite, we were divided into groups of twenty "pioneers," gathered on the assembly ground, and given detailed instructions for all planned activities for the two-week period.

The mornings started with assembly, assuming formations, roll call, raising the flag, and announcing the schedule for the day. Then we ate breakfast, followed by meetings, training, rehearsals, lunch, and rest. In the afternoon—cleaning and landscaping the grounds around the tents, the barrack, the cabin, the mess hall, then more meetings, rehearsals, training, evening assembly, assuming formations, roll call, report on the daily activities, lowering the flag, some social activities, and, finally, to bed.

The first time at assembly, I fainted.

At the very beginning, we were also divided into "athletes" and "artists," and each group started preparing in earnest for the grand celebration at the end of the two weeks. The athletes worked on a routine of jumps, exercises, and pyramid formations; the artists prepared posters, formed a choir, and started working on a *montage*. The posters usually had a background of a golden semicircle, representing the rising sun, its golden rays reaching all the corners of the cardboard. The word *socialism* or *communism* was inscribed along the semicircle—depending on how far in the future one was led by inspiration to look into. The montage was a combination of songs, recitations, chants, and movements. It had no prescribed format. However, it was subjected to the same requirements: not to violate the principle of "unity between form and content" and to convey a clear ideological message. Any art form not conforming to these rules was considered decadent and reactionary.

On Sundays, parents paid a visit. We were allowed some free time, which we spent with them, roaming around the camp or exploring the hazelnut grove.

At the beginning of the second week, trouble started brewing in our tent. We had created a sort of a mentoring system, in which the older girls "adopted" the younger ones and assumed responsibility for their behavior. It started as a game, but in fact, we took it quite seriously, and when two of the younger ones had a disagreement, the older ones were affected, the so-called "mothers".

I was one of the mothers.

The arguments ended up in a wrestling bout, accompanied by screams. It did not last long, but it did not take long either for the director of the camp and the komsomoltsy in charge of the different activities to hear about it. Immediately an emergency meeting was held, shortly after which we were informed of the decision: Our group was to be dismantled—we were branded as rotten bourgeoisie—and were to be dispersed among the rest.

The director called me aside. "I have information that your grandfather is in prison. Tell me about it." I could not and would not tell her anything. She sent me to sleep in the barrack till the end of the stay.

The girls who slept in the barrack were from Hadji Dimitar, a suburb with a blue-collar working-class population. The youth of the neighborhood had a reputation for toughness. As it turned out, I had nothing to worry about; they had accepted me more than I had anticipated. In some ways, they treated me as a minor celebrity in need of protection.

The last day of the two weeks came. The athletes did their routine; there were recitations, singing, and the montage at the end for the grand finale. My greatest contribution was to the creation of the montage.

After supper, we had a huge bonfire. Everyone sat or lay around it. In the darkness and stillness of the warm summer night, the large, looming flames were mesmerizing. There was a sense of harmony and tranquility. Somebody started to sing an old mountaineer's tune; the rest joined in. Another song followed. The feeling of camaraderie and bonding set in.

Suddenly, a partisan march resounded, then a favorite song of one political leader or another…

The magic was gone.

Back at home, my parents asked, "How was it? What did you do?" As I went on describing all I did, they listened in silence, asking only, "What is a montage?" and "Didn't you go to the moraine?"

"No, I never went anywhere. There was a berry-picking trip, but I could not go. I was busy with the montage." After a pause I blurted out, "I don't want to go to camp again."

The summer was over.

In early fall, on a lovely autumn day, Mother, a friend of hers with her young son, my best friend and me took Streetcar 5, alighted at Kniajevo, the last stop at the foothills of Vitosha, and continued on foot along the rocky path up to Bialata Voda, usually the first stop for most hikers on the way to all the mountain lodges. After a brief rest there and a couple of hours of steady, silent march up the road, we reached the Golden Bridges.

The campsite was empty.

We walked over the wooden bridge and asked a tourist to take a picture of us standing by the railing, the background a mass of rocks. Then we stepped off the bridge and started climbing the moraine.

Each one went her own way.

I found my boulder, climbed to its flat, smooth top, stretched myself out on it, and pressed my arms and legs against its warm surface. Then, I closed my eyes, feeling the gentle breeze and sun softly caressing my hair, my face, and my bare skin…

At the age of thirty-three, Mother was diagnosed with a heart condition: valvular stenosis. It did not mean anything to me at the time. What prompted the visit to the doctor was a sudden fainting attack that left her listless and pale as a ghost, her fingers cold and stiff.

When a renowned heart specialist, Dr. Razsolkov, saw her, he used somewhat harsh comparison to emphasize the seriousness of the state of her health. "My dear, you are like a house with a beautiful facade, but in a state of decay inside." This comment brought to mind the bombed American embassy, with its almost intact exterior and completely destroyed interior. The sturdy walls that had survived the destructive power of war continued to withstand the elements, and the facade remained for as long as I was there.

Mother also withstood.

Her condition, though, was untreatable at the time, and living and coping with it was not always easy.

All his life, Father never took a vacation. He loved his work and his native city—Sofia. Staying away from one or the other made him restless and uncomfortable. When Mother and I went on a holiday, it had to be close by, so he could come and visit us on Sundays.

In spring, summer, or fall, we went on excursions to nearby places along the River Iskar, or we hiked in Vitosha. We went with Uncle Otto and Aunt Desha, Uncle Peko and Aunt Blaga, and a number of other friends and acquaintances. There were always children. Everybody was in good spirits with plenty of laughter and picture taking. Looking at some of the surviving photos now, it is hard to recognize almost anybody. Most were group shots of ten or more, all sitting in the high grass of a meadow with smiling faces, long woolen skirts, kerchiefs around necks, knitted pullovers, and heavy mountain shoes with socks folded over the edge; some in striking, self-conscious poses.

The same summer, at the end of grade six, Mother decided that it was time to go on a trip around the country to see more of it. I had never been to the seashore and was very curious about it. Besides, we could afford it.

Of course, Father was not coming with us. He was working now at Collective Firm 13.

It was July. We started our trip by going to Vidin, a town on the River Danube, north from Sofia. This was an old city, famous for its fortifications. At one point in time, it became a semi-independent city-state, printing its own coins. But that was in the past. The town we saw was a small provincial backwater where people looked somewhat puzzled when asked about the historical sites. That did not discourage us, and we continued with the search until we finally found them. There was little to see. The ruins had been so neglected that we wondered if we were in the right place.

The next stop on our trip was Lom, a town east of Vidin, also situated on the river. It was an even smaller place, without any sites of interest, the only claim to fame being its watermelons. So we spent some time in the market, enjoying the colors and smells of it.

Most of our travels were by train, except for the journey from Lom to Russe, which we made on board one of the two ships cruising up and down the Danube, between Bulgaria and Romania. The ships were named *Alexander Stambolyisky* and *Georgy Dimitrov*. We embarked on one of them, proceeding downstream on the sluggish, murky waters of the Danube. Most of the time we spent on deck, observing the slow-moving banks of the river. Occasionally, the ship navigating the shallow waters moved close to the Romanian shore, which thrilled me. I thought, "I can say I was abroad!"

On both sides, there was nothing but nature—nothing to disturb the monotony of the indolent flow of the waters or the serenity of the landscape.

It took only a day or two to reach our destination, the city of Russe.

Russe was a clean, pleasant town, touted as the doorway to freedom or self-imposed exile for Bulgarians during the nineteenth century, when the country was still under the Ottoman Empire and Romania was an independent state. We took a room in a hotel in the center of the city, opposite a park. It was a pseudo-baroque building with an air of past elegance about it. The place was almost empty, so we ended up in the best corner room on the second floor. It had a curved balcony protruding over the street below and the best wide-angle view of the city. We spent a couple of days there, exploring the town, meandering along streets we picked on whim. One of those walks resulted in our getting lost among a crowd of busy shoppers in an open market, somewhat away from the hotel. Mostly though, we enjoyed ourselves by sitting on the balcony for hours, observing the almost nonexistent traffic and the pedestrians leisurely going about their business. A lasting memento was a picture we took, posing in front of a monument in the park, a huge lion crouching on his hind legs, his head covered in resplendent mane, and a broken, heavy chain hanging from his mouth—the symbolism inescapable.

Our next destination was Varna, renamed Stalin. It was only a short ride by train from Russe. There we took a room in the city, some distance away from the sea. The beautiful beaches by the Black Sea had not yet been turned into the resorts that would spring up only few years later. Vacationers usually took lodgings in town and went to the public beaches or traveled for a day to a nearby seaside.

Varna was, and is, a beautiful, modern city, its beginnings hidden in antiquity. Then it was known as the Tracian city of Odessus. There are no impressive remnants, however, from those ancient times to remind the present-day traveler of its past; they are buried deep in the ground. The tourists that flock to the place are drawn by its natural beauty—the combination of open sea vistas and the Balkan

Mountains, gently sloping toward the Black Sea before disappearing into its depths. At the time of our visit, the most famous spot in Varna used to be its Seaside Garden, where people went for a promenade to enjoy the splendid view and to take in the sea air. But the most popular place was the public beach. We went there daily, arriving early in the mornings and leaving around noon, before the heat became oppressive.

Mother did not swim and avoided the sun. She spent her time hiding under the shade of the pier, absorbed in a novel. On the other hand, I had recently learned how to swim at the public pool in Sofia and felt confident and eager to show off.

The waves were gentle, the water was shallow for quite a stretch into the sea, and there were no dangerous fish except for the slimy jellyfish that swam in schools after ships and big boats. So one day, instead of waddling along the edge of the water with Mother holding me by the hand (and after some pleading), I was allowed to go into the sea a bit farther, alone. The buoyancy of the salt water took me by surprise. I felt as though I could swim for hours without ever getting tired, or just float restfully stretched on my back, letting the gentle undulations carry me off with the drift. Lost in this new experience, I must have also lost track of the time. Suddenly, I noticed a few girls and boys waving at me, fixing their gazes on my swimsuit.

"Hey, girl, does your swimsuit have red and white flowers?"

"Yes, it does."

Hearing that, they started yelling at me almost in a panic. "Your mother is looking for you! She is very upset! Hurry back to shore!"

My God! It was a disaster. I knew how dangerous any anxiety was for her; I knew also how explosive her reactions were. Slowly, reluctantly, heart palpitating, I approached the shore until I saw Mother standing at the edge of the water, frantically waving toward the sea. She was surrounded by a few women also looking in the same direction and talking to her. It was ominous! I waited until she spotted me, standing quite away from the dry sand, sure that she couldn't reach me. Then I started carrying on negotiations, shouting as loud as I could to overcome the rumble of the breakers against the shore. It took a while, but eventually Mother promised that I was not going to be punished, at which moment I rushed into her arms.

After this incident, the waddling resumed, and the story was included in our family folklore, always related with heavy emphasis on Mother's fear and my disobedience. I liked it because it painted me as a rebel.

The excursion that I remember best was to St. Konstantin, a small peninsula where the only attraction was a chapel, dedicated to the patron saint. It was a lonely place. Not many tourists came to visit this tranquil, rather run-down, somewhat melancholy piece of land, jutting into the sea, surrounded by rocks.

On the way to St. Konstantin, or, as it was called then, Drujba, meaning "friendship," the bus passed by Evsinograd. The road, winding along the seacoast, took a shortcut inland, leaving the sea and the palace almost hidden from the traveler's view. Evsinograd's palace used to be a summer residence of the tsar's family and was now a vacationing place for the new elite. Its wine cellars, stocked with exquisite white wines made from grapes grown at the surrounding hills, were famous. Of course, the wines, as well as the palace and the terrain around it, nationalized and proclaimed as property of the people, were out of the reach of anybody but the privileged few—for their exclusive use.

From afar, Evsinograd looked like a palace from a fairy tale.

Soon, the vacation was over, and we had to head back home. Before we left, we had to collect the few pictures taken by photographers on the beach and in the park. And there it was—a most poignant photo: Mother and I in the forefront, striding in the shadow of a white, oversize statue of Stalin standing high on a monolithic pedestal, dominating the landscape.

In a few short years, Stalin would have died and been discredited. The statue disappeared, and Varna was given back its old name.

That summer we made yet another trip. This time Father came with us. Our destination was the remarkable and spectacularly situated monastery of St. Ivan Rilsky. Nestled in the bosom of Rila Mountain, it was built close to the cave where the hermit Ivan, called Rilsky, lived at the end of the ninth and the beginning of the tenth century. The first structures were erected in the fourteenth century by the despot Hrelyo. The medieval tower, standing next to the church within the compound, was the only reminder of that time. The building, encircling the stone-covered courtyard, was formidable and unapproachable; indeed, it looked like a fortification from the outside. On the inside, the multistory facade displayed horizontal rows of wooden arcades, from one end of each floor to the other, all connected by wooden staircases. All rooms could be accessed only through this multilevel thoroughfare.

Inside the church, built in the nineteenth century, much later than the rest of the buildings, was the burial place of Tsar Boris the Third. When we visited, the body of the tsar had been dug out and removed. There was nothing left to mark the spot.

This was our last trip together. We had company: Father's colleague and his wife and two sons—one of them, a few years my senior. I forget their names, though, thanks to a couple of pictures that we took, I still have their faces fresh in my mind. In the photos, Father looks somber and tense. Nobody is smiling, and the older boy and I are standing as far as possible from each other. Still, I remember the trip fondly.

That was the first time I visited Rila's Monastery. We started our journey by boarding a train in Sofia, then switched halfway to a narrow-gauged railway, riding on a slow-moving, smaller train that sneaked among endless woodlands and climbed up and up for what seemed forever. At the end of the railway track was the monastery, and still all around it there were more steep, dark green slopes shooting upward towards the skies. The white, red-roofed compound was nestled among the peaks, hidden and isolated from the rest of the world.

Inside its walls, another world existed.

We spent the day touring the monastery, marveling at the frescoes in the arcade surrounding the church, exploring the nature around it. We climbed as high as we could, then stopped and stood overwhelmed by the magnificence of the view, had a picnic in a meadow covered in sweet-smelling grass, drank from the fast-running river water, so cold that it made me sick. At dusk, we went back before the monastery doors were closed and stayed for the night. Back inside, it was like stepping into another time: listening to the ringing bells and watching the monks in their long, black habits, eyes lowered, hands folded and pressed against their chests, noiselessly and quickly moving like shadows.

We spent the night in a room on the top floor in the highest corner of the building. The view from the small window was of a bottomless precipice. It was like a place suspended in midair, somewhere between Heaven and Earth. It made one feel exhilarated and humble, completely alone and at the same time perfectly united with the whole universe.

On its way back the train maintained a slow descent—squeezing through dark forests, its brakes screeching—until it reached a clearing with many fallen trees, piled up, ready to be transported...This was the end of the vacation.

It was also the end of August 1950.

On my next trip to the monastery, years later, the monks were gone. They had been banished, and, with them, the soul of the place was gone too.

Busloads of tourists were arriving throughout the day, mainly foreigners. At any time, there were a few groups of them walking around the grounds, following loud and anxious guides, telling them about the history of the monastery, dates and events, pointing out Hrelyo's tower, commenting on the frescoes on the ceiling and walls of the church. On the outside, they were taken to the Partisan's Meadow, where we had our picnic years ago—we were not aware of its political significance then; we chose it only because it was a beautiful, sunny place.

The tourists were appreciative, even impressed with this charming spot and its pristine nature. They were invigorated by the fresh mountain air but usually did not linger long. The destination was close, a one-day trip—long enough to get there, take a few pictures, and get back to Sofia. Besides, there were more soulless places to be seen.

Neither did we linger in the monastery more than a day. Early the following morning, just a day after we arrived there, the four of us collected our backpacks, inquired about the way to a lodge higher up the mountain, and started slowly climbing up a steep, winding path, in search of a place closer to Heaven.

11

MARA

Early, sleepy afternoon on a summer day: outside, the streets were quiet. There was hardly any traffic, and only a few people were walking along the sidewalks. The doorbell rang a few times before Mother opened the door. In front stood a nice young man. He was wearing a homemade knitted sweater; his manners exuded politeness. Mother, hand on the doorknob, was looking inquiringly at him, while Mara and I, peeping over her shoulder, observed carefully.

"Is this the residence of the lawyer Konstantin Grigorov?" asked the young man.

"Yes. Can I help you?" answered Mother, looking a bit perplexed. No clients ever came to look for Father at home.

"I am the brother-in-law of Vassil Vassilev, your husband's colleague, and I have come straight from Mr. Grigorov's office. My brother-in-law must have told your husband that I am leaving for a village to buy cooking oil; Mr. Grigorov sent me to ask if you would like me to bring one demijohn of oil for you. Only there is a problem: I don't have a spare demijohn and I will need 2000 leva. All the money I have, I am going to use for the purchase of oil for ourselves."

Mother was distressed.

"Demijohn, that I have and I will give it to you right away, but money…Oh, I don't have any." She was getting desperate.

"Mara, will you go to the neighbors? Go to Denkovs'. Explain the situation, and ask them if they can lend us the money till tomorrow, please."

While Mara was out, the nice young man waited outside, refusing the invitation to come inside the apartment. He was very concerned that he was wasting too much time. His bus was leaving in a short while, and he was in a hurry.

Finally, Mara came back, money in hand, and said that Mrs. Denkova asked whether Vassilev's brother-in-law could buy some oil for her too. She would provide the demijohn and money right away. Unfortunately, he couldn't; he was running out of time, and he would miss the bus. Mother was smiling—what luck! She thanked him profusely, and he rushed down the few steps leading to the exit of the apartment building. The moment Mother closed the door, Mara started fidgeting nervously. A couple of minutes later, she flung the door open and flew out into the street. She was very fast on her feet, and, when, bewildered, we ran after her, she was already far down the street, waving her hands and yelling. There was no trace of the nice young man.

Finally, Mara turned around and started to walk back. Tears were streaming down her cheeks.

"He robbed us! He robbed us!" That was all she could say.

"But he is Vassilev's brother-in-law. He knew our name, he knew us…"

"Auntie Olga, he did not know us. He read the sign on the door. He probably read Mr. Vassilev's sign somewhere!"

Mother had to sit down.

There was a large brass sign on our door, displaying Father's name and occupation. It was customary to place signs like that on one's door or to the side of it, on the wall. When Father came home in the evening, he could not even remember a lawyer named Vassil Vassilev.

The following few days were very exciting for the whole neighborhood. The main topic of all conversations was the nice young man with the attractive homemade sweater, who seemed to have called on quite a number of households and impressed everybody favorably. We began to feel a bit better, discovering that we got off relatively lightly.

The story that created the most stir and impressed us most was how he swindled the wife of a chauffeur working for the Ministry of Foreign Affairs. A couple of hours before he rang our doorbell, the young man had gone to the chauffeur's apartment, a few buildings away from us. The wife was there, and somehow he convinced her that he was sent by her husband, who had to leave immediately with his boss for Egypt and needed some things for the trip. She was very obliging and handed him everything he asked for: her husband's new suit, as many good shirts as he had, a couple of woolen blankets—which was a bit odd, considering where he was going. All was packed in a suitcase worthy of traveling abroad with.

The story elevated the guy from the position of crook to that of daredevil. It was one thing to dupe a bourgeois's wife; it was another matter to swindle a spy.

I was very fond of Mara. Her full name was Maria Shteriou Kapnidou, and she was born in Kavala, Greece, but when was not quite clear. She had no official documents and, not being sure, kept changing the date. For a couple of years she simply refused to grow up and stuck to the age of sixteen; nobody could make her understand that this was unacceptable. She must have been about six years older than I.

At home, we called her "peresteraki," which means sparrow in Greek. She was good-hearted, romantic, and gentle. I was very attached to her. The three of us loved her.

Mara came to us as the last stop of a long and tortuous journey.

Her mother had passed away when she was very small; she did not remember her at all. Her father remarried but shortly afterward died from consumption—that was her guess—so Mara ended up living with her stepmother. Her memories of that time weren't bitter. She did not begrudge her stepmother the punishments she received for disobeying her by going to take a dip in the sea without permission. She considered the situation as a challenge. At first she wondered how her stepmother knew that she had been swimming, until it dawned on her that it had something to do with the strange licks her stepmother bestowed on the skin of her arms and hair following her prolonged absences from the house. She tested the theory by starting to wash herself completely with tap water after every escapade to the sea, and, sure enough, she never got caught again.

When the Bulgarian Army advanced on Kavala, Mara was alone in the house. Her stepmother had abandoned her, fleeing in a boat carrying military personnel; to Mara they looked like officers.

She must have been a sorry sight. A Bulgarian family living in the outskirts of the city took her in, and, when, at the end of the war, their fortunes turned around and they had to flee to Bulgaria, they took Mara along. The family must have fallen on hard times and had to part with the extra mouth to feed on their hands. Somehow she ended up in Lialintsi with my Grandmother Lia, who used to spend her summers there.

This is where we saw her, on one of our short trips to visit Grandma. It must have been 1947.

Lost and out of place though she was, Mara still seemed cheerful and unperturbed. However, Mother got upset. Mara was learning the strange dialect of the region, which, with her heavy accent, made her sound almost incomprehensible. Her hair was a mess, partially hanging in front of her face; her eyes appeared crossed. She dismissed any suggestion that she comb the mop on her head or that it was affecting her eyesight.

Mother thought that Lialintsi was not a place for Mara, and, shortly after, she came to live with us.

The chairman of the tenants' committee for our apartment building approached me with a request to make a poster a meter high and as long as the width of the building. It had to be displayed before the ninth of September for the annual celebrations of the victory of the Communist regime in 1944. It had to reflect our hopes for the future, and our dedicated efforts and commitment toward their fulfillment.

On the one hand, it was a daunting task: it was a large canvas, over fifteen square meters, to be covered with drawings. On the other hand, it was easy: it did not require creativity; the message and the form were prescribed, and we were all very well drilled to remember them. We had chanted so many slogans, sung so many songs, and beaten the pavement so many marches—all inspired by the same message—that all it took to depict it was technique. The images were bright sunshine; blue skies; stacks of tall chimneys bellowing thick, black smoke; endless fields of wheat, tractors and combines running merrily through them; trains crisscrossing the countryside; dams shimmering in the sunlight…and people. Happy, smiling, enthusiastic people, workers and peasants, shoulder to shoulder…children with smiling faces, soldiers inspiring confidence…The message had to be forceful, the images bright, optimistic.

My only problem was that I could not draw people very well. The chairman reassured me that this did not matter, since nobody could do better. So I drew tractors, combines, dams, fields of wheat bent by the gentle breeze, chimneys. And when I got tired of drawing them, I filled the empty spots with ribbons and rolls of black, endless smog.

The project was a success. The chairman, the committee, and the rest of the residents of the apartment building praised me lavishly for years to come. I was flattered, but not for a moment did I think that it was my talent they were praising; rather they were thankful I took a task that nobody wanted to undertake.

The poster was ready on time. It was spread across the breadth of the building, above the parterre floor. It remained there for a couple of months.

One of the projects of the Five-Year Economic plan called for the construction of a railroad track between Pernik, a renowned coal-mining town, and Voluyak, a railway station along an already existing track. It was to be built by brigades of young volunteers called "brigadiers," a term that entered the vocabulary at that time and became one of the symbols of the period. For a vast majority of young people, though, it had nothing to do with choice, as the term suggested. The brigades were organized by the Dimitrov Union of National Youth. This was the organization of all young people between the ages of thirteen and twenty-five, a precursor of the Komsomol, an organization that bore a different name but had the same agenda and mode of operation. For all practical purposes, membership was mandatory. In order to attend daytime school or university or to get employed, one had to be a member of this organization. Expulsion from it, inevitably, led to an expulsion from all educational institutions as well as dismissal from work.

When the representatives of the organization came to our door to call on Mara to join the brigade they were organizing, there wasn't any enthusiasm on her part and a lot of reluctance on Mother's. Building a railroad required heavy physical work. Most of the tasks, the digging and removal of materials, were done manually. The living accommodations were poor: barracks and tents put together in a hurry. The working days were long, and free time was filled up with political education activities. Each shift lasted for a few months.

In her teens, Mara was rather tiny and shy. But she was of the right age, and there were consequences to be considered: the dossiers that we were already aware of being compiled on each of us. They were permanent records of even our smallest *mistakes* or *transgressions* to haunt us for the rest of our lives.

So Mara became a *brigadier* and went to build a railway.

When she came back, she was changed. The cheerful and energetic young girl had been transformed into a melancholy, phlegmatic young woman. She spent a lot of time just sitting in a chair with her feet stuck in the kitchen oven, warming them just like an old lady. It did not help at all to ask her questions or try to distract her in any other way. Before, she used to confide in me, tell me *secrets* and stories from her childhood. I never betrayed her trust and was fascinated by everything she told me. She also taught me some Greek, but, unfortunately, not having the opportunity to practice her native language, Mara was beginning to forget most of it. Being romantic, she remembered a love song, which she shared with me. It began with the word *tamatia,* which she told me meant "eyes," and had a refrain starting with the words *saga po, saga po,* which meant, "I love you, I love you." I learned the whole song, but except for these few words, the rest was meaningless.

Back from the brigade, pensive and aloof, Mara did not tell me any more stories, but, when Mother was not around, she would softly sing "Tamatia." For quite a while, this was the only clue she gave me about her new experience and the feelings she had discovered when she was away.

Slowly, Mara returned to her old self, except that she had grown up, matured. This was the result of the most natural thing that happens to all young girls: she fell in love. It turned out that she did not know much about him, did not even think about finding him or seeing him again, so, to my disappointment, it seemed nothing more than a crush.

Oh, well, things came and went, life marched on…However, there was a difference: it happened while Mara was on a brigade—just like in the new movies.

Life moved along, in many ways, as before. On the rare occasion when we had company for dinner, the children and young adults had to provide the entertainment at the end of the meal by putting on a show to entertain the guests. Usually I recited poetry and Mara sang "Tamatia." Not long after the first words, she would grow emotional, and the tears would start streaming down her cheeks. Before she got to the end of the song, everybody's eyes would grow misty, and, when the song was over, a deep silence would reign for a while.

Mara never received a formal education. Eagerly and enthusiastically, I took the initiative to teach her. Unfortunately, she became bored easily. Mother wasn't much help either. After dinner, we would go and sit in one of the rooms. Mother would settle with her knitting, and Mara and I would hit the books. Shortly after I'd begin lecturing and asking questions, Mara would start throwing pleading looks around, and sooner or later, Mother would say, "Stop torturing her. Not everybody likes to study. I, myself, did not enjoy it much."

That would usually vex me, and I'd start arguing, pointing out the advantages of education. Meanwhile, Mara would disappear and leave me frustrated and angry, staring at Mother.

Eventually, we had some success. She learned how to read quite well; writing was another story—all to her credit.

In a couple of years, Mara got married.

After the ceremony, we had a little party at home. All sat around the dining table. There were toasts, and the best man read some poetry. It was a nice party. When all the guests left, Mara also left with her husband.

She had left a few times before, trying to become independent by getting a job and making some money, but, every time the going got tough or she became discouraged, she would come back home. This time, she left for good.

She had two daughters. She named the first one Olga, after Mother.

Around the time Mara got married, a devastating blow altered our lives. Father was disbarred and remained jobless for the rest of his life. From then on, we never knew whether or whence our bread would come the following day. Father never stopped going "to work" early in the morning and coming home "from work" late at night.

The insecurity and vulnerability were unbearable at times and had their effect on the three of us. The rest of our lives would be defined by this event.

12

THE TURNING POINT

In the fall of 1951, I started high school. Life had changed completely for the country, and soon it was going to change even more for my family.

Two categories of people were established: "the progressive" and "the reactionary." Peasants and their children, proletarians and their children, or those belonging to the Party were the "progressive"; the kulaks—a term used to identify "wealthy" peasants—the intelligentsia, or professionals, and the bourgeoisie were "reactionary." To cross the line required undergoing a *political reeducation*, and proving that one had reached the necessary level of *consciousness* by a tremendous amount of *activist work*. Yet those who did it seldom gained the trust and acceptance they were seeking.

Everybody had a dossier. Snitching was encouraged, and anybody could go to the militia and accuse anybody of anything. How this information was processed depended on the category one belonged to—for the "reactionaries," every little bit of gossip was treated as evidence; for the "progressive," it was complicated. The only loyalty that counted was to the Party and the Communist State.

There were no sacred family ties. In school, a Soviet child-hero, Pavlik Morozov, was touted as a role model. His great deed was the betrayal of his parents, who were kulaks and did not cooperate with the Soviet authorities. Pavlik provided the evidence needed to make the accusation stick, and, as a result, they were eliminated. The orphaned hero was killed by the counterrevolutionaries, so, in the end, the whole family was wiped out. Pavlik Morozov was the true pioneer (member of the Pioneer's Organization), glorified in songs and movies, thus turning him into a legend for posterity.

Fear slowly created a paranoid society: "the walls had ears." Sometimes a meaningful look expressed the opposite of what was coming out of one's mouth. Deviousness, secretiveness, and selfishness found fertile ground. As a matter of fact, for many, this was the only behavior that could guarantee survival or success, depending on the category to which they belonged.

Shiny personalities were allowed to exist or prosper only if they shined in the right direction and could be controlled. Individualism was condemned as decadence and obstructionism.

Navigating the dangerous waters of the new reality was becoming an art.

It never occurred to my parents that an adjustment in behavior was necessary. They refused to compromise in the slightest degree, never joining any organization, even the virtually mandatory Unified Organization, claiming a membership of nearly 100 percent of the general population.

Close to fifty years later, the fruits of more adaptable behavior and upbringing tailored to ensure survival astonished me. Many of the young people, born and raised into this reality, answer the questions "How are you?" or "How are things?" with the nonrevealing, almost-military response, "Normal." After hearing it many times, it still startles me and almost impels me to respond, "What do you mean by that?"

The face of the city was changing, and so was the face of its population.

A new law was enacted: it required that everybody be registered as a citizen in the place of his/her residence and had no right to live anywhere else in the country. As a start, one's citizenship was fixed as the place of one's birth, but changes could be made. This law opened another avenue for granting privileges or dispensing punishment. The *desirable elements* moved to the cities of their choice, and the *undesirable elements* were banished from theirs, their citizenships revoked.

An influx of people from the villages and small provincial towns flooded Sofia. They were quite visible. The migration to the big cities was nothing new. After its liberation from the Ottoman rule, Bulgaria was a country with a large peasant population—most of its city-folk had very shallow urban roots. The difference between natural migration and the new, forced one was that newcomers in the past had come to the city in search of opportunities, to acquire an education, eager to adapt to the urbane lifestyle, to blend in with the more sophisticated milieu of Sofia; whereas the new citizens arrived with powers and privileges, which they owed to their peasant, proletarian background and showed no inclination to change whatsoever. As far as they were concerned, it was the old bourgeoisie, steeped in decadence and self-importance, that had to *reform*—or else! The arrogance of these new citizens evoked a resentment in the old ones that they learned to conceal and bury deep in their hearts.

A new code of behavior was taking root.

Superficial changes were imposed for no other reason than to eradicate the past. Some even made sense, like the new form of addressing the mail. The new way required that the country of destination go on the top line; the city destination on the next line; the street, house or apartment number on the line below; and finally, the name of the addressee on the bottom line. This new order was supposed to make more sense for the sorting of the mail. The fact that the mail was destined to somebody rather than to someplace was insignificant. Recognition of the individual was another remnant of the decadent past, a hindrance to our march toward the bright future. This new, efficient and ideologically correct way of addressing the mail was a step forward.

Big, small, profound, and superficial changes all led to one unshakable truth: one should always remember that we lived under the system of the Dictatorship of the Proletariat.

Meanwhile, hidden from the eyes of the people, behind high fences, in numerous residences, a new class was emerging. The children of the ruling elite, former proletarians and peasants, raised in unprecedented privilege and affluence for this small country and relieved of any sense of responsibility, were becoming more corrupt and decadent than any other segment of society the country had ever seen.

In the fall of 1951, Father was disbarred from the College of Barristers. This meant not only that he could not practice law anymore, but that he was branded as an enemy of the regime, something that made him unemployable for life. It took me a couple of years to find out about that, almost by accident. I also believe that Mother was in the dark for quite a while. Father was able to hide it by following the same routine as before, getting up in the morning and coming home late in the evening at his usual time.

He was not the only one, just one of the many victims of the purge of the intelligentsia, especially targeting lawyers as natural enemies of the ideology of the new regime. He made a living by working on the fringes of the law: giving legal advice, preparing documents, acting as a middleman in buying and selling apartments, doing the leg-and paperwork for completing all kinds of transactions, and writing pleas for practicing lawyers. In fact, he continued doing everything he did before except appearing at court. Thanks to his large clientele and reputation among his colleagues, it was not the lack of work that made things tough; rather, he was at the mercy of his clients when time came to receive payment for the services he had rendered. On a few occasions he felt lucky to have escaped with no more than a bruised ego. Sometimes he would relate to us an incident of that kind, when, after an initial expression of indignation in solidarity, I would suggest to him in earnest a scheme for revenge: I would collect a band of my buddies, and we would find the despicable swindlers and bestow on them the retribution they deserved. Father always declined, pointing out at the absurdity of my proposal, ending the conversation on a light note by joking about the entire episode.

And, there was also the aggravating matter in regard to his office—he was not allowed to use one. All year round—sunshine, rain, or snow—he used to stand for hours on a street corner in front of a cinema or in a city park where his clients could find him. He made light of that, referring mockingly to a particular bench in the park or particular spot on the sidewalk as his office. Since what he was doing was illegal, he could not stick for long at the same location. He had to keep moving.

It was a meager existence. Every morning he would usually leave just enough money for Mother to buy food for the day, but there were times when he did not have any. Then he would leave with the promise to come back at lunch and bring some. He never broke his word.

Another matter of concern was clothing. Father found all kinds of reasons, except the lack of money, for never buying a new set of clothes for more than a dozen years. When his old winter coat wore out, he stopped wearing an overcoat, claiming that, since he had *iron health*, he did not need one. When his suit started turning to tatters, he proclaimed that he was launching a *silent protest* against the regime by wearing his shiny, worn-out pants and jacket with dignity and pride, which he ironed often and mended himself as well as possible.

In this struggle, Mother did her bit, but, unfortunately, she could not claim iron health.

A year after Father passed away, and Mother had been gone for over two years, Father's sister, Aunt Tina, gave me the following documents. I did not know about their existence until that moment.

PROTOCOL #36

18 September 1951

In attendance: chairman: Konstantin Dimitrov; vice-chairman: Boyan Stefanov; member-secretary: Atanas Armyanov; member-treasurer: Todor Petrov

Members: Boris Avronev, Peppo Coen, Dr. Seraphim Miloshev, Stefan Dlugnikov, additional members: Astruk Kalev, Kiril Christov, Slavcho Stoyanov, Tsako Todorovski

The protocol from the previous meeting was read.

43) In today's sitting of the Council, after dealing with the situation of the lawyer Konstantin Mirkov Grigorov, the council RULED: It disbars Konstantin Mirkov Grigorov from the College of Barristers on the strength of Article 24 in relation to Article 2, letter "zh" of the Law for the Lawyers.

This decree is not final and is subject to appeal within two weeks from receipt before The High Council of Lawyers.

MOTIVES: The Council has at its disposal positive information that the lawyer Konstantin Mirkov Grigorov is engaged in demoralizing activity, actively disseminating slanderous rumors about the leading comrades of the C.C.* of the B.K.P.** The same spreads rumors of impending war between the USSR and the USA, creating a war psychosis amongst his acquaintances. The same is making statements against the USSR and is proclaiming that soon the Anglo-Americans will come and liberate us.

The Council of Lawyers considering as inadmissible, at the present times, a lawyer having such an attitude toward the progressive forces and especially towards the USSR, is disbarring him on the strength of Article 2, letter "zh" of the Law for the Lawyers.

CHAIRMAN: (signature) Kon. Dimitrov

VICE-CHAIRMAN: (signature) Boyan Stefanov

MEMBER-SECRETARY: (signature) At. Armyanov permanent members:(signed) Tod. Petrov, Bor. Avronev, Peppo Coen, Dr. Ser. Miloshev, St. Dlugnikov, additional members: (signed) Ast. Kalev, Kir. Christov, Sl. Stoyanov, Tz. Todorovski

TRUE

MEMBER-SECRETARY: (signature)

* Central Committee

** Bulgarian Communist Party

TO THE ESTEEMED

HIGH COUNCIL OF LAWYERS

WRITTEN DEFENCE

from KONSTANTIN MIRKOV GRIGOROV, lawyer,

from the city of Sofia, bul. "Stalin" # 1ª

re: lawyer's case #4/1952

examined on 17.IV.1952

RESPECTED COMRADES,

I am requesting that the appealable decree of The Lawyers Council of Sofia be abrogated and a decree be issued against my disbarment from the College of Barristers of Sofia.

The Lawyers Council of Sofia disbarred me on the strength of Article 2, letter "zh" of the Law for the Lawyers on the grounds that I am engaging in demoralizing activity, actively disseminating slanderous rumors in regard to the leading comrades of the C.C. and the B.K.P.; that I am spreading rumors of impending war between the USSR and the USA and creating a war psychosis amongst my acquaintances; that I have made statements against the USSR and have proclaimed that soon the Anglo-Americans will come and liberate us.

Those charges brought against me are not substantiated by any evidence; the Lawyers Council of Sofia was satisfied to justify the decree by the expression: "THE COUNCIL HAS AT ITS DISPOSAL POSITIVE INFORMATION." None of the procedural codes, nor the Law for the Lawyers, relieves the local Lawyers Council of the responsibility to issue decrees for disbarment based on evidence; furthermore, it is obligatory that all evidence be appended to the file in order for the lawyer himself to take a stand, as well for the higher authority—in this case The High Council of Lawyers—to pass a judgment on how correct the assessment of the substantiveness of the evidence is.

Thus issued decree puts me in a very burdensome situation since it deprives me of the opportunity to challenge the evidence of the sources from which the local Council has collected its information, as well as to challenge the substantiveness of the sources. It would have been a different case if the file had been appended with data identifying the persons, agencies or places used as sources of information. In this case, if the persons who provided the information had been named, I would have presented counter-evidence to establish successfully that these persons are motivated perhaps by personal animosity towards me, perhaps to satisfy some personal ambition, perhaps at the cost of my disbarment are trying to build up a credit for furthering their personal agenda; whatever the case may be, this anonymous *information does not reflect the truth. On the other hand, if the Council has referred, unknown to me, evidence in the form of written reports or confessions, etc., it is impossible for me to challenge them or to question their evaluation and interpretation. Socialistic legality, though, does not condone this manner of procedure; it outright rejects it.*

But, regardless of this, in essence the decree that I am appealing is unlawful and unfair.

Without going into a detailed discussion of all evidence collected by you, it is easy to understand my attitude towards the people's regime, towards its undertakings and institutions, as well as my attitude towards the previous regimes. The witnesses questioned in this case are not just random citizens, without social consciousness, but persons holding positions of responsibility, with the names and reputations of honest, objective citizens, whose Party affiliations is enough to guarantee that they will tell nothing but the truth. Added to the testimony of these people, that of Nikolai Trakiev, whose heroic life in the struggle against fascism has brought honor to the Party and the working people, as well as the testimony of Grigor Ostrovski, I think, leave no doubt that the alleged charges against me are not truthful.

Furthermore, respected comrades, I think that when the case for my disbarment is brought up for discussion, which is equivalent to determining my fate and the fate of my family (since the consequences of disbarment are well known) it is absolutely necessary to consider not only one fact, as the alleged statements attributed to me, but to examine my character and the circumstances that ordain my place in society.

All verbal testimonies establish that in the past, before the 9th of September 1944, I was not a member of any political party, though from my personal conduct and deeds during the university years, in the army and as a lawyer, though not officially, but actually (and that is what really matters) I was on the side of the progressive forces.

I have been practicing law close to twenty years and even though I have not led an extravagant lifestyle I do not own my living accommodations. After the 9th of September 1944, I was not affected by the undertakings of the people's regime, nor was I affected by the Law concerning the large-scale city properties, the Law for nationalization of mines and large-scale industrial businesses, the Law for confiscation. In general, I was not affected by any laws or decrees of the people's regime.

Also, for a period of about two years, I served as a Deputy Secretary of the former Lawyers' Collective #17, in collaboration with its Secretary P. Philev, actively assisting him in the spirit of the Law for Lawyers. In case of absence of the Secretary took charge of the collective: representing it, carried out the assigned tasks in accordance with the instructions issued by the authorities. Hereafter, on the basis of the facts and the law, and placing my trust in your experienced hands, I implore you to grant my appeal.

City of Sofia, April 24, 1952

Respectfully: (signature)

DECREE

#53

City of Sofia April 17, 1952

The High Council of Lawyers on April 17, 1952

consisting of:

Chairman: Alexander Papanchev

Vice-chairman: Prof. Dr. Joseph Fadenheht,

Members: St. Notev, Sv. Karadjiev, St. Rashenov, E.Benatov, Nayko Naykov, Jordan Bakalov, Dimitar Russev, Georgy Panev and Ilya Balev.

After examining the report of Comrade Georgy Penev, Lawyers' Case #4 of the caseload for 1952, initiated by the appeal of Konstantin Mirkov Grigorov from Sofia, against the decree issued by the Lawyers' Council of Sofia on September 18, 1951.

RULED:

It confirms the decree of the Lawyers' Council of Sofia of September 18, 1951 and rejects the plea of Konstantin Mirkov Grigorov.

This decree is final and can be appealed within two weeks in the Supreme Court.

Chairman: Alexander Papanchev

Members: Dr. Jos. Fadenheht, St. Notev, Sv. Kiradjiev, St. Rashenov, E. Benatov, N. Naykov, Jord. Bakalov, D. Russev and Ilya Balev.

MOTIVES:

The Lawyers' Council of Sofia has disbarred from the College of Barristers the lawyer Konstantin Mirkov Grigorov from Sofia, with Protocol #36 of 18. 9. 1951 on the strength of Article 2, letter "zh" of the Law for the Lawyers, on the following grounds: The lawyer Konstantin Mirkov Grigorov was engaged in demoralizing activity, in disseminating slanderous rumors about the leaders of the C.C. of the Party. He was spreading rumors of impending war between the USSR and the USA and creating a war psychosis amongst his colleagues. The same had made statements against the USSR and was proclaiming that soon the Anglo-Americans would come and liberate us.

Dissatisfied with the decree of the Lawyers' Council of Sofia, Konstantin Mirkov Grigorov has lodged an appeal with the High Council of Lawyers within the time limit, requesting a reversal, which would allow him to continue working as a lawyer. In his appeal, the plaintiff indicated oral testimonies.

The High Council of Lawyers allowed the questioning of all requested witnesses and also conducted a thorough investigation into the ideological-political profile of the plaintiff.

The thorough investigation made into the political profile of the plaintiff regarding his attitude towards the progressive people in the past, before 9. 9. 1944 and especially his attitude towards the people's regime after 9. 9. 1944, and from the information supplied by the civic establishments and organizations, fully established the facts, supporting the motives of the Lawyers' Council of Sofia for disbarring the plaintiff.

It is true that the questioned witnesses—Nikolai Trakiev, Grigor Pop Georgiev Ostrovsky, Venko G. Velikov, P. Dimitrov, Natchko Nikolov Gyorev, Panyot Filev and others have said that before 9. 9. 1944 Konstantin M. Grigorov had progressive ideas; that during his military training he sympathized with the poor and opposed his commanders before 9. 9. 1944; that he even undertook the defense of Ostrovski in Bitolya but could not appear in court due to the fact that he was mobilized, that he, the plaintiff, even lent his typewriter for writing underground literature that defended in court somebody by the name of Kosta Belev etc.

The High Council of Lawyers, after considering all testimonies together and separately, concedes that it is possible that the plaintiff Konstantin M. Grigorov had, before 9. 9. 1944, engaged in some progressive activities, but after the 9th of September took a completely negative attitude towards the O. F.* This was established, as mentioned before, by a thorough investigation, as well by the facts supplied by other civic establishments, which positively confirm the hostile statements made by him. The fact that even now, four years after the formation of the Fatherland Front as a united social-political organization, he still has not joined it and that he is outside the ranks of the mass political organization shows that he really did not embrace the people's regime and is assuming the position of waiting for the Americans to come and "liberate" us; and now, at the threshold of the Third Congress of the O.F., when all necessary measures have been taken for mass popularization of O.F., Konstantin M. Grigorov is outside its ranks. A people's lawyer, under the present Fatherland Front's regime, can not just look calmly at the great economic and cultural transformation occurring in our country; he has to participate actively in the building of socialism. A lawyer can not be only a professional; he has to be also an activist.

Such a lawyer can not remain in the ranks of the College.

Based on these considerations, the High Council of Lawyers confirmed the decree of the Lawyers' Council of Sofia.

CHAIRMAN: Al. Papanchev

MEMBERS: Prof. Fadenheht, St. Notev, Sv. Kiradjiev, St. Rashenov, E. Benatov, N. Neykov, Jor. Bakalov, D. Russev, G. Penev, Il. Balev.

SECRETARY: (signature)

(seal)

---

* Fatherland Front

There were no more documents. Father did not appeal the decision of the High Council; it would have been futile. Probably none of the disbarred lawyers, about 60 percent of the total membership of the College of Barristers, did either.

I was completely unaware of the useless battle that Father was waging, trying to retain the right to practice his profession. I certainly knew about the purge carried out; so many people had been affected. However, this was a topic that was never discussed at home—as if it were a dreaded decease.

A brief entry in my dairy describes how I learned about it, by accident. It was a painful moment. The shock of it was so great, that we, as a family, never recovered from it.

> June 15, 1953
>
> Monday
>
> Father has been disbarred! At home, big commotion! It all happened in this way: Mrs. Nikiforova came and brought in some kind of a bill—she found it left by the door; it was addressed to Mother. It was for taxes of 140600 leva (old money) or about 1570 leva now. Mother went into a frenzy. She has been threatening to create a public display in the Taxation Office, telling them that Father is jobless, that we are having financial problems, that we are in a crisis.
>
> I could not imagine such a shameful exhibition and told her that she should just go to find out what the penalty is for late payments, etc…and to keep her cool, and when she calms down to consider the alternatives. Besides, I said, the taxation officers must be confronted daily by complaining and crying customers, but if she wants to make a scene, that is her business. That did it. She turned on me, screaming: "What? Do you presume to teach me? You silly girl." Nothing upsets me as much as calling me names, but I kept my cool.
>
> Also, that "advice" to Mother got me a slap in the face. It did not faze me at all.

This is how the story of Father's disbarment came to light for me. It demonstrated the consequences of our reduced income, something that did not happen overnight but in a steady and relentless decline over the course of the last couple of years. From that moment on, at least I knew the reason for it and became aware of the permanency of the predicament we were in.

After this incident I had to face an unforeseen problem stemming from Father's new situation. The specific challenge was how I should answer the ever-asked question, "What does your father do?" It was not an idle concern; we were all treated not as individuals, but as extensions of our parents and grandparents. Their backgrounds were a determining factor in all aspects of our lives. My father's occupation was of vital importance to me. He advised me to answer,

"Labor reserve." From then on, this is what I put on all documents and forms, and that was how I answered the question when asked, and always felt uneasy and afraid that somebody would look at me in disbelief and suspicion and think, "It is a lie! What is she hiding?"

There was one occasion, though, when I slipped. It was during the exam of History of the Communist Party of the Soviet Union. Our exams were oral, and the topics were determined by lots. My lot happened to be Lenin's views on the question of war. It was a relief not having to talk about the Congresses. There were too many of them, too many dates, resolutions, and decisions in each one that were hard to memorize and distinguish one from the other. It was much easier to talk about the *defensive* and *liberation* versus the *aggressive* and *imperialistic* wars, which actually meant to present the *good* versus the *bad*, and one must have been living on the moon for the past ten or fifteen years not to know all about it. We were told that over and over and over! Something about my presentation must have impressed the professor, rather than the depth of my knowledge, I am sure. It was just one of those days when I seemed to be on top of everything; the words were just flowing effortlessly and confidently. At the end of the exam, when I finally finished, the examiner gave me a funny look and asked, "What is your father's occupation?" and before I even knew, I heard myself saying, "Lawyer."

"Ah, this is where you got it from, a lawyer's mouth." It was not clear to me whether the professor meant it as a compliment or a reprimand, a good or a bad thing.

Already I was regretting my lack of caution and wondering, "What made me say that: vanity or stupidity?"

13

HEARTBREAKS AND HARDSHIPS. MOTHER. END OF STALIN

In May of 1952, I began keeping a diary. Almost every evening I would spend close to an hour scribbling away.

At home things had changed profoundly. On the surface everything seemed the same, but the uneasiness and worry were there to stay. The three of us withdrew into ourselves. We started hiding things from each other to avoid inflicting more painful feelings, to ration emotions.

The diary was my outlet and escape. At times my preoccupation with it seemed to go so far that Father started wondering, "Is your diary a reflection of your life, or are you living for the sake of the diary?"

At times I couldn't tell.

Perhaps what triggered this desire to record my life, to analyze and reflect on it, was the death of my favored uncle Liubomir, or Liubcho, as everybody called him. He was Mother's younger brother, who had passed away only a few days before the first entry in my diary. Until then, I had never experienced the loss of somebody close to me, someone I loved.

It was hard to cope with it—even harder in the circumstances at the time.

Uncle Liubcho was in his teens when I was born. I was told that he often babysat me. Since I was a crybaby by my parents' accounts, it must have taken a lot of persuasion to make him do it over and over. One of the ways Mother succeeded was by bribing him. He loved going to the cinema, and for a couple of tickets was willing to take care of me, as well as endure my whining for a while. As long as I can remember, I thought that he was the most handsome man in the world and, naturally, I had wanted to marry him since I was three years old.

He was very slim, over six feet tall, and very dark. He had a triangularly shaped face and wore his high school cap tilted to one side. Grandmother, Mother, and everybody else in the family seemed to be worried about his health. They felt he was wasting his energy on movies—running from one cinema to another, sometimes seeing three or four different pictures a day. Later he acquired a big, heavy, dark green bicycle, which he rode around the city, always in a hurry, always busy.

At first he had weak lungs, then dark spots appeared on them, and finally he developed tuberculosis. There was no cure for the disease; it was a hopeless diagnosis. He never showed any bitterness or fear. When visiting us (and this was a few times a week), he would ask for his own fork, his own plate, and his own spoon when having a meal, and he would push me away when I got too close to him. Except for this, he acted like a healthy, happy person. When Uncle Manol was there, the three of them (Mother and her two younger brothers) would start singing, imitating old teachers or characters from their childhood, composing poetry, and laughing loudly. The three had good voices and great imagination. Sometimes they would poke good-natured fun at Aunt Nina, who was the oldest and seemed to have given each one of them a hard time on one occasion or another during their childhood. Also, they had nicknames for everybody, as well as for themselves, and used them to tease each other.

When Uncle Liubcho's illness progressed to a more advanced stage, he was sent for rest and treatment to a place called Iskrets, close to the small town of Svoge. The large white building of the sanitarium was located in the hills of the Balkan Mountains, surrounded by a forest of pine trees. There the air was fresh and light, so it was easy to breathe. For a couple of weeks of the summer he spent there, Mother and I stayed in a rented room in the nearby town. During the day we would go up to the sanitarium and spend some time with him.

The treatment he was undergoing included the standard procedure of filling the cavities in his lungs with oxygen.

He met a girl there, and for a while they were very close. Back in Sofia, they used to visit us.

Spring was considered a bad time for those sick with tuberculosis. Surviving this critical season usually meant one more year of life. The last couple of years of his life, Uncle Liubcho used to spend the spring months in bed, more or less, waiting for the summer. He lived in my grandparents' house at the other end of the city, a good distance away from us. To get there, we had to ride two different streetcars. Besides, this last spring, Mother was bedridden, her heart condition worsening.

Finally, the cold and rainy weather was replaced by the warmth and sunshine of longer days and clearer skies. On one fine afternoon in May, my best friend Dessy and I went to Aunt Nina's place to pick up a dress she had made for me. We walked along the boulevard by the river, crossed the Eagle Bridge, and continued until we hit Gurko, the street where Aunt Nina lived with Uncle Hristo and her two small boys. She had closed her atelier on Graf Ignatiev Street and had moved to an apartment in a new building. We climbed to the top floor of the seven-story building—there was no elevator—and rang the doorbell.

Aunt Nina opened the door. She had been crying. A few women were sitting or standing in the living room. The mood was somber. Auntie pulled me to one side, led me into the bedroom, where she made me sit down, then disappeared for a minute to return with a glass of water in her hand. Looking intently into my eyes, she said, "Your Uncle Liubcho passed away this morning."

She waited for a while, and after the critical moment passed without my fainting, screaming, or even saying anything, she continued, "He kept asking for you. He wanted to talk to you."

After a pause she added, "Your mother does not know, and let us keep it that way."

I took the glass of water from her hands, drank it, went to the living room to pick up my friend and the dress, and left. I felt completely numb; it was as though my emotions were turned off somehow. Inside I felt nothing.

Outside I told Dessy what had happened. Then we fell into a silence that went unbroken for the rest of the way back. The whole time I kept thinking that something was wrong, that I was acting strangely. There was only one overwhelming thought that I could not put out of my mind, "What did he want to tell me? Why did nobody tell me about it? Were they trying to spare me or what?"

On the day of the funeral, Mother stayed in bed and cried quietly. I went about my school business, and, when Father came home, supposedly from work, nobody said anything, pretending that this was a day like any other. I was sure that Mother knew, though I had no idea how and kept wondering if Father had delivered the eulogy.

He would have said the right things.

When Mother's condition stabilized and she got back on her feet, she went to church. Even though Easter, Christmas, and the rest of the holy days were celebrated at home in the traditional ways, we were not a church-going family. From the time of Uncle's death, that changed as far as Mother was concerned. She started attending services regularly, frequently read the New Testament, and surrounded herself with friends, for some of whom, the church was the focus of their existence.

For the rest of her life, Mother drew tremendous strength from her faith. In church she would find a spot to stand, usually in the shadow of a column or next to a wall, and lose herself in the service—sometimes listening with eyes closed and mouthing the words of her favored texts or following the singing of the choir. She went most frequently to Alexander Nevsky, one of the most beautiful cathedrals anywhere, with a vast and open interior, walls covered with richly painted frescoes and marble columns and floors that resounded with every step. There it was easy to shut the world out and to let your spirit soar, especially if one happened to enter the cool, spacious interior when the choir was singing. The sound reverberated as though coming from all sides; it felt as if you had entered heaven—tears involuntary filled your eyes and feelings of serenity and peace slowly enveloped you.

After Uncle passed away, I developed a habit—in moments of reflection or before falling asleep, especially when I felt troubled—of telling him things. It brought me comfort.

For a while Mother's entrepreneurship helped carry us through the difficult times. It was out of the question to find work as an accountant or as a bookkeeper, an occupation she had trained for at a reputable school of commerce, Minerva, and had a couple of years of work experience after graduating. Instead, she seized the opportunity created by the shortages, which lingered for a long time after the war, and, in some areas, continued till the very end of the regime.

Mother drew the inspiration for her ventures from the inexhaustible need for simple articles, staples of everyday life. Many of these items did not require much skill or special tools for manufacturing, except—as Mother saw it—initiative. And she had plenty of that.

Her first enterprise was making children's garters. The basic materials—elastic, ribbons, and buttons were available. Once those were purchased, all that remained to do was to cut the pieces, put them together, and sew them. Since we had no sewing machine, Mother had to do it by hand. She took the finished garters to small private stores that still operated along Pirotska Street. There was no problem whatsoever of selling them.

The next project was making stuffed rabbits covered in white and pink flannelette. Parents did not have much money to spend on such nonessentials, so it was important to make them as affordable as possible. However, this presented a challenge: making the toys involved a lot of sewing, and doing the operation manually made the task too time-consuming and inefficient.

Soon after, all private businesses were outlawed and Mother had nowhere to sell her merchandise. This brought an end to her previous endeavors.

The most successful idea Mother had was to make colorful, noisy, cheap toys, which she kept making for years and sold in fairs. By then she had a Toy Maker's Certificate. With Father's help, she had applied and received the papers, which were sort of useless but at least gave her some legitimacy by keeping her from operating totally outside the rules and regulations.

The toys were basically cylinders made of cardboard, about five centimeters in height and five centimeters in diameter. They were decorated with shiny, colorful paper cutouts pasted all over its surface. A couple of bright, fluffy feathers, dyed by Mother herself, protruded from the sides, adorning the simple toy further; and, most importantly, there was the functional part: a horsehair stuck out from the top of the cylinder and looped around a groove in one end of a wooden stick. The main appeal of the toy was not in the looks of it, which was attractive enough to grab the children's attention, but in the squeaky noises created by the friction between the horsehair and the head shaped out of asphalt. In order to produce them, the child had to swing the stick as fast as he could, so that the flying cylinder would pull on the hair. The harder the pull, the louder the noise, its pitch rising higher and higher.

Each one of those fascinating, bright, noisy toys was made by hand, and it took about twenty steps to complete. Mother devised a mass-production method that made the process a lot faster. I knew every single operation of the entire manufacturing procedure and loved performing some: cutting the glossy paper, combining all the shapes and colors to create different designs, or selecting and attaching the feathers. We took pride in trying to make every toy different and dazzling, challenging ourselves, comparing and competing with each other. Sometimes Mara came to help, too. The most important operation, though, was done only by Mother—that was the dipping of the sticks into heated asphalt and forming the groove along its circumference. It was a stinky, difficult task, which Mother performed on the balcony as fast as she could in order to complete it while the asphalt was still pliable. The quality of this operation determined the effectiveness of the toy.

Mother made hundreds of toys, which she took to fairs in small towns or villages around Sofia. She traveled by bus or train, carrying suitcases or bags full of merchandise. The trips were hard on her. She never took me along, but sometimes she took a friend, Mrs. Nikiforova. They turned the whole affair into a game, pretending that it was fun, sort of an escapade or a picnic; except that, instead of baskets of food, they were carrying bags of toys to sell.

At the fairs she sold the toys in bulk to vendors, who, in turn, displayed and sold them from their stalls. Sometimes I think she sold some directly to the customers, though she never told me so.

She always came back very tired, never brought back any toys, and never said anything. Within the next day or so, she would start getting material for the next batch—the cardboard strips precut to size, the glossy paper, the feathers, the horsehair, the wooden sticks, and the black raisin which, when melted, turned into soft asphalt.

Eventually this private enterprise, like all private businesses, came to an end.

The only employment Mother could get afterward was as a *reclassified laborer*, a category for disabled workers. To qualify, she had to be examined and approved by a committee of doctors. She was certified on the basis of her heart condition and given a job in a factory outside the city. Her job was filling up paper bags with powdered lemonade. Mother worked there for over a year, commuting by train.

Every day she left the apartment early in the morning, rushing to the streetcar worried about missing the connection at the train station and getting to work on time. In the evenings she came back on the same crowded, noisy, dirty train, exhausted physically and spent emotionally. The job was tiresomely monotonous. The workers had to wear masks to prevent the lemonade powder from getting into their lungs. That was the most burdensome aspect of her work; it made breathing difficult.

For the first time ever, I had to spend most of my time at home alone, enduring the oppressive weight of loneliness, making decisions about the small details of daily life. Mostly, I occupied myself with reading—in my favorite way, lying under the covers. So, there were days when I did not get out of bed at all—unable to put down a novel, totally immersed as I was in the lives of the characters, transported into times gone by and faraway places.

Growing more independent and self-sufficient, those were the compensations for the lonesomeness, for those miserable moments when I yearned to have my mother around.

My best friend was Dessy. She had curly red hair, green eyes, freckles, and long legs. She was very pretty.

We met when we were in grade four. She lived at number 34, and I lived at number 24 on the same street. On the day we met, we both were hanging around on the sidewalk, in front of our respective apartment buildings, waiting for somebody to come and play. Dessy had just returned from the provinces, where her family had moved during the war. They remained there for a few more years after the war ended until she came back with her mother and brother, leaving her father behind, working. He joined them later.

I don't remember who approached whom, but we went through the usual ceremony of getting acquainted: "What is your name? My name is…" Her reply to the question was: "Dessislava Vladimir Shipkova." Instantly, I was impressed by the way she announced her patronymic—omitting the suffix "ova"—as well as by her given name. It was an unusual, old, medieval one—very rare at the time—associated with Sevastocrator Kaloyan and his wife, Dessislava, from the fourteenth century. I liked it a lot. For my part, I said, "Radka Konstantinova Grigorova." And thus, our long and fast friendship was established.

We became inseparable. We went to school together, we played together, we liked the same boys, and we were planning to live always that way—together. Our parents got to know each other. They did not become close friends, but we felt at home at each other's place and felt comfortable with each other's parents. Dessy's mother was working as an accountant or a bookkeeper, and they also seemed to be going through hard times.

During the school year we wore uniforms: black frocks with white collars, woolen skirts underneath, and cardigans on top. By the time we reached high school, we both had outgrown our clothes—coats, stockings, and the rest—except for the memorable matching tops made by our mothers a while before. The brown knitted cardigans with front panels of ribbed velvet and zippers instead of buttons presented nothing short of a rare fashion statement that went a long way toward mitigating the stark deficiencies of our daily garbs.

I can still see us walking on a cold winter day, shoulder to shoulder, our clothes showing in layers: skirts first; then the black frocks; coats on top about four fingers higher, sleeves too short to cover the wrists; white knee socks reaching only mid calves; and the exposed legs covered with bluish cold spots. To keep the sleeves from running up, we would cross our arms and keep our hands in each other's pocket. We would push the other hand as deep as it would go into our own pockets. Then we would lift our shoulders, trying to protect our necks from the cold and keeping up in step we would move as one, talking and talking and talking. Most of our conversations were *confessions*. We would tell each other our *dreams*. Actually, I don't think I have ever had a single dream as fantastic, as exciting, or as surprising as the ones we shared. We did not dream them; we just made them up, and kept the pretense. Also, we read books, all kinds of books, and we discussed them.

Everybody had lots of books. On birthdays or name days, they were the only presents we gave to each other. Almost always they were old ones, but that did not matter. As customary, we wrote dedications on the first page, and, more often than not, we had to scratch one already there in order to write a new one.

The high school curriculum was arranged and rearranged all the time. Popular authors that were studied at school before had been denounced, suddenly rejected and sometimes just as suddenly brought back. That happened to foreign as well as Bulgarian writers. We did study Shakespeare, Byron, Tolstoy, Pushkin, Lermontov, Hugo, Homer, Botev, Vazov, Smirnensky, and Vaptsarov; but we also read Stefan Zweig, Jack London, Vicki Baum, Pearl Buck, Daphne du Maurier, Zola. Forbidden books we couldn't get enough of were the detective novels of Edgar Wallace, the adventures of Sherlock Holmes, and Arsène Lupin. Our reading habits became an issue for the Komsomol Organization, which called a general assembly in the school gymnasium. We were criticized and accused of being *willing conduits of the decadent, rotten capitalist's culture, lacking in social consciousness.*

The most daring act occurred when someone brought *Lady Chatterley's Lover* to school. We dismembered the book into quires that fit neatly in our notebooks and would read them in the back rows during class—with flushed faces and complete absorption. The other students would keep watch and make sure that the teacher's attention was elsewhere.

And then there is the story about my old coat, and more...

November 1952 was a very cold month. There was a shortage of coal, and some of the schools, including mine, had to be closed for the duration of the inclement weather. Meanwhile, arrangements were made for the students to attend other schools. The one I had to go to was located quite a long walking distance from our place.

Suddenly, what at first appeared to be a mere inconvenience turned into a disaster. I had outgrown my worn, old coat to the point that it had become useless. My parents had to find a solution in a hurry, while I stayed at home. To make things worse, we had also run out of coal, so it was freezing in the apartment too. The kitchen stove, as well as the heating stove in the living room, were so cold that they gave me the shivers to the touch. The only warm spot was in bed, under the thickly quilted covers. For a few days I stayed there reading, all wrapped up to keep warm, until, finally, I got a new coat and started attending school again.

Well, this sounds like a story with a happy ending, though that is not entirely true. While my previous coat was made from Father's old one, completely restyled and with the cloth reversed, it was rather nice. The good quality of the material was obvious, even from the underside. In contrast, the new coat was made of poor-quality material and the color was an unidentifiable hue. Somebody must have spilled a bucket of gray dye into the original dark brown tincture. For the next few years, at the approach of the cold weather, I would start experiencing mild anxiety attacks at the thought of having to wear the ugly garment. And this was not just in my head; even now, looking at winter pictures of that time, I see myself as a mouse of undeterminable color.

In contrast, the next coat I got was an attractive wraparound with a loose belt keeping it tightly fit about my waist. This time Mother did not even bother to look for a material in the half-empty stores. Instead, in a fit of imaginative inspiration, she bought a vivid jade-colored blanket and took it to the dressmaker. The bright, eye-catching garment weighed a ton on my weak shoulders, but it looked great hanging on my skinny frame. However, I had to be very careful not to get it wet—then the weight became almost crushing, and it took ages for the fabric to dry.

Looking at pictures from that time, I see an elegant young woman. Ah, the magic of clothes. Not enough can be said on that topic: they can transform even a mouse into a wench!

In conclusion, from the more superfluous to the essential...

January 6th, 1953. Christmas Eve. We had our meal on the floor, as was the custom.

Mother had prepared traditional dishes: meatless cabbage rolls, beans, banitsa, homemade bread with a coin inside. There were also apples, walnuts, and dried fruit. Before the meal, Father cleansed the house with the censer, swinging it like a pendulum, reaching into all corners and resistant spots, spreading the exotic smell of the burning incense all over the place. Then we said the Lord's Prayer, and Father broke the bread. Whoever found the coin would be lucky throughout the year. I did not record in my diary who the lucky one was, but I made a point of the fact that observing religious holidays, celebrating them in any fashion, was forbidden.

The leftovers from the meal were left on the floor where we ate, till the morning, as required by tradition.

On Klement Gotvald 20, at the juncture of Gerlovo Street, lived Mrs. Nikiforova. She was Mother's best friend—a widow who lived with her daughter, Margarita, and her mother in one of the rooms of the same apartment they occupied when Mr. Nikiforov was alive.

Stoyan Nikiforov was one of the victims of the People's Court. He had been a deputy to the National Assembly for many years and for a while in the thirties a cabinet minister. He had been arrested after the ninth of September 1944 and put on a trial with over a hundred deputies. In October or November, Mrs. Nikiforova and her teenage daughter were interned in a small place far away from Sofia, never to see or hear from their husband and father again.

At the beginning of 1945, they learned that all deputies had been executed, with no exceptions. Stoyan Nikiforov had to have shared their fate. But, without any official notification or confirmation, without a grave, with no last word or letter from him, Mrs. Nikiforova seemed to have chosen to cling to the slight hope that perhaps not all were killed—that some were sent to Siberia and someday might return. She did not talk about her hopes, but we felt that this was the case.

All their properties were confiscated. On their return from internment, however, they were allowed to live in one of the bedrooms of their apartment. Mrs. Nikiforova's mother fixed herself a bed in a closet off the entrance hallway.

I felt very close to Mrs. Nikiforova—not that this would have been obvious to anyone. The depth of the affection, trust, and loyalty we felt for each other were difficult to detect; they emerged to the surface of our daily lives only in exceptional circumstances. We still lived in a society where formality and lack of demonstrativeness were the accepted norm of behavior. This was reflected in the way we addressed each other. For a child or young person, it was unacceptable to address an adult in any other way except with the formal you. Neighbors, even friends, addressed each other in the same way. Civility and good manners were not promoted, though. In most cases they were considered the stamp of the old, decadent society. It took a few years to eradicate what had taken generations to build. Eventually the behavior based on formality and reserve, instilled during upbringing, was replaced by one reflecting the paranoia and secretiveness created by fear. Casualness replaced ease and politeness in daily interactions. And the faces of the people lost their smiles.

But back in the fifties, there were still plenty of good manners to go around. I never even imagined addressing Mrs. Nikiforova in any other way but the formal. So did Margarita to my parents, and, finally, so did Mother, Father, and Mrs. Nikiforova among themselves. That did not, however, bring coldness and remoteness in our relationship.

There was a considerable difference between Mother's and Mrs. Nikiforova's age. In this respect she was closer to my father, who liked her and had a lot of respect and empathy for her. On the other hand, her stable, even temperament and Mother's warmth and sensitiveness seemed to satisfy their individual needs and deepen their friendship. They were very close.

In some ways, for years, we lived like an extended family.

Every time Mother had a fainting attack, I ran upstairs to fetch Dr. Shopova or next door for Dr. Denkov. Whoever was at home would rush to our apartment and revive her with a shot of cardiosol. If both of them were away, I would run up and down the streets, looking for any doctor I could find, searching out the signs all professionals displayed on their doors. I would ring the bell of any doctor's residence, and, if any one happened to be there, he always came running after me, small leather bags in hand. Usually that was all that was needed to bring Mother back to life. In more serious cases, we would call an ambulance.

On one of those occasions, we were standing around Mother—pale and listless lying on the bed. There were Father, Mrs. Nikiforova, and Dr. Denkov, who looked helplessly at Mother after giving her the shot of cardiosol and seeing her not responding. All was quiet until she opened her eyes and motioned that I should be taken out of the room. Immediately, someone grabbed me by the shoulder and shoved me outside the door, leaving me in the hallway alone to stare at the closed door, filled with apprehension that slowly turned into dread.

Shortly an ambulance arrived. Father left with it, accompanying Mother, who was carried inside it on a stretcher.

When everything turned quiet again, only Mrs. Nikiforova and me were left in the apartment. This was the worst attack I could remember, and Mother's wish to have me leave the room had left me petrified.

We did not linger there for long. Mrs. Nikiforova took me to her place and made me sit in one of her big leather armchairs. For a while she kept walking around the room, busying herself with who knows what, then stopped in front of me and said, "Everything will be all right, but, if something happens with your mother, I will take care of you. Relax and try not to worry."

She stood in front of me, short and plump, her soft gray eyes looking down on me. A sense of calm and hope slowly started to replace my anxiety, desperation, and fear.

Those were not her exact words, but they are the gist of what she said. I did not doubt for a moment that she meant it.

After this incident, every time I went to the Nikiforovas, I felt good, comfortable, and secure—almost like being at home.

There is a special piece of music that always takes me back to a particular moment—surrounded by the familiar furniture, the leather chairs, the low round table, the comfortable, large sofa, the beautiful buffet with embossed doors, Margarita's piano, and the two beds, all crowded in this one room; Mother and Mrs. Nikiforova seated in the chairs, eyes closed; Margarita curled on her bed, the radio next to her and the music of Bruch's *First Violin Concerto* floating in the air. No harsh lights inside to dispel the magic; only shadows thrown on the wall by the streetlights shining outside the window through the trees.

The most powerful symbol of this time was the omnipresent image of Stalin. It was not the person himself—we knew nothing of him except for a few facts about the place of his birth, his early education, and his feats before he became *the greatest* and withdrew behind the Kremlin's walls. It was his portraits, statues, and name that dominated our world. There was one particular portrait that startles me even to this day. It was the one that appeared on the first page of every newspaper every day, the one that hung on the walls of the schools and all public places, behind every desk occupied by a person of authority. It was the portrait multiplied hundreds of thousands of times that had to be carried over the heads of the marching masses during the demonstrations, the one adorning the tanks at military parades. It was the face of the man we had to refer to as our *father*, the man who was compared to the life-giving sun, who was called *the peacemaker, the messenger of peace*, the *genius* who wrote books and chartered our future, who approved of our accomplishments and disapproved of our failures.

This was the time later referred to as "the period of the cult of Stalin's personality."

Meanwhile, we studied his books, sent him telegrams for his birthdays, wrote stories, poetry, and plays dedicated to him, erected statues of him, renamed our old cities and streets after him, rebuilt our destroyed cities in a new architectural style bearing his name.

And he was not even one of our own.

March 3, 1953

Tuesday

The class on political information was canceled, and we were allowed to go home early. Went for a walk with Detelina. She invited me for tomorrow to go to her place to study together.

March 4, 1953

Wednesday

Spent the morning studying at Detelina's. Back home for lunch; mother told me that it was announced over the radio at 12 o'clock that yesterday at 2 o'clock, Stalin had a stroke—hemorrhage of the brain. Complications followed: albumen, problems within the respiratory system and blood circulation, became paralyzed, lost his speech, lost consciousness, etc.

At school, hardly any mention of that. Faking ignorance.

March 5, 1953

Thursday

The dominant topic for discussion now is Stalin's illness. Everyone is interpreting the news as it suits him.

At school an interesting thing happened. While Raina was being examined by Gitcheva, some of the questions stumped her, and she fell silent. The teacher became enraged, screaming and yelling so hard that we started throwing frightened glances at each other. Gitcheva is prone to outbursts, but had never had one as ugly as that. It really shocked us. We all shut up and slumped over our desks.

All of a sudden it got so quiet that many could not take it and began to shake from a silent laughter. A few could not suppress it and from time to time let out all kinds of funny noises. One could see only backs and shoulders, rocking.

Gitcheva noticed our reaction; she was embarrassed. By way of apology, she let us go fifteen minutes earlier.

March 6, 1953

Friday

This morning, as I was walking along the street, I suddenly noticed the black flags. At first I did not understand the meaning of it all and, even after it dawned on me, couldn't take it in until I heard the loudspeakers on the Public Bath announcing: "On March 5 of this year at 9:50 in the evening, Comrade Joseph Vissarionovitch Stalin passed away."

I could not believe my ears. It felt like this was impossible. The world we live in, the political state of it, peace, war, it all was connected with his existence; he was so firmly crowned with the halo of immortality that for a moment I was overcome by panic that everything would go out of its order, that the world would turn upside down. It gave me such a sense of insecurity that for a moment, it seemed tomorrow wouldn't come.

There were hardly any classes at school. We were taken to a demonstration.

March 7, 1953

Saturday

The day passed in heavy studies; only the French teacher gave us a break.

We just had to read our homework and something from the textbook before she let us go. That made us happy and we started dancing.

March 8, 1953

Sunday

Spent the day at home. Toward evening went out with father to buy some food. Had visitors: Aunt Violetta with Bobby and Tony. The radio is playing non-stop funeral music. "The country is swept up in sorrow…"

March 9, 1953

Monday

Today was an official holiday: the burial of Stalin. Exactly at 11 o'clock (local time), all sirens, locomotives, and factories started to hoot. Everything ceased for five minutes of silence. Meanwhile the gun salutes began to resound.

I was at home and watched from the window.

In the afternoon went with Margo to Kniajevo and climbed up almost to Bialata Voda searching for hellebore. Did not find any.

14

HIGH SCHOOL

Life did not change; everything went on just as before. I was in grade nine.

There were, however, the continuous changes in the curriculum. The latest was the introduction of state exams at the end of each year and the introduction of more political subjects. Reading the entries in my diary, I am reminded of some of the clichés we were using. The political ones guaranteed a passing mark, regardless of the topic or the depth of the essay. A particularly colorful phrase was *the predatory clutches of capitalism*. Sometimes it took a lot of creativity to squeeze them into the text.

In spite of that, our fascination with the capitalistic West, and especially with America, grew. The echoes of the Korean War found its way to inspire us to create exciting entertainment. We did not have clear ideas about many things concerning life behind the Iron Curtain. We were intrigued by Coca-Cola, one of the symbols of America and the American way of life. What kind of a drink was it? Was it the highly potent alcoholic brew we were led to believe it was? During class recess, we acted out sketches of American soldiers, drunk on Coca Cola, dressed as gangsters in black leather jackets, dark glasses, and, for some reason, scarves thrown elegantly around their necks, driving in jeeps all over the Korean countryside and abducting innocent Korean girls. The school benches arranged one behind the other represented the jeep; four boys perched on top of them making all sorts of noises—imitating the sounds of the engine, the squeaking of the wheels, and the bangs of the machine guns and pistols, all depicted by gestures rather than objects—represented the soldiers. After a few minutes of noise and wild acting on their part and tense anticipation on the part of the girls standing by, they would pull one of us up; there would be screams and more noise, and it would all end with a small group of us chanting an advertisement for Chat Noir, a French perfume. The commercial was played on a radio station in Novi Sad, Yugoslavia. Advertising was not allowed in Bulgaria; it was another capitalistic practice that fascinated us.

During these performances, there was always somebody standing by the closed door watching, making sure that nobody from the administration or teacher would surprise us. Delegates from other classes were allowed to attend the show.

A couple of years later, at the end of high school, the most ardent of all participants, Valentin, found his way out of the country and ended up in the American army. He became a Green Beret and served during the Vietnam War.

On May 10, 1953, Kiril from Plovdiv was elected as Patriarch of the Bulgarian Orthodox Church. In my diary I wrote:

May 10, 1953

Sunday

Today is a great day for our church. Finally, once again, we have a Patriarch.

The government sent congratulations to the Holy Synod. What hypocrisy! On the one hand rejecting religion and vilifying the church, and on the other congratulating it. What a dirty business!

By now, the church played a very important part in our lives. Mother and her friends, Mrs. Nikiforova and Mrs. Gorianska, were part of a group, mainly women, whose lives revolved around it. These were people who drew strength to carry on with their lives from the only source left to them. Almost all had lost something or somebody, and all refused to surrender to the new order. All day long they went about their lives with their eyes dry and their bodies erect; and only in the darkened church would they let sorrow take over, and one could see the tears rolling down their cheeks.

Vera Pavlova Gorianska was a Russian émigré. She never talked about her past. The few facts that we knew were that she was from Moscow, left her native land as a young woman after the revolution of 1917, got married to a Russian somewhere, and later moved to Bulgaria. I have a vague memory that her in-laws were opera singers who happened to be in Italy during that time. That is probably where Vera Pavlova met her husband. From time to time, she gave us a glimpse of the life she led in Moscow, telling us about how she used to enjoy skating outdoors during the winters.

Her husband used to work as an administrator at the opera in Sofia. The day the Red Army entered the city, Mr. Goriansky did not return home from work;

he just vanished. His fate, as well as that of a number of Russian émigrés who had disappeared without a trace during those days, remained a mystery.

All inquiries were in vain; nobody could or would tell her anything. Was he killed? Mrs. Gorianska preferred to think that he had been taken to Siberia and was alive.

She refused to learn to speak Bulgarian and kept talking in her native tongue to everybody, sometimes snapping in Russian at strangers on the street. That was met with glances of resentment from the people who often mistook her for being one of the same ones who had brought all the misery to their lives.

She carried her head high. Her eyes were clear and blue; her chin showed almost stubborn determination. There was an air of refinement and haughtiness about her.

Mrs. Gorianska had her circle of Russian friends whom she invited to her place, usually on her name day, and then we could have a peek at them. Some were more aristocratic than others, some had an excellent education and were at the top of the academic ladder in the University of Sofia, some were older, some younger, some stately, some flippant, all foreign, and, so I thought, all fascinating.

She supported herself by taking care of old or sick people, sometimes only for a few days while they recuperated after a hospital stay or, as she liked to put it, as a private nurse. Since nothing *private* was allowed, she was working outside the protection of the law, her survival depending on people not much better off than herself.

One of my favorite pictures of Mother, Mrs. Nikiforova, and Mrs. Gorianska is the one showing them standing in front of the south side of Alexander Nevsky, looking their best: their postures straight, shoulders pulled back. The three are smiling. Mrs. Nikiforova is clutching a small bouquet of flowers, and Mrs. Gorianska is wearing a raincoat, buttoned right up to her chin. It is the one I left behind, and Mother had given it to her.

On the back of the photo there is an inscription: "First of May 1967, Sofia, on leaving the church of Alexander Nevsky." It was my thirtieth birthday. The flowers, the raincoat, the smiles—all were conveying a special message to me on that special day of my life.

Sometime in the seventies, I learned that Vera Pavlova Gorianska had been killed in a traffic accident. She had been run over by a van delivering food to the homes of the Party elite. By that time, the Party's agenda to eradicate all vestiges of the old had been accomplished, while the privileges and corruption of the new "red bourgeoisie" had reached unprecedented levels. The supreme Party oligarchy, originally created by rough-cut, semi-educated peasants and now led by the dictator Todor Zhivkov, resembled more and more a caste divinely endowed with the supreme right to rule—a far cry from the proletarian class they were supposed to have sprung from. And while the regular Party members were still trying to determine how far they had progressed along "the triumphant march toward socialism," the elite had already arrived at the final stage of the *transition*: Communism.

They were already living by the motto, "From everybody according to his ability, to everyone according to his needs." And their needs, by any standards, were prodigious: ten, twenty, thirty, forty residences, a lavish life-style: flying to a hairdresser at Paris; fresh food for a reception flown straight from Maxim in Paris. As far as contributing according to ones abilities went, the so-called *old guard* felt entitled to all that, having proved themselves in *the struggle*. But most of their children, the offspring of heroes, pampered, spoiled, and irresponsible, only took from the system; they had little, if any, to give. Surprisingly, the ones demonstrating some abilities turned out to have developed refined tastes and appreciation of subjects like the history of art and poetry. The sensitivity and tenderness of heart in those children of propagators of merciless cruelty was quite unbelievable. To the ordinary people, the tales of Liudmila Zhivkova's *salon*, the daughter of the dictator, with her poetry reading soirees and required attire, provided a mild distraction, peppered with a strong dose of resentment, from the hardships of their daily lives—a topic to be discussed while waiting on a queue for toilet paper, salami, fresh bread, or some of life's other necessities. But most of what was going on, the corruption and abuses of power, were hidden, away from scrutiny.

Though some were hard to conceal, and one of them were the vans rushing through the streets of the residential district around the Doctor's Garden, delivering the daily food to the privileged who have moved to new, exclusive, well-protected homes.

It must have been there, along one of the pleasant, quiet streets, that Mrs. Gorianska had crossed the path of one of the speeding vans.

But now, back to the fifties.

Mother was working once again at home. She was knitting pullovers for export by a cooperative called Trud. Mrs. Nikiforova, Dessy's mother, as well as a few other women from the neighborhood, were employed by the same establishment for the same job.

On nice summer days, they sat on the benches of the small parkette by the river, eyes fixed on their work, fingers deftly manipulating the needles, pulling on the yarn at regular intervals while the conversations went on and on.

During the cold weather months, we would sit around the high coal-burning stove in the living room. Mother and Mrs. Nikiforova sat comfortably in the armchairs knitting, and, on rare occasions when he happened to be home on Sundays or other holidays, Father joined in with a newspaper in his hands. The cat would be sprawled out on one side, front and hind legs stretched luxuriously. I would be seated close by, doing homework or reading a book.

The pullovers had a strip of colorful designs in front. Sometimes, I would knit them. I could never start the loops and was not very good in the plain parts, but I had the patience for knitting the intricate patterns. I also found enjoyment in doing it.

The fronts, the backs, the sleeves, and the collars that were knitted separately had to be finished to size and then put together. With the approach of the deadline, tension and ceaseless activity replaced the calm and peace of prior days. The air in the apartment would be heavy with the smell of steam and wet wool—every piece had to be ironed, measured, and brought to standard size. And this was impossible to accomplish without stretching or shrinking. Armed with the measuring tape, the iron, and a bowl of water, Mother would spend hours hunched over the ironing pad, pulling and pushing the woolen pieces in all directions. She hardly ever slept the night before submitting her work. The next day she would pack all the pullovers, put them in a bag, and carry them downtown. In a couple of hours, they would be back, Mother and Mrs. Nikiforova, tired but relaxed.

On occasion, they would relate stories they had heard from other women whom they had met at the store or at the warehouse, and they would chat about them.

Then the cycle would start anew, paced slowly at the beginning with the steady, calm period of knitting, and finished with anxiety and sleepless nights at the end.

In spite of the sadness and the hard times that befell us, the indomitable optimism of youth and the unshakable trust in my parents' love kept me from brooding too much, losing hope, or being afraid of the future.

May 1, 1953

Friday

As you can guess, there was a march followed by a dance at school. Did not dance much. Older by a year.

I am already sixteen!

June 17, 1953

Wednesday

My dear diary, I have been going through your pages, reading and rereading them while listening to the waltzes being played over the radio. And I have been daydreaming about the future.

How much I want to be happy. And that isn't to say that I am complaining about my life, only that I am so eagerly waiting for the moment when all my happy dreams, born in my imagination, will come true. My present life, and everything that is going to pass till that time, is but a prelude to that wonderful moment!

June 18, 1953

Thursday

Noontime. Mother went on a trip to a monastery (forgot its name) with friends from church.

Did some cleaning and than sat down to read a bit.

It is so beautiful! I am reclining on the couch, gazing through the window.

A curtain of foliage obstructs the view outside. Not a single spot is left uncovered by the leaves. I can hear voices drifting in: the guys from the neighborhood are sitting on the benches outside, talking. The music from the radio is drowning out their conversation. It is relaxing…

Somebody rang the bell. It was Zhana looking for Lilli. She had forgotten which floor Lilli lives on and stopped at our place to ask. Lilli had promised to lend her a book.

At the moment I am reading The Sea Tower by Hugh Walpole. Dessy is reading Marion Alive by Vicki Baum.

How jolly! Everybody is reading!

June 19, 1953

Friday

Oh my precious diary! I am so glad I have you to share everything with without fear. My ability to keep my cool under pressure was put to the test today.

A while ago the doorbell rang. At the door were Kapitanova and another woman, collecting money for the dues. Even though I was aware of the purpose of their call, I still asked what they wanted. Did it on purpose. Neither of them likes me because I never pay any attention to them, simply because Kapitanova is a Communist who came only recently from some village and is particularly arrogant and pushy and the other one is a Fascist who had changed her colors after September the Ninth. Disgusting cow!

Called Mother. She started crying, giving explanations.

Oh, how I hate those sniveling scenes! Can't stand it when Mother loses her composure!

In the evening, called on Dessy and we went for a long walk along our street lined with whispering Canadian poplars.

Saw Rudy, Vesko, and Mitko. Had a nice conversation. Made an arrangement to meet a bunch of kids tomorrow morning at ten o'clock in front of our apartment building to go to the public swimming pool in the park.

I am so excited! There is a small problem though—the old swimming suit is falling apart, but it will hold for a day. After that, we shall see…

And now "Good Night." Tomorrow have to be up early in order to get ready and be off to the pool!

June 27, 1953

Saturday

Dear Diary. Today Dessy left (for Varna), and you will know how I am going to spend my days from the letters I shall be sending her every day. I am going to miss her, but there is nothing to be done. If Mom and Dad find some money, maybe I will be able to go and visit her, but I don't think that is going to happen.

As you know, Father is unemployed as well as Mother. So probably under the date of every entry you will find "Sofia" written in a different handwriting: sometimes neat (eligible), or angry (illegible scribbles), all depending on the kind of mood I am in. And therefore, my only true friend (since Dessy left), there will be a new chapter on your pages: "Letters to Dessy in Varna."

I did keep my promise and wrote diligently, every day, telling her that I was lonely and went to bed with my favorite doll, Silvia. I told her about all the books I read, like *Sons* by Pearl Buck, *Carthage in Flames* by Emilio Salgari; also, that I saw a white collar for my dress and went for a walk with Mother and Father in Boris' Garden (originally named for the tsar, but the name was changed to the Park of Freedom, a name we never used); that it rained on the day of our outing there, but we were not deterred and continued with our walk. I told her about a visit by Mara with her little girl Oli and that I made her scribble on the letter challenging Dessy to read her message. I informed her also that all of us, Mother, me, and Mara, made a dress for Oli, noting that I did the cutting and "it turned out very cute." The letters read like a catalog of all the things that we did or lived through in our daily lives. Nothing was too trivial or irrelevant to mention. So I wrote about Mrs. Nikifirova's visits, about Bulgaria's loss to Romania (3–1) at a soccer match and told her—it sounds more like advice—that she should not despair since there is going to be a return match, etc., etc.

Oh, and I almost forgot to mention that on Sunday, June 28, we were called to pass on a message to Dessy's family that their electricity has been cut off.

Finally I wrote a note:

Dear diary, seems I have lost most of the copies of the letters.

Anyway, they were full of whining!

Closing this chapter.

With Dessy's return from her holiday, things returned to normal. I stopped whining and started spending more time actually living my life rather than observing and recording it.

July 24, 1953

Friday

Today was Mother's name day. We received guests: all of the women from the neighborhood came to visit.

My cat got a bit sick and I started crying terribly. Mother got very cross with me because I was crying on her special day. But I could not help it.

Went out with Dessy and bought a bouquet of flowers for Mother. She was delighted, as well as touched. That made me happy too.

It turned out to be a nice day! The kitten is also fine.

Every morning, Father kept going "to work" and returned home late in the evening. One memory about him from this period, which I did not share even with my diary but found hard to forget, was veiled in secrecy and silence.

Father received a summons from the militia. I did not see it and was not even told about it until I overheard a conversation between him and Mother. Mother sounded very disturbed and worried. In turn, that made me feel so uneasy that I began to think that something awful was going to happen. A thought crossed my mind that there would be a search of the apartment and that they would be looking for subversive literature.

In my mind, the only printed material that could have been misconstrued as such was an old calendar with the picture of Little Simeon, as well as a few magazines with photos of the tsar's family. We had kept them hidden in a drawer for years, taking them out when we wanted to remind ourselves of happier times. Now I saw them as a danger. I had to remove them from the apartment.

At the end of each winter, the pipes of the stove used for heating the bedrooms were dismantled, cleaned, and stored till late fall, when they would be needed again.

It was summertime when the summons arrived, and the pipes were piled up in the cellar, forgotten for a while. My idea was to hide the dangerous papers in one of the sections of pipe; the straight pieces were too long, but the angular piece, connecting the vertical to the horizontal section, was small and suitable for that purpose. I buried the pipe stuffed with the folded and rolled calendar and magazines in the backyard in the strip of dirt by the fence, close to the window of our apartment.

A few days went by and nothing happened; that is until the night Father did not come back from "work."

That was so unusual. I remember lying in bed and listening for him to open the door, waiting, unable to fall asleep. There was no use asking Mother where he was. I knew that she would only say, "Who knows?"

The next day, when I got back home from school, Father was there. It was only the afternoon, still daytime, and he was already in bed. As I entered the bedroom, he pulled the covers up, close to his chin. He was lying stiff on his back, and the way he was looking at me was almost defiant—his face taut and his eyes hard. It was almost as though he was seeing and reacting to somebody else.

I stepped back in the corridor and closed the door. During the couple of days he spent in bed, I stayed away from him; I was sure that this was what he wanted me to do.

Later, I heard Mother talk to Mrs. Nikiforova about the night he did not come home. He had spent it in the basement of the militia headquarters. The most bizarre thing that I heard her say, and that stuck in my mind, was that he had been forced to climb stairs painted on the wall.

It was over, and it was time to retrieve the hidden calendar and magazines. The cold weather was approaching; the time for assembling and mounting the pipes was almost at hand. During the summer, the backyard was a favorite playground for the kids from the neighborhood. Lots of feet would have trampled over the ground on both sides of the fence; it was impossible to detect the spot where I had dug and buried the angle pipe. But it was a small area, and I did not give up easily. For days I kept waiting for an opportune moment to go behind the apartment building, surreptitiously digging and poking the hard earth by the fence, refusing to accept the possibility that I would never find the pipe and the pictures. In the end, when there was no dirt left unturned, I had to go to Mother and tell her what I had done and why, so she could stop searching for the missing pipe and be less upset about it.

Streetcar 5 ran from the center of the city to the foothills of Vitosha in the village of Kniajevo. The terminal station, at the square opposite the church Sveta Nedelia, was a roofed, enclosed shelter with number of wickets on the two far sides and a labyrinth of rails running along its length, keeping the multitude of passengers lined up between them moving in an orderly manner.

The station was always crowded on Sundays and holidays.

The crowd of young people, children, and the young at heart were noisy and cheerful. It made a pretty picture. In summer, the men dressed in shorts or light pants, the women in colorful cotton dresses, huge backpacks hanging over their shoulders; in winter, all sporting woolen pullovers and ski pants, skis sticking over heads covered with knitted caps topped by colorful pompoms, bending forward under the weight of even larger backpacks.

The trams moved slowly and noisily between the neat hedges running along both sides of the rail tracks. Before the war, during summertime, some of the cars were open on both sides and could be mounted anywhere along their length. During the slow, leisurely ride, the breeze sweeping through was gentle and invigorating. Fewer people were living in the city then, and even Streetcar 5 was not crowded.

Beyond Kniajevo, only dirt roads or paths winding through woods and meadows led up the mountain. A number of mountain lodges offered sleeping accommodations to the hikers. Usually they consisted of a couple of large rooms: one lined with rows of plank beds where men and women slept next to each other and another common room, furnished with tables, chairs, or benches, where people ate their meals, drank, sang, and danced in the evenings. The entertainment was provided by the tourists themselves, since everybody who could play guitar, accordion, or harmonica brought them along.

One early sunny afternoon, Dessy and I took Streetcar 5 and got off at the last stop to join the rest of a group of classmates going skiing for a couple of days. The itinerary specified that all gather at Kniajevo and wait for the guide, who was supposed to lead us and serve as a chaperone, in a way. Most of the guys and gals skied regularly; some were even training in clubs attached to the army or other government establishments. Dessy was one of them. That afternoon, she carried her cross-country skis and looked smart in a yellow and blue pullover. I had my aunt Nina's old pair of skis. One of them had been broken and fixed with a tin patch. The repaired ski was shorter than the good one, but the bamboo poles were fine.

The trip had a shaky start: the guide did not show up till late in the afternoon. By the time he arrived, dusk was falling. Tired and frustrated, we started to climb up the foothills of Vitosha. After a brief stop at Bialata Voda, a small lodge with a sort of a convenience store, we entered the longest stretch of the hike. It was already dark. Fresh snow had covered the ground and the tall majestic evergreens, obliterating paths and tracks. The moonlight, reflected by the whiteness all around, lit our way.

We moved in a single column in complete silence, following the guide in front. The deep snow made every step of the way more difficult. Some kept dropping back, reaching the point of exhaustion at which one could hardly lift one's legs, until a surge of new energy wiped out the fatigue.

It was a long hike with exhaustion and exhilaration alternating constantly till finally, late in the night, we reached our destination: the Lodge of the Military. To our dismay, we were turned away. We were told that the lodge was full; there was no sleeping space available, and we were advised to go to the closest lodge: Phonphones.

In an hour or so we got there, only to find out that there was no room there either.

All the other lodges were too far away and it was very late, well past midnight.

Finally, we were allowed to spend the night in the Phonphones in a decrepit attic room with broken windows and coverless plank beds. It was cold and uncomfortable. We managed to find some protection from the elements, however, by squeezing ourselves between the mattresses and the planks. In the morning, we were surprised to wake up under a blanket of snow that had drifted through the openings of the broken windows.

Most of the following day we spent skiing on the popular slope known as the Ophelias. The track was wide and not very steep, good for beginners and for people who enjoyed more leisurely skiing. Since there were no lifts, most of the time was spent climbing to the top, a drudgery that also made the whole experience more relaxed. Many stopped for a rest on their way up, getting into conversations, watching the ones going downhill, cheering and encouraging them. or poking fun at the ones who rolled over or slid down on their behinds, backs, and tummies.

One of the items on the agenda was to attend a slalom competition scheduled to take place close by the Military Lodge. By the time we arrived there, the event was well under way.

As we approached the slope, before we could join the crowd of spectators, we observed a commotion surrounding an injured skier being carried away on a stretcher. There had been an accident, and one of the competitors was hurt; rumor had it that the injury was quite severe, a broken spine. Nobody wanted to watch the competition any more; we all went to the lodge to have some tea. Inside, the conversations that followed revolved around the injured skier.

Accidents, crime, or personal tragedies were never reported by the press. We lived in a society where things like that were not supposed to happen, or, if they happened, it was to the bad guys. Every time an occurrence came that could shake our faith in our own invincibility or evidenced the fickleness of human destiny, we were deeply affected. Every crime, every tragedy that somehow became public knowledge, we discussed with passion from all possible angles. In the end, the arguments raised were always about right and wrong, about ideology and, indirectly, about the system we lived in.

Before starting the trip back home, we went to a room off the lodge to pick up our skis and poles. My poles were gone. I had to ride all the way down the mountain on the back of the skis of one of my classmates, holding fast to his jacket.

By the time we got to the city, it was very late. The apartment was empty. My parents had gone to Dessy's place to share their worries and anxieties with her mother and father. There we had to face all four of them.

The trip that had started somewhat badly did not end any better.

In the fall of our last year of high school, a group of classmates, accompanied by my mother and Dessy's, spent over a week on a hike in Vitosha. There are quite a few pictures of the trip in my album.

We roamed all over the mountain, moving from place to place, sleeping at Edelweiss and Brock, our favorite lodges, and preparing meals from the provisions we carried in the big backpacks hanging over our shoulders.

We walked late at night across a moor with the moon shining and its light reflecting on the surface of the smooth, flat stones we were treading…

We walked across wooden bridges flanked by thick growths of raspberries, clutching heavy sticks ready to fight off the ever-dreaded snakes that inhabited the thickets and hid under the warm rocks…

We felt like explorers and adventurers, keeping an eye open for a good photo opportunity.

We also reached the highest point of the mountain, Cherny Vrah.

The peak stood rocky and bare at the end of a climb through a terrain covered with blackberries and low-spreading junipers. It was a mysterious and inhospitable place, especially when fast-moving clouds descended over it, enveloping it in their white, sticky mass, the hissing wind sweeping waves of heavy moisture, the sharp, fresh scent of the junipers permeating the air. The smells, sounds, and loneliness one experiences in moments like that come back hauntingly in the remembrance of the "black" peak.

Blending in with the bleak surroundings, among the gray rocks stood the gray stony building of the weather station.

The girls in the group were Dara, Tzeni, Valia, Dessy, and me. A few years later, we spread all over the world: Canada, South Africa, England, West Germany. Only Dessy remained.

When I saw her after many years, she was living close to the lift that went straight up Vitosha, to the Aleko lodge, just below Cherny Vrah. She told me then that whenever she had time and wanted to get away from it all, she took the lift and climbed up there to smell the junipers, to listen to the wind, to feel the mist of the clouds.

I look at the pictures from time to time.

15

END OF HIGH SCHOOL

May 20, 1955

Friday

Last day of school; the graduation ball in the evening!

It felt like going to a party.

In our homeroom, all school desks were pushed aside; somebody was playing an accordion. In spite of that we had two hours of instruction. When it was over, we all decided that we had enough, and, even though we were supposed to have chemistry, the whole class went down into the schoolyard.

Somebody was taking pictures.

Inside the school, preparations for the ceremony were going on. The staircase was covered with runners and carpets; flowerpots were placed along both sides of the steps.

I felt giddy from excitement; couldn't stop clowning and running around.

Dara and I put on a show: I climbed on the water fountain, and with Dara stretching her arms toward me, we played the balcony scene from "Romeo and Juliet". Then we sang an array of parodies of folk songs. Somebody took pictures of us girls with berets on our heads and belts tied below our waists, striking poses like flappers from the twenties. Finally, we went back to the classroom where the other graduating class was brought in. We were not to leave the room until told to do so.

The students were getting restless; some of the girls started crying; Dara and I went on performing on the podium in front of the blackboard. I started thinking that my flippant behavior was inappropriate but couldn't stop.

We were arranged in a double file of gals and guys. The door opened, and we stepped into the hallway. In front of us, a three-colored ribbon was stretched across the top of the staircase, and a cordon of younger students holding flowers had lined up along the four flights of stairs.

There were speeches. Doneva, our Bulgarian teacher, was crying; half of the girls were in tears also. I was grinning. Eli delivered a speech on behalf of the class; the three-colored ribbon was untied. The school band started playing; the music thundered. The children were shouting and throwing their bouquets. Soon the staircase turned into a flower path we tread on the way down.

All the teachers were standing on the steps along the wall. They hugged us one by one. As Doneva gave me a hug and a kiss, I heard her whisper, "I have scolded you on many occasions. Hope you are not cross with me."

"No! No!" I began to repeat and suddenly broke into tears.

From there, I ran over the steps as though propelled by a rocket. Some kids were shoving flowers into my hands; others were squeezing my arms; all were shouting farewell.

In the foyer, at the bottom of the stairs, there was a crowd of pupils from the primary school. They kept screaming and obstructing my way.

Finally I shot out the door.

It was sunny outside.

It was over!

Slowly we started drifting toward home. We felt almost like adults.

By the school fence, a group of graduates had surrounded Mr. Tomalevski, our physics and astronomy teacher. We joined in and heard him delighting in the good weather, joking, and inquiring about our plans for the future.

Eventually I got home, hungry.

Mother congratulated me and asked, "Are you sad?"

"Oh, no!" It was not sadness, but gladness and tenderness that had overtaken me. I was full of faith and anticipation: all the promises to be fulfilled. All the discoveries to be made.

Later went to Aunt Nina's to pick up the dress she made me to wear to the graduation ball; pale blue taffeta, very stylish. Then met Dara, to go have our hair done. Mother accompanied us. From the hairdresser, went to Dara's place to fix our nails. Meanwhile her mother was working on her black-and-white-checkered dress, doing the finishing touches. To complement the outfit, Dara had a matching necklace and barrette, as well as silver bracelets.

At about seven o'clock we all returned home, where I got dressed.

Niuney came too, dressed in a blue-checkered dress, looking terrific. Our neighbor Mrs. Spasicheva, Zhiva (a friend), and her sister were also there.

It was a mad house.

Then, all of us walked to the restaurant in the park where the graduation ball was held.

The tables were set; the music was playing. The dinner started after a long delay. We were dancing; the time flew by.

Finally the music stopped. All the students gathered around our teachers, Munkov and Tomalevski. We started singing old patriotic songs from the Bulgarian National Revival. The teachers were surprised and thrilled. Many did not want to come to the ball, afraid that we would misbehave and they would end up feeling disappointed. Instead, here we were dressed like young ladies and gentlemen and behaving accordingly. Velichkov (our Bulgarian teacher from grade eight) pulled out an old notebook and went down memory lane, recalling our grades from years ago.

Outside on the terrace, a couple of guys were drifting into a drunken stupor.

May 21, 1955

Saturday

A new day had begun.

Some of the teachers had left; the music had started playing again. It was the rumba. After three o'clock, more graduates arrived, students from other schools who had been kicked out of the restaurants their balls had been held in.

Dawn was breaking.

We watched the sky from the verandah, imagining ourselves on the deck of a ship in the middle of the sea.

Nobody was leaving. The tipsy guys kept everybody laughing.

At about six o'clock, the foursome: Dessy, Dara, Niuney, and I, headed home. All had swollen feet; we could hardly walk. So we selected three benches close to one another to stretch ourselves on; only Dara stubbornly continued walking. After a rest, Dessy and I accompanied Niuney to the streetcar, then continued walking till we reached our street.

Mother was waiting for me, leaning from the window.

In the parkette in front of our apartment building, some of my former classmates were dancing and singing in a celebratory mood.

They were still there—the noise and laughter drifting through the window—as I dropped into bed, exhausted from the longest day of my life.

"Good morning. Rache! What are you doing here? Waiting for somebody?"
The voice of my math teacher, Mr. Munkov, startled me. I did not hear or notice the approach of this slightly stooped figure clad in the invariable brown suit. As usual, his hands were clutching a pipe, and he was looking at me with gentle, good-natured eyes. It was a fresh, sunny morning, perfect for a stroll along the riverside boulevard. It was also the day of the math entrance exam at the end of a long, hard summer.

First, there were the matriculation exams—there were no exemptions. All tests were oral. The students drew lots and, after a brief interim to contemplate the answers, were called before a small committee of teachers to deliver their verbal responses or solve problems on the blackboard.

The pressure was relentless. About 90 percent of us had applied to continue our education at different universities. The academic criteria for acceptance were called "bal." The bal was calculated on the basis of diploma grades and entrance-exam results. Consequently, it was mandatory to pass the matriculation exams with top grades.

Once that was over, the graduation ceremony kept us in a state of exhilaration for a while. It was held in a nearby theater, with all parents and teachers attending, thus filling the salon to capacity.

Hardly a month later, the entrance exams began.

It was not an easy task to choose one's future profession, even for a top student. Money was never a consideration. Tuition was low and soon afterward was abolished altogether. Potential earning after graduating was irrelevant—all salaries were about the same. There were however, all these other important questions to ponder, like: "After graduating, where am I going to be sent for the three years compulsory work?"

The answer: "Preferably in a city."

"Now, where are my best chances of getting in considering all requirements?" The answers varied.

I had always thought, rather assumed, that I was going to continue my education at a university; that this was expected of me. But bogged down in the present as we were, the moment to fill the application forms for admittance to university caught me almost by surprise. Suddenly, I had to face the facts: the limitations beyond the simple requirements of grades, the quotas for the privileged, and their effect on the opportunities for the rest—myself included.

In the first place, there was no way that I would have been accepted to study journalism, a vague idea that had taken hold on my imagination for a while or would become a practicing professional in the field ever.

It was time to ask myself the questions everybody was asking. It was time to be practical.

> May 23, 1955
>
> Monday
>
> I chose my future profession, electrical engineering. Not quite sure if this is for me, but what does it matter since I can't be what I want to be? Wishful thinking is not enough to get me into journalism. One needs connections, and I have none...
>
> The present institutions of higher education are nothing more than incubators for fools parading as professionals. Most of the students ending up there had probably tried just to get somewhere—anywhere, since for most, their preferred choices were out of reach.

Actually, most young people were not as cynical as I sounded in that entry. Neither was I, most of the time. The realization that my choice was out of reach must have made me bitter for the moment.

When I tried to discuss the matter with my parents, my first question was a tentative: "How about law?" It was meant partially as a compliment to my father. His reaction, though, told me it was not taken as intended.

"Law! What do you think you will end up doing? Writing posters on a cooperative farm?" Father seldom snapped at me like that.

The closest to advice I got was from Mother. "Why don't you study medicine?"

"And why should I do that?"

"Perhaps you can become a heart specialist."

And Father's lukewarm suggestion: "How about dentistry? Maybe pharmacy?"

It was hopeless. Mother wanted me to become her doctor; Father could not even come up with an original idea. It simply irked me. I wanted to shake them, to show them that I could do something challenging, something unusual.

"Engineering!"

That got the desired effect; both were nonplused. I took their reaction as overwhelmingly impressed.

And that is how the direction of my life was determined.

Never mind that I had no idea what engineering meant, what kinds of engineers were out there, that I had no idea what the difference was between a bolt and a nut, or was there any?

There was one last decision to be made: exactly what kind of engineering to apply for. Since the first one at the top of the list on the application form was electrical-radio engineering and the rest sounded just as obscure as this one, I settled for it.

One person who encouraged me to go into engineering was my math teacher, Mr. Munkov. So it turned out to be a lucky coincidence that he happened to pass by the bench I had been resting on the morning of the entrance exam in math, feeling overwhelmed, fearful, or merely too tired to go on with the race. Three days earlier, I had already written an exam in Bulgarian and a couple of days later would write exam in physics.

His voice was soothing. "It will be all right. You will do well. No need to worry. I think they might give you a question to prove Newton's binomial theorem. Good luck, Rache!"

It was my nickname he was calling me by. It made me feel good. A surge of energy and confidence came over me; the fatigue disappeared.

As my teacher turned around to continue his walk, I jumped up from the bench and darted in the direction of the school where the exam was held. Earlier I had wandered somewhat.

It was a beautiful day, and it did not take me long to get there on time.

On the twentieth of July, the exams were over and the tense period of idle wait for the results began.

August 12, 1955

(recorded a couple of weeks later)

Sofia

According to some notes, this was the day the lists of the successful candidates were to be posted at the university. Previously, Aunt Raina visited us and told us my grades in the exams; she had access to the records in the university office. My total was above the cutting point. I was in. There were congratulations, which I accepted calmly and went out, feeling almost like university student.

Alas, my joy was short-lived. On August 12, the lists came out and around ten o'clock in the morning, Mother went to check them. I stayed in bed at home. When she came back, she was beside herself.

My name was not on the lists!

Mother was on the verge of collapse.

I remember that it was a cloudy, dismal day.

What happened afterward is somewhat hazy in my mind; I got up and started wandering about in the apartment. The only thing I remember for sure was the sensation of my head going empty, vacant.

Later went with somebody, I forget who, to see the lists for myself (maybe it was Panka), came back home, and for a couple of days walked around in a daze, floating in space…

Damn the Communists with their privileged "proletarian" children!

Now I have to get used to living with the thought of going through the same exams, anxieties, and fear again.

It was a great shock, but I survived. Somewhere, however, there must have been a lesson in all that.

Nothing was left for me to do but wait till next year. Then try again.
Telling myself that I was not the only one did not bring me consolation, but it did soften the blow some.

Many, trying to get into one of the more desirable programs or into one of the arts-related programs, spent half of their youth trying, year after year, to succeed.

Quite a few could be seen hanging around the drama school all day long, all year round, just wasting time between entrance exams, while others concentrated their efforts on taking endless lessons in the hope of improving their chances, stubbornly refusing to give up.

It was hard to change direction at this point in one's life. There were no other opportunities besides the ones offered by a good education. The only employer was the government. Initiative, entrepreneurship had no place in this society; only qualifications counted. They could offset, to a certain extent, the most powerful disadvantage: the stigma of being born into the wrong class.

In the fall of 1955, I simply went into a state of stupefaction that lasted almost till the next spring. While others in my situation were studying and preparing themselves for the entrance exams the following year, I just drifted, living day by day.

My parents simply left me alone.

There was one dramatic moment, though, when it seemed that all my worries about getting into university might as well have been completely immaterial.

Dessy did not get into chemical engineering, the program of her choice, either. And we both failed to register in the neighborhood chapter of the Dimitrov Union of National Youth. Since we had been enrolled en masse in school, it had not dawned on us that, being out of school, we had to register somewhere else. We had assumed that, once we were in university, our membership would be automatic. We had assumed wrongly, so it was a great shock to receive a notice that we had to attend a meeting. The main item on the agenda had to deal with our expulsion from the organization. Devastating consequences would ensue, and we knew it!

The meeting was held in a place on a street just behind ours. Quite a few people attended and, among them, some older guys whom we recognized as alumni from our school. They lived in the neighborhood and must have already graduated from university.

We knew that the question would be put to a vote, and we knew also that voting was never an expression of free will; it was just a formality. I felt doomed, and I guess that Dessy did too. On that occasion, though, something extraordinary occurred: just as the vote was to be called, one of the guys stood up and suggested that, since this was our first misdeed, a reprimand and a show of criticism on the part of the membership combined with heartfelt self-criticism on our part might be sufficient punishment for now. After a moment of stunned silence, another guy got up and expressed his support for the idea, then a few others said more or less the same, and, before we knew it, the motion was put to a vote and we were saved!

I remember distinctly that on that evening we felt not only happy, relieved, and grateful, but for some strange reason, a trifle heroic.

We ran around the corner to tell our parents the good news.

The following year, both of us were accepted at the universities of our choice: Dessy into chemical engineering and me into mechanical. I simply did not have the stomach to retry the same program as the previous year. I just wanted to forget the whole thing.

16
THE SECRET

There was a family secret that for a long while was of an almost overwhelming significance in my life. Its shadow hung over the lives of a few people, but it was central to mine, because it was about how my life began in the first place.

I was born out of wedlock. At the time and place of my birth, this was the stuff that secrets were made of. It was shocking, unacceptable, and therefore shameful. Living a life with a secret like that was, at times, dreamlike. Then I would feel as though I was just playing the role of a "regular" child and would wish for the impossible: that I had been born at least nine months after my parents were married. As it happened, I was born two years and a month before the wedding.

At the time, many people knew the story, and, later, Mother brought it to life by occasionally talking about the past with her friends. And that is how I heard most of it. It seemed that she never treated the subject as a big secret, rather as an unsettled, emotional issue that she did not like to remember often but could not stop dwelling on. It seemed that she still needed to vent frustrations built up long ago that were still simmering deep inside her.

I never talked about it and, needless to say, never told anybody until I grew up. But I thought about it and feel certain that it influenced the development of my outlook on morality to a great extent. My feelings of compassion and empathy for all social outcasts, my passion for fairness and justice for anyone wronged, probably stems from the realization that I could have easily become one of them if people only knew. Intuitively, as a child, I was aware that if the secret were revealed, I would pay a price, even though, as blame goes, I had nothing to do with it.

On the other hand, I always thought that it sounded like a fascinating romantic novel. Nobody told me the whole story. Mother was reluctant to talk to me about it, and I was afraid even to mention it to Father, sure that his reaction would have been only embarrassed silence. So my secret was ridden with secrets of its own. But the parts that I know read like a movie script.

Mother is twenty-one years old: fair, slim, and elegant. She has graduated from business school and is now employed in the pension department at the Ministry of the Interior. A portrait of her from this time shows her with hair in a tight roll at the nape of her neck; her smile reveals a row of large, bright, perfect teeth. Her face has an open and wholesome look.

She has an admirer, or rather what was called, at the time, a simpatico, working in the same department. He leaves tender notes in the drawer of her desk. They are quite innocent.

At twenty-one, all Mother wants from life is to get married well and have a family. Her work is one way to meet a "good party." As a matter of fact, in spite of being a working girl, she is far from being independent; indeed, her father collects her salary and keeps her on an allowance.

I can almost see her through the eyes of my mind, in the morning, waiting for the streetcar all dressed up for work, young, fresh, innocent, and eager, clutching a purse in gloved hands, darting flirtatious glances from the shadow of her hat.

We had no pictures of Father from that time. He had already been thirty years old and working as a lawyer in his father's office. He had been a dandy. Earlier pictures show him with thick, somewhat-unruly curly hair, a rather intense and serious countenance. In his thirties he must have looked much the same, except for his hair, which he started to part slightly on one side and keep greased flat as was the fashion at that time. He had already had a relationship with a woman his age; his family had known her well. It had not, however, developed into a permanent one. Father had not been the marrying type.

Mother and Father meet at the streetcar stop, waiting for the same tram to take them downtown to their respective jobs. Every time they see each other, they exchange glances. This goes on for quite a long time until they are introduced almost by accident. By then they have fantasized so much about each other that they are ready for a romance.

It is New Year's Eve, 1936. Mother has had a falling-out with her simpatico and is in the mood for revenge. Her sister Nina plans to go to a celebration with a fellow who has a friend and is looking for a date for him. The idea is to spend the evening as a foursome.

Mother and Aunt Nina were quite different. They had distinct tastes of their own and almost opposite ideas about life. Mother was romantic and waited for things to happen to her; Auntie did not waste time in wishful dreaming but went after what she wanted and lived life to the full. Grandfather had been mindful of her willfulness and tried to bridle her. On the other hand, Mother had never given him any problems. There had also been the usual competition and petty jealousies between siblings. They had not chummed together.

On the eve of 1936, things are to change dramatically. Almost on a whim, Aunt Nina asks Mother to go with her on a blind date with her boyfriend's friend. It is a mystery man, and Mother is hesitant. But anger toward her own boyfriend and the prospect of spending a dull evening at home on such an occasion makes her accept. It is destiny. The blind date is the man from the streetcar stop, the one she remembers well.

At the time Mother had thought that it really was fate, but I have heard her also say that she would not have been surprised to learn that it had been cleverly arranged by Father.

How and where the four of them spent the evening, I don't know, but I know that Mother had been completely fascinated by him on that very first date. Throughout the years she often pondered, "I liked tall men. He was short."

"I loved to dance. He did not even try."

"How did I fall for him? He overwhelmed me with that mind of his! He was so extraordinary!"

She never said that he was only talk and no substance. Even in a state of utter disappointment and anger with him, when love seemed to have been completely wiped out, she remained in awe of him. And on Father's side, no matter how old she became, how ravaged her face was by bitterness and hardship, he always saw her as the most beautiful woman in the world.

So, in their life together, full of conflicts and extreme emotions, what kept them together was her endless fascination with "that mind of his" and his everlasting enchantment with her looks. And for both of them, these sentiments had been permanently and firmly established on their first date, New Year's Eve, 1936.

Their courtship sounded to me like a fairy tale. Mother told me about it many times, reminiscing about the good old days when there were no comrades, but Miss, Mr., and Mrs., and there had been gaiety in life.

Sofia is full of small restaurants with quaint names: the Wild Roosters, the Three Constrictors, the Blind Dog. Father has reservations for a table in one of them every evening. He and Mother spend hours after work there, dining and talking, just the two of them. Father buys her bouquets of white drops, lilies of the valley, violets, and roses from the flower girls making the rounds every evening. Mother loves flowers. At the end of these evenings, he takes her home to her parents' house. His own parents' home, where he lives, is not far from there.

Their fathers know each other. They belong to the same party, and both are active politicians. But there is no love lost between them. When Grandfather Vassil becomes aware that his daughter is dating Mirko Grigorov's son, the reaction is swift: the suitor is unsuitable, the girl has a lot to lose, the whole thing must stop. He goes so far as to lock Mother in the toilet to prevent her from going on a date with Father.

It had not worked. It had gotten worse. Sometime in the end of summer, Mother had gotten pregnant—according to my calculations. She never talked about that, never said anything implying accusation or excuse.

What happens afterward is at times heartbreaking and at times even comic. Mother tries to hide her pregnancy by fastening her girdle tighter and tighter. There is a picture of her from this time, walking along a street with Uncle Manol. She is so thin and emaciated that she looks much taller than she ever was; her face exudes tension and apprehension.

Father refuses to get married. In particular, he does not want to be married in a church. He wants only a civil ceremony; at this time, there is no such thing.

From the moment the two sets of parents learn of the situation, they insist on an immediate wedding. Great pressure is exerted on Father by his family. But he will not budge. Both he and Mother leave home and "move" to Father's office, where they spend the nights, but how and where Mother spends the days, I don't know. To the chagrin of everybody, she goes along with Father's ideas.

There are promises of rewards from the grandfathers if only the two will get married, and there is the question of honor. That is when things turn almost bizarre. In Grandfather Vassil's life, guns play a prominent role. He always goes armed on his travels, for protection, and he looks at these weapons as a way to restore his honor. One day, somehow he drags Mother to a shooting gallery at some sort of a fair. Here he produces a gun, sticks it in her hand, and orders her to start shooting. He tells her that she must learn how to use the gun, because she has to shoot the villain who has taken her honor and covered them all with shame.

Mother drops the gun and runs away from her father as fast as she can.

Just before my birth, they move to a house in the foothills of Vitosha. By all accounts Father is full of anticipation. But there is a problem. Since they are not married, Mother has to go to the wing for unwed women, and, for some reason, this is unacceptable to Father. He arranges for her to be admitted to the regular wing, where I am born and registered under my father's name.

I have been told many times by Mother and different aunts how Father behaves during this time. Due to a flu or some other epidemic, the hospital is restricted to visitors. Father, who comes every day bringing baskets of fruit and bouquets of flowers, is barred from coming inside; but the security people always take the presents, which he assumes are being delivered to Mother. In fact, they are not. But as she is leaving the hospital with her baby, she is showered with thanks and praises for Father. In the estimation of the hospital employees, there has never been a happier or more generous father than he.

Our first home is a small room in a suburban house. The furniture consists of a double bed and a wooden washbasin where I sleep. Even though right after my arrival Father's sisters bring gifts for me, blankets and dresses they had knitted themselves, there is not much contact or help of any kind, nor does a close relationship develop with the new family. Mother and Father are on their own. They must start from scratch.

It turns out that I am a handful of a baby. Father spends entire nights pacing the small room, carrying me in his arms, trying to keep me from crying. Mother almost drowns me while giving me a bath until finally Zorah, the landlady, takes pity and assumes some of the chores. Mother is especially appreciative that Zorah undertakes the delicate task of bathing me. In later years, after we move away from Zorah's house, Mother keeps taking me there for visits and makes a point of reminding me of her goodness by saying, "Zorah is your second mother. Without her, I don't know how we would have survived."

There is family contact from Mother's side. Her two brothers, both younger than she and students at the time, visit us, but it is her parents' support that she misses and longs for. The hardships and the unresolved matter of the marriage have taken their toll, especially on her. Later I gather that, at one point, she packs me up and goes back to her parents. It does not last; only a couple of days later we are back in the small, empty room. Cold and unforgiving, Grandma Lia has not given her the sympathy and understanding Mother is looking for.

Life has not only been all gloom and doom, though. There is warmth and love in the small household, and, later I will hear many stories about that time from Mother's and Father's reminiscences attesting to that. Most of them are about me. They are doting parents, and, as I outgrow babyhood, I become a happy child.

In a year or so we begin moving from place to place, never acquiring much furniture, just the bare necessities, living like people in transition.

Finally, in June of 1939, without much ado, Mother and Father get married. I am over two years old. I think their wedding is my earliest memory. It is a picture I carry in my mind—of Grandmother Lia's house in Sofia. I am dressed in a pink dress, holding her hand. We are standing in the garden, on the pathway outlined by flowers. I am waving at Mother and Father, who are standing by the gate with a couple of people. Mother is dressed in a tweed manteau and Father in a dark suit. They look elegant, urbane, and I adore them. They are on their way to a small monastery outside Sofia where they are going to get married. The best man and the maid of honor are Father's colleague and his wife.

The wedding is a very simple affair, no big gathering of relatives and friends or celebration. I don't think anybody from Father's side attends; maybe they had not been invited.

And, as far as romantic novels go, that should have been the happy ending of the story.

Grandmother Raina and Grandfather Mirko, ca 1905

Father (front middle, kneeling) with law school chums. ca.1928

Enjoying the show sitting on Grandfather Vassil's knee at the annual get-together organized by the Association Liubash. Also pictured: Grandmother Lia (all dressed up in the traditional costume of the district of Trun), Mother, and Aunt Nina

Grandfather Mirko's funeral, 1941. Kneeling, front row: Uncle Liubomir, Grandmother Raina, Aunt Rada, Aunt Tina, and Mother. Standing behind them: Uncle Angel, Aunt Julia, Uncle Alexander (Sanyo), Aunt Bojana, and Father.

Mother

A portrait of Grandfather Vassil as a Permanent Member of the Sofia's Regional Council 1930–1932.

Uncle Manol

Father

A Sunday outing with Aunt Blaga, Milcho, Darcho. Not pictured: Uncle Pecko who was taking the photo

To the movies with Mother. (Can't take my eyes from the new Bata shoes!)

Sunday promenade in Gorna Bania with Aunt Desha, Uncle Otto, Chris, holding hands with cousin Bobby.

The choir at the middle school #10 (V.Aprilov), 1950. I am the girl without the uniform in the middle of the second row.

End of high school, May 20,1955. From 1965–1978, half of the girls left Bulgaria and settled in England, West Germany, Italy, South Africa, and Canada. I am pictured in the first row, second from the right.

At the monastery of St Ivan Rilsky, with Father's colleague and family, 1950

At the Golden Bridges, with Mother and Dessy

A *student's brigade* at the village of Mirovtsi, Novi Pazar, October 1957

Mrs. Nikiforova, Mother and Mrs. V. Gorianska, at Alexander Nevsky 1967

Mother and Father, 1949

Welcome to my world! (Mother and I).

With Mother, Father, and favorite Uncle Liubcho

17

UNIVERSITY. MATURING

The formidable Hungarian soccer team of the fifties was bringing glory and pride into the drab world behind the Iron Curtain. Pushkash and the rest of the players elevated the small eastern European country to height in the sports world reserved only for the mighty Big Brother. Sports had already been politicized, turned into a powerful propaganda tool. Already the athletes of the satellite countries were made to understand that sometimes winning a sport event meant jeopardizing their future or even losing their freedom. A very popular Bulgarian bicyclist disregarded the rule, winning over a Soviet rival, and ended up in a labor camp. Personal ambition, national pride, there was no place for any of that in the socialistic states.

In light of that, the Hungarian soccer team was an affront to the supremacy of the Soviets, as well as a boost to Hungarian nationalism. It was almost impossible not to view the players as more than athletes; they were heroes.

And then came the Hungarian Counterrevolution—the official label given to the events in the fall of 1956 by the Communist governments—but referred to as a Revolution by the people who rejected the false notion that these socialistic states were established as a result of Communist uprisings rather than by occupation by the Red Army. It is tempting to draw the conclusion that, in some way, the great soccer team contributed to the onset of the uprising by lifting the spirits and building the confidence of the Hungarian people.

It came as a surprise to most. It brought excitement, admiration, and, for a very short while, even hope. It also brought a disbelief in the failure of the West to help the Hungarian people, abandoning them after years of encouraging dissent, of implicit promises broadcast daily from the West.

The revolution in Hungary reached us like thunder from afar. The distance was not great, but the event itself was so inconceivable in Bulgaria; the restriction of travel even within the socialist camp created a feeling of claustrophobic isolation that made the world beyond our borders very distant. The news was coming again from the West through the broadcasts of the BBC, Voice of America, Deutsche Welle, Free Europe—all, of course, jammed and hard to hear over the interference.

In Sofia, there was no visible reaction, no unrest to speak of. But there was no doubt that the government was prepared with contingency plans for action in case of trouble. The officials of our university issued a list of names of the students who were going to be expelled in case of any activity inspired by the events in Hungary. The days were filled with a great degree of hidden tension and anticipation, but there was no sense of urgency, rather an attitude of "wait and see."

When it all ended with the Soviet tanks rumbling through the streets of Budapest, crushing short-lived illusions and high hopes along their path of destruction, the only thing left was admiration for the brave fighters. Also, from that moment on, the intensity of the anti-Russian feelings among the Hungarians soared.

At home, Father went into a state of denial, looking for excuses for the Americans and the rest of the free world for letting the Revolution down. It was hard to give up hope altogether.

The exodus following the end of the uprising claimed most of the famous soccer players. The Western teams swallowed them up, and some of them became stars who went on to build new careers and fortunes. We kept hearing about Pushkash's success in Spain. The tales were tall, spread by word of mouth and therefore out of proportion, turning them and their destinies into legends. The ones that failed simply faded away into the past. The dream team was no more.

The Hungarians excelled in another sport: fencing. A couple of years after the events in Hungary, a friend from university who was a Master Champion of rapier took me to a fencing tournament held in Sofia. The participating athletes were from the Soviet Union, Hungary, and elsewhere, probably Eastern European countries, which I don't remember. As a matter of fact, I would have forgotten the event altogether if it had not been for the final match between a Hungarian and a Russian.

There were several games going on at the same time on the floor of the huge hall. Each couple of competitors were fencing on a platform surrounded by a retinue of officials and teammates on the floor below. Time was passing slowly; the afternoon was dragging on without much excitement until my friend prompted me. "Watch these guys. It is going to be an interesting game."

Two men stepped onto the platform: one tall and strapping, looking composed and confident; the other, smaller in stature, tense and restless, exuding almost palpable nervous energy. They looked mismatched.

As soon as they were wired to the scoring board and the signal for the start was given, it became obvious that this was going to be an extraordinary show. The Hungarian lounged at the Russian with a ferocity that was startling. He kept coming after him relentlessly, with anger defying any sportsman's resolve and an energy drawn from such intense and powerful emotions that it had to be personal. What made the scene so riveting was the fact that the opponent's persona seemed irrelevant to the Hungarian; he might have been fighting a windmill.

The hall was electric with tension. We all felt touched and moved by the drama played out on the platform.

The match went on for a long time. The Russian, with his cool and accomplished skills, was holding his own. It was impossible to compare the two competitors; they were playing two different games.

Finally the Hungarian won. The spectators were on their feet. On the platform, the winner collapsed.

Later, at the ceremony, still pale and dazed, he stood on the podium, tears streaming down his cheeks. Exalted, transported, he was not simply an athlete winner in a tournament; he was a crusader who fought and won an epic battle.

Many years later, I was reminded of that time, of the great Hungarian team, in a most unexpected way.

It must have been around 1983. The incident occurred in the drafting studio of the college where I was teaching—in a large, bright room filled with rows of drafting tables all occupied by students busy with their drawings, absorbed in the challenging task of manipulating the drafting mechanisms.

It was at the beginning of the semester, and I had not yet had time to learn the students by name. Standing on the high platform in front of the blackboard, keeping an eye on them in readiness to respond to any request for assistance, during a quiet spell I decided to get through the class list, calling each student, trying to match names to faces.

It was still a long while before the events of 1989 and the flood of emigrants from Eastern Europe, or, for that matter, before the few other waves of emigrants that would completely change the face of our college. I had never been back.

Even the possibility of this ever happening was elusive. The memories were the only bridge connecting the halves of my live, my two countries. No matter how hard I tried to bring them together, they seemed to drift farther apart.

That is why when I came across the name Richard Szigetti I felt almost jolted by the familiarity of its sound.

"Szigetti?"

A tall, fair lad, fresh from high school, raised his eyes. "Yes."

The urge to inquire further was too strong. "Is this a Hungarian name?"

"Yes. My father is Hungarian."

On an impulse I continued, "In the fifties, there was a famous Hungarian soccer team. One of the players had the name of Szigetti."

"Yes. It was my father."

I was so startled by what I heard and my reaction must have been so revealing that, at once, all the students stopped their work and fixed their attention on Richard and me. Some probably misunderstood my obvious agitation, assuming that I had known his father personally. An explanation was in order.

It was not easy, though. Remembering the great Hungarian soccer team stirred feelings in me that had nothing to do with the game and everything to do with a time in my life. I felt the blood rushing to my head; my heart rate quickened. It took an effort to keep my emotions under control. And I started talking about the game…

In the land of hockey, it was mystifying for students to hear that in Europe soccer players were stars, much like the hockey players here; that I remembered their names and that I spoke about them with an enthusiasm they probably found hard to understand.

Richard told us that his father had left Hungary after the events of 1956, got married, and eventually immigrated to Canada. I don't remember what his occupation was then, but I am pretty sure that it was not connected with the game of soccer. During the break, our conversation continued in the hallway: Richard and I, surrounded by a throng of students.

There were more chats during the time he attended the college. And every time I would spot him in the classroom or bump into him somewhere along the hallways or in the cafeteria, my face would inadvertently break into a smile, as though I had just received a letter from home.

Most of the songs and poems we were taught to sing and recite in primary school had to do with the beauty of nature and our love for the land, the changing of the seasons, and the joy of toiling the fields and gathering its fruits. The last sentiment must have been a carryover from the time before the collectivization of the land and the transformation of the peasant population. There was no enthusiasm for working in the fields, especially on the part of the men in the villages, and no matter how many books were written, how many movies were made, glorifying the success of the agrarian policies of the Party, their failures were obvious.

The plowing and the sowing were done mainly by machines, but in summer and fall, when fruit and vegetables had to be picked by hand, the crunch came. Much of the crops would have been left to rot in the fields had it not been for the students. The practice was developed originally for the benefit of the latter, as part of the curriculum for their political education.

Every fall we were transported to all corners of the country to do a variety of tasks for which we had no skills or even basic preparation. We also lacked the motivation, and the resentment was ubiquitous. The benefits to everybody involved—students, as well as peasants—were, at best, dubious.

In October, at the beginning of my second year at the university, the students from my specialty, Technology of Machine Building, were assigned to a village in the northeast, approximately 400 km from Sofia. Three females were supposed to be included in our group of about thirty students. I was the only one, however, who showed up at the train station. The other two were absent, excused for valid reasons. The autumn weather was unpredictable; a flu epidemic was spreading all over the country. People were getting sick. It was not hard to get out of the dreaded brigade duty. I never tried; participation in these activities was to balance, to a certain extent, the inherent shortcomings of my bourgeois origin.

It took a daylong ride to reach the village. At dusk we were dropped off in a square where a small crowd of locals were waiting to meet us and take us to our accommodations. No prearrangments were made; the allocation was done on the spot: we had to stand and wait until somebody stepped forward and told us to follow.

I was chosen by the leader of one of the labor units in the cooperative called "zveno." She looked nice enough and appeared to be of Mother's age. I felt relieved that she had chosen me. The house she took me to was a new, two-story building with an outside staircase that led to a single large room on the second floor. While she was showing me around, she explained that I was to share it with her daughter, who had just graduated from high school and was a couple of years my junior.

The room was neat and clean and furnished like any city room. Besides the two beds, there was a wardrobe with rows of quinces lined on top, the giveaway of village living. Their presence and the air, sweet with their aroma, created a comfortable feeling associated with a certain kind of life. I liked the room a lot. This was, however, only a place to spend the night. For breakfast and dinner, I had to go to a designated hall in the village to join the rest of the group.

The next morning we were taken in open trucks to a vast cornfield quite a distance away in the country. The stalks were high and heavy with corncobs. The crop must have been good.

It was a cold, gray day. To keep ourselves warm, we had taken all the cloths we had brought out of our bags and put them on our backs: raincoats, knitted pullovers, corduroy pants, and long woolen scarves wrapped around our necks. Most had covered their heads with a variety of caps and berets. I wore a kerchief. Mittens and gloves protected our hands from the cold. We were a motley group, totally out of place among the green stalks. The appearance aside, the footwear was a disaster. The leather shoes we all wore did not provide much protection—if any—from the moist loam we trampled upon all day long. My feet felt cold and wet and hurt constantly.

The field was huge; the work was daunting.

Short instructions followed: we were to spread out among the cornstalks, each taking a place between two rows. The working tools were distributed: long nails hanging on a rope, which we had to tie around our wrists, making sure that the string was long enough to allow the nail to be held by its head and used as a device for splitting the foliage covering the cob. Then the foliage was to be pulled back; the bare cob was twisted until it broke at its base and was thrown into a basket. The maneuver had to be repeated to the left and right of each path, advancing as fast as possible along the endless rows stretching straight ahead till we got to the end of the field. Then we would turn around and start all over again.

It was all done in a spirit of competition. The group of thirty or so students were divided into several competing teams. At the end of the day, the winners received a bottle of plum brandy.

The work was hard and painful. The gloves wore off at our fingertips and made them sore. Restricted by uncomfortable and unsuitable clothes, we moved clumsily along, surrounded by the sounds of the whistling wind and crushing foliage. To cheer ourselves on, we would sing.

The only break we had was at noon, for lunch. The food was brought to the field where we ate, sitting under the trees or sprawled on our bellies, elbows dug into the ground for support.

Toward evening, the trucks returned to pick us up. A large red flag was given to us to display on the return trip to the village. Being the only girl, I would end up right in front of the open platform, leaning against the cabin, the banner stuck next to me, flapping in the wind that lashed at my face and brought tears to my eyes.

After a couple of days, many succumbed to the flu and had to be sent to the nearest hospital. Soon the hospital was filled to capacity with sick students, and the new cases had to be sent farther, to facilities in the neighboring towns.

I did not see much of my roommate. She stayed out late at night and came back when I was asleep. She was still sleeping when I got up and left for work in the morning. Then I could see only her head buried in the pillows, hair covered in rollers, and her watch left on the table. Once I asked her mother why her daughter was not coming to the field with us. She gave me a startled, incredulous look. "She has an education. She just graduated from high school. Do you see this watch? Her father went to town a while ago and bought it for her—a graduation present." Clearly, it was a stupid question.

In the center of the village was a tavern. It was open all day long, and there were men always in there, but never any women. The women were busy working, taking care of things; the men, on the other hand, seemed to have a lot of time to spare. They sat in groups, leaning forward at the tables, talking or silently observing the goings-on while reclining leisurely against the backs of the benches and chairs. They drank brandy, "mastika," or "menta"—a green, mint-flavored liqueur—smoking slowly, deliberately. The air was heavy with smoke and smells of earth, wood, and damp cloth.

The students avoided the tavern. We felt like strangers there—unwelcome, looked upon with suspicion.

The people in charge of the students tried to keep us entertained during the evenings. Once they treated us to a movie, brought especially for this one projection. On a couple of occasions, they organized dances. Unfortunately, there was a shortage of girls. The few who came were in great demand. At the end of the evening, they were exhausted; whereas most of the guys grew bored from standing around and staring at the dancing couples. My roommate was a great success. Her freshly curled hair bounced off her shoulders with every turn of the waltz, and her new watch sparkled on her wrist reflecting every ray of light.

My best friends from the university, Ivan and Stephan, were also there. We met at the very beginning of the first year in mechanical engineering classes the three of us were attending. Immediately we became fast friends—sharing notes, helping each other with assignments. Our friendship extended beyond the university walls. We confided in each other and even sought advice from one another in personal matters concerning the opposite sex. This was especially true in my relationship with Ivan. We had a lot in common, and I trusted him.

One day, the three of us went to the tavern. I guess we did it on purpose, to assert ourselves and to show we were not intimidated. So we sat at a table, ordered three glasses of brandy, and lit cigarettes. The reaction was instantaneous: all eyes were on us, most of the attention directed at me. I did not flinch. As uncomfortable as I felt I sat there, flanked by my buddies, drinking plum brandy and smoking a cigarette, just as slowly and deliberately as the men did. After the last drop of liqueur went down our throats and the cigarette butts were extinguished and squashed in the ashtray, we stood up and crossed the room at a leisurely pace, through the thick smoke and heavy smell until we reached the door and burst out into the fresh air.

The ride back was just as long as the ride there, but the *brigade* was over and time passed faster. I felt happy. For hours I stood by the open window, head stuck out as far as I could, the wind beating my brow. It was invigorating; it was cleansing. I had survived!

The next day I woke up with a terrible headache. My sinuses were inflamed; my eyebrows felt heavy, giving me the sensation they were going to fall off my face. It was hard to see through the pain. For about a week, I remained in bed, sick and miserable.

The fact that we lived behind the impenetrable Iron Curtain, cut off from the world, that all news that reached us was carefully prepackaged into propaganda and delivered by the government-owned press, did not preclude us from demonstratively and forcefully expressing swift reactions—rather, outrage—to all kinds of events played on the world stage.

This is how it was supposed to look to the world outside: like a part of the struggle against the *dirty imperialism and capitalism* for the glory of the only perfect system—the one we lived in. Fake indignation expressed through telegrams of protest and choreographed demonstrations were always in support of causes and events far from our hearts and minds. The utter arrogance in the face of all failures of this unjust system made those expressions of righteousness look and feel preposterous.

Every time we were herded into a crowd, forced to protest against a war, a conflict, or some Western policy, I felt embarrassed, humiliated. Most of the time we had no idea what it was all about or even where the action was. Sometimes during the French-Algerian conflict in the late fifties, a show of protest was organized in our university against the treatment of Raymonda Dien, a heroine of the Liberation War of Algeria. There was something so absurd about the occasion that the event and her name remained etched in my memory.

A telegram of protest was to be sent to the French Government.

Lectures were canceled, and all students were taken outside into the square in front of the building, under the monument of Vassil Levsky. The president of the university, Professor Sazdo Ivanov, appeared on the steps holding a piece of paper in his hand. It was a telegram, which he proceeded to read slowly and haltingly, lacking pathos and conviction. In his short address to the crowd, he had difficulty with the name of the country fighting for independence. This provoked surreptitious smiles and giggles that lasted for quite a while. We did understand, though, that Raymonda Dien was a courageous woman, who expressed her opposition to the war, facing danger, ready to sacrifice her life by lying down across the rails in front of trains carrying arms to the French soldiers. For that she was arrested and jailed. But instead of feeling outrage for her treatment, I felt sorry for us. At least she was doing what she thought was right; whereas we, manipulated like marionettes, were too scared or too cowardly to give voice to our true views.

Besides, there were too many heroes, too many enemies, too many great causes to cheer or condemn on demand, and perhaps this was one of the roots from which sprouted the cynicism that corrupted later generations.

In their extreme, the demonstrations led to the overturning of cars, the chanting of slogans: down with this or that. The favorite location for conducting these shows was the American embassy. Those were carefully choreographed with the main actors responsible for special effects like screaming, climbing walls, or overturning the cars, while in the background, the students brought here from the universities, under the threat of expulsion, as in any mass scene of a movie or like any disorganized mob of extras, crushed on all sides, in a fit of claustrophobic anxiety, kept pushing and shoving each other.

The Mechanical Electrotechnical Institute I attended from 1956 to 1962 was known and referred to usually as MEI. It was a first-class university with high academic standards and a curriculum that was challenging and heavy on the theoretical, while somewhat weak on the practical side. Was this imbalance due to a deliberate theoretical framework or simply from a lack of facilities? It is hard to say. The program was rigidly structured, and that inflexibility made the six years required to complete it quite stressful.

Moreover, it was not a place of enlightenment, of broadening horizons, of enriching a young person's life; it was strictly for grilling students in engineering knowledge, accompanied by a compulsory political education that was organized into a number of common subjects delivered in all universities. The environment it provided for the students was boring and uninspired. Going through school was a drudgery.

MEI had somewhat of a reputation as a stronghold of true and loyal future communist cadres. Engineering was in fashion; it had great relevance to the goals set by the Party for the progress of the new society. A graduate from this university, with the right background and the correct ideological orientation, had the best of opportunities ahead of him or her. For some programs, though, this statement should rightfully end with the exclusive "him." In general, there was a preponderance of males.

The second and third years were particularly challenging. It was crucial to survive them. The second year was probably the most important one: a psychological barrier, a hurdle many students tripped on, falling behind. But determination was hardly ever a casualty of such an experience. People hung on. Dropping out of university was an anomaly. There were no better options.

For me, those were very difficult years. Pressure was building from all sides: besides the demands of school, some foreboding sense of imminent disaster was surging like a powerful undercurrent hidden by the mud in the sluggish flow of our domestic life.

My personal life was turning into a nightmare. I was looking for an escape, for strength and harmony in the wrong place.

Some of the entries in my diary from this period, mundane or confessional in content, echo the struggle between disillusionment and hope that began tormenting me then and continued to afflict me until, finally, I turned my back on everything.

October 22, 1958

Wednesday

Just in from lectures. Feel elated! After a quick bite will go out, back on the streets. It is so heavenly!

Lately was sick, felt miserable, all my strength depleted. But today, suddenly, felt wonderful! My spirits lifted! Brighter, comforting thoughts filled my mind.

At the end of classes, leaving through the doors of the Institute, saw throngs of people streaming out, all in a hurry, all in pursuit of different destinations, all absorbed in their worries and joys. And an overwhelming sense of relief came over me. Who am I, with my petty sorrows and bad moods in this sea of humanity? Just looking at the multitudes, being surrounded by them, brought me comfort and a sense of resignation, and the thought that acceptance is all that one needs to find the strength to carry on with life. Perhaps even to be happy.

Got more relief and a sense of joy—from nature—from treading over a carpet of fallen leaves covering the sidewalks, from breathing the air—so pure and fresh tonight, filled with all kinds of wonderful smells. The scents of autumn, of damp earth, of village hearths—all portents of snow, of Christmas, and New Year. The magical air of fairy-tales.

I wished that I could take a really deep breath, one that would reach every fiber of my body, from the top of my head to my heels. The wind was lashing at my face, pinching my cheeks, making me feel alive, joyful.

So I will go out again and will keep on breathing the marvelously scented air that lifts moods and chases bad thoughts away.

December 5, 1958

Friday

Neglected you for a while. Happy people are self-absorbed and egotistical. They like to keep all to themselves. And for a little while I was happy.

I can't write about it now. It is in the past. Besides, how can I write about "endless happiness" and "boundless joy" when I am on the verge of going crazy, battling an urge to jump in the middle of the lecture hall.

Don't want to think about anything, or feel anything.

Don't know what is happening to me. Never felt this way.

Horrible shivers are running all over my body; my head hurts as though squeezed by an iron ring.

And I am afraid to go home.

Last night, Mother had an attack; kept bending over, pressing her chest with clamped arms. It must have been her heart.

It was scary.

The shivers are unbearable; creeping down my spine and legs, up to my face...

When will this lecture end? Feel so bad—wonder how I am going to survive.

Can't hold the pen between my fingers any longer.

Can't listen to the disquisition on "martensite" and "austenite."

March 18, 1959

Wednesday

Again I have ignored you for a long time. Nor am I going to try to recapture the time gone by.

This morning skipped lectures—nothing new these days. On contrary, it happens quite often. And that throws me off balance, provokes all kinds of feelings of guilt and pangs of conscience.

Tomorrow have to submit a project in thermodynamics. It is not finished yet—a diagram and a sketch remain to be done.

Only, I am running out of steam. Meeting the deadline is becoming quite problematic.

April 5, 1959

Sunday

The remarkable event today was the election of "people's councilors" and I don't know what else. Actually, it was not an election; rather a mockery.

There was only one ballot with the names of the anointed candidates; therefore, no choices. Could not even drop in an empty envelope—the ballot boxes were carefully observed by the "activists."

The weather is very nice. It would have been quite warm if it had not been for the wind.

Had plans to do some drafting today, but had to go and vote in the morning; then, with a group of students from the Institute, had to go to different polling stations to perform folk dances! To top it all off, was drafted for an hour's duty from 4 PM to 5 PM.

I am slacking off in my work and feel stressed.

How I am going to complete all these projects just blows my mind. Hope tomorrow I will be able to sit down and start taking care of all that work.

And now it is time to get ready and go to the club and take care of my "civic duty." Bye!

18

THE LOW POINT

Ever since the end of the war, Sofia was in an official state of housing shortage. The problem was never solved.

A snapshot of neglected dwellings with crumbling plaster walls, inhabited by a multitude of tenants with dour faces, along with the rest of tarnished hallmarks of glorified socialist's achievements would provide an instant authenticity to the depiction of urban life of this period. Though not all of the dwellers would be renters; the ownership of apartments was not abolished entirely. It was restricted—to one residence per family. The restrictions went further: the owners had no authority over whom the place was to be rented to in the event of vacancy or over the rent. They were subject to the same limitations when it came to the number of occupants; the law stated that it was two people per room. All residences were registered with city hall, and control over them was in the hands of the bureaucrats. A rent control was established. At the end, what was accomplished by these measurements was the practical elimination of all incentives for ownership and, ultimately, the perpetuation of the housing shortage till the end of the regime.

Most of the apartment buildings in the city had been constructed in the mid-thirties. In the aftermath of the war, no new ones were erected to replace the homes destroyed by the raids or to provide for the increasing needs of the population. In spite of the requirements for citizenship in Sofia, due to the influx of apparatchiks, or merely of people with connections for whom anything was possible, the city kept growing.

The only way to manage the situation was by enforcing a policy of sharing the existing accommodations—often by more than one family and a number of singles. New families were put on long waiting lists that, once filed, seemed to be forgotten.

The apartment we lived in was rented. It belonged to a widow who lived in a town along the Danube—at least this is what I think. All of that never mattered to me, one way or the other. I felt secure in the apartment and loved it. It was my home.

In the spring of 1959, however, this was about to change.

Quite a few years had elapsed since Father's disbarment. During this time our lives had been transformed—from the once comfortably stable and secure existence to one of extreme vulnerability, lived in a state of perpetual crisis. And yet, in the spring of 1959, faced with a new, dramatic, and painful calamity, we found ourselves completely unprepared for it. In some manner, we never survived it; we just endured it.

From then on, even the occasional lulls of calm that occurred from time to time were underlain by anxiety borne of the doomsday hopelessness that had grown deep roots in our psyche. One might say we felt like convicts.

It was a shock to hear, barely a month before it happened, Mother telling me that we were going to be thrown out of the place. And it was even harder to believe, nothing short of incomprehensible, that we had no right to be put on a waiting list or to be put up in a room somewhere.

We were to be left on the street.

One thing that did not surprise me was that Father had failed to pay the rent for a few months and, of course, kept it a secret from Mother. This made it easy for city hall to evict us from the apartment without trouble. In such circumstances the authorities were not compelled to provide emergency accommodations or hope for the future. Already, somebody well connected liked the place and wanted to move in. It was of no avail that Father knew his name. We did not stand a chance to fight it; for that matter, neither did the owner.

May 11, 1959

Monday

On May 6, one of the rooms was emptied and locked. They are coming back on May 22 to empty the rest and lock us out.

All of the nightmares that each dawn would dissipate and bring me relief have become a reality. It is final! The decision to evict us from the home I grew up in is final. The sense of security I felt here has evaporated, blown away like smoke. I have the feeling that I will never regain it, that I will never be sure of anything, that I will never experience happiness.

On the 21st is the final exam in Lifting and Transportation Machinery and fifteen days later, in Thermodynamics, the heaviest exam this semester.

Homeless in exam week!

Is Father to be blamed for this? How much more punishment can he take?

Can't bring myself to utter harsh words against him.

Maybe we will not be able to live together anymore.

Maybe we will not be a family anymore. I don't know!

I need somebody to talk to, somebody to comfort me. I can't describe the anguish, the hopes, and the disappointments I am going through. The other day was cheerful and full of hope; last night, despondent; today, at noon, happy, and then, again, depressed. The reasons for these ups and downs: the other day Grandfather promised to help us and that brought joy; the next day it became clear that nothing was going to come out of what turned out to be no more than good intentions, and that brought disappointment and pain. For a day it seemed that I might be able to live in the storage room in the attic of Uncle Manol's apartment building; then this turned out to be impossible...

Oh, how hard it is! I wish I could wake up and find that all of this is just a bad dream...

At the end of May we lost our home, but I passed the exams.

On the day we were evicted, Mother and Father told me to stay away—to spare me the humiliation of the spectacle.

Father had succeeded in persuading somebody with influence in the right places to help us get a roof over our heads. He still had a lot of connections: many people who knew and thought highly of him, however, most of them were in positions without much power.

In a small truck piled high with furniture, we moved to a house not far away from the apartment. We were given a single room on the second floor with bathroom privileges to a common washroom, but no access to the kitchen.

Mother had to find storage for the rest of the furniture. Some of it was put in friends' cellars; a few things got lost, forgotten somewhere, and I never saw them again. It was a thrill, however, to discover an old Viennese love seat and a chair in Lialintsi thirty-eight years later.

Our new home had room enough for only three single spring beds (arranged along the walls), a wardrobe, and two armchairs. A hot plate was placed on a small, low table pushed into a nook next to the door. It was cramped, it was miserable, but we were not alone. The house was full of people who were in the same boat.

The two-story, turn-of-the-century house, once a handsome edifice, now covered in a crumbling, dirty yellowish plaster, was a home to all kinds of people who came in and went out like shadows—all trying to preserve some personal space around themselves, avoiding conversations, acknowledging each other only by a nod or a curt hello. Somewhere among these people must have been the owners, who had retreated to a corner inside their once-comfortable home to make room for the slew of invaders.

The place reminded me of an anthill.

There must have been some lighter moments to recall while we lived there. Only, it was a time of such hopelessness and despair that any attempt to bring a ray of sunshine or cheerfulness to the memory of it feels like a sacrilege.

Mother's health deteriorated. She was completely overwhelmed by the insecurity and stress we were living with. Father withdrew so deeply within himself that he became almost invisible. I struggled to handle school and an unhappy personal life, to maintain some optimism and faith in something, anything…

The radio provided an escape and a vague hope. During the night, when Father was asleep and Mother pretended to be, I would stick to the radio, fiddling with the tuner, trying to catch some of the sounds of the outside, free world. I would strain my ears for hours, listening to the faint, intermittently audible music, the incomprehensible mumbo-jumbo of foreign speech, and hear a promise.

We spent two and a half years in that place.

An entry from my diary, written about five months after our move there, refers to the state we were living in, which remained unchanged till we left a couple of years later.

October 24, 1959

Saturday

For the last few months we have been living in a state of "high alert," expecting at any time to be thrown out of our present home. All of our portable possessions are readied for moving, stuffed in sacks, packed in boxes and briefcases. Only the absolute essentials are left unpacked.

In spite of the circumstances, life goes on, my studies also. I find myself constantly looking for books, drafting tools, etc. And while rummaging through my "private" box, I came upon you. So let me tell you how I feel.

Ten days ago, on the fifteenth, Grandfather passed away. It is sad! But it is even sadder that already there is discord among the family about the inheritance.

These days, everything turns into a mess.

Besides that—nothing…

Now, I shall put you away again, probably abandoning you for a long time. Until things get better!

19

LIVING UNDER DICTATORSHIP OF THE PROLETARIAT

A year or two earlier, the dispensation of justice in the present system was demonstrated in a case that started as a criminal one and ended up, as usual, as a political show, that had less to do with the misdeeds of the accused than with the message it was sending.

It did not take long for the rumor to spread that two of our classmates were taken into custody, accused of attempted robbery. Events of this nature were not reported. Trial would follow soon.

One of the accused was in my section in the Mechanical Engineering Department. Three years before, the day he learned of his acceptance at university, had been a joyous one. We met on the street; he was happy and excited, and he gave me a hug and a kiss. Both of us were thrilled to be colleagues; it was going to be great to have a friend, a familiar face, in the unknown, crowded, and intimidating world of the university.

The other one was a student in civil engineering. Both were from our neighborhood, and the latter one had been my classmate throughout high school. He was what could be described as a completely nice guy; no rebel in any sense of the word. He was a well-bred lad who preferred the company of girls to the camaraderie of the rowdy teenage boys. I was fond of him.

The news of their arrest shocked me.

The story that was circulating was more or less the following: the two of them ambushed the cashier delivering the payroll to the university in the passage connecting the street to the inside court. There they assaulted him by striking him over the head with a baton, demanding he hand over the briefcase with the cash. What exactly happened next was not clear, except that they bolted, leaving the screaming cashier clutching his head. One of the assailants ran for shelter to his aunt's, who lived nearby, and was apprehended from her apartment; the other surrendered later.

It was hard to believe that these two guys, who had never even participated in a push-and-shove game in the schoolyard, would have done such a thing. Or if they did it, why they did.

At the opening of the trial, the courtroom in the Palace of Justice was packed. To attend, I had to skip classes. The reasons to go were two: first, I felt skeptical about the story, and, second, I had always been intrigued by the workings of the courts, mainly due to Father and his love of his profession. Unfortunately, I was too young when he was practicing, and after his disbarment I did not care to go.

For a couple of days I went, listened, and observed. I could see the accused a few meters away from my seat, at all times trying to read their faces, hoping to hear them testify. They never took the stand while I was there, and it probably would not have made any difference to the outcome of the trial if they had.

As the trial went on, I became sickened and alarmed. The direction the prosecutor was moving foretold only bad things ahead for the two accused. The crime was not attempted robbery; it was becoming clear from the prosecution's case—something that was impossible to prove but oh, so familiar—that the crime was who these two guys were.

The motive for the robbery, presented by the prosecution, was to obtain money for the purchase of a motorbike, specifically the model Triumph, for the purpose of running across the border to the West. Two of the points that were made in justifying this scenario were that a number of detective books had been found when the homes of the accused were searched, and several sheets of paper with pages covered with doodles of motorbikes had also been found somewhere. Those were presented to the court. The strength of the prosecution's case lay in presenting the accused as obsessed with the West, perverted by its culture. It would be only natural to assume that the end purpose of the actual crime was to run away.

There was no defense against such an accusation.

Was there any truth in it? It sounded improbable, but was it inconceivable? People were running away on foot, across the mountains, crawling under bushes, jumping over ditches, waiting, counting the minutes of the intervals at which the armed soldiers patrolling the border were passing. But across a road, on a motorcycle, through barricades and a slew of guards? Did they really contemplate such a desperate action? Were they ready to risk their lives? Their future? What future? Some of it made sense; most of it didn't.

It was too disturbing. The questions raised in my mind were not the ones I came to find answers for in the first place.

I stopped going to the trial.

A couple of months later, I heard the trial was over. The punishment was a long, stiff prison sentence. I wondered: was that a penalty for their crime or the price for a dream?

Years had passed since I saw Aunt Blaga, Uncle Pecko, Milcho, and Darcho. Some time, in the beginning of the fifties, they disappeared from my life. Father and Mother kept mentioning them with concern, discussing their fate with bewilderment. For some unexplainable reason, they were interned in a place far away from Sofia, and, a few years later, Milcho and Darcho, just teenagers, ended up at the famous labor camp in Lovech, a place where anybody labeled an *undesirable element, enemy of the people*, or any other category of people created by the paranoid Internal Security, could be sent without due process.

The family started to fall apart.

Father kept in touch with the children, assuming the role of their guardian. In case of need, they could find him at any of the different street corners where he spent his days waiting for clients. I don't recall a single occasion of them ever visiting us.

Then, one day, unexpectedly, Milcho showed up at our apartment door. I could hardly recognize him. He was a grown man, looking even paler and more delicate than the child I remembered.

It felt strange and awkward: I was a university student, and he had just been released from a labor camp. We asked about Darcho. He told us that they were together in the camp, but, while he was released, Darcho was kept behind. There were no questions about why they were sent there, when, and for how long. Since the reasons were usually manufactured and the decisions arbitrary and unpredictable, all discussion seemed useless, irrelevant.

Milcho looked subdued, pensive, lost.

He had come to the neighborhood to look up a friend who lived nearby, but missed him. On his way back, he happened to pass in front of our apartment building and, realizing that this was where we lived, decided to come up and look us up instead. He had been away for a long time; he was out of touch with his old friends. He must have felt lonely.

And we had been close once. But now it was impossible to have a normal conversation. We had nothing in common any more. We were moving in different worlds, though we tried to get to know each other again.

Milcho told us that he wanted to start a new life—perhaps get married or find work. All that sounded so normal. On impulse, I suggested that he accompany me to one of my classes. Maybe—I was hoping—the university environment would motivate him to look for a way to continue his education. Of course, it was quite unrealistic to expect that this could really happen, but I guess it was the only thing I could think of. Surprisingly he came and endured a couple of hours of complete boredom, unable to concentrate.

The worst moment for me came when, in one of our conversations, I learned that in the camp he had developed a sort of disability, the result of brutal beatings about the head, inflicted on him by the guards. He suffered from fainting spells and terrible headaches. There was nothing to be done.

Again he disappeared from my life, but not from my mind, especially after Father told me in 1985, that a few years after I left Bulgaria, Milcho came to see him at one of his favorite spots to say good-bye. He was planning to leave the country, too.

As he was relating the story, I observed Father's face tightening, his jaw stiffening. He never saw Milcho again.

Somehow, Milcho made it to West Germany.

So we both ended up in the same world after all, in search of the one taken away from us.

On the same occasion that Father related the story of his last meeting with Milcho, I asked about Darcho: what had become of him? How was he doing? Father became his usual cautious self and said very little in a vague, reluctant fashion, obviously careful not to divulge any information.

Darcho was the younger of the two brothers. From a cute, spirited, curious, and adventurous little boy, he grew into an attractive and strong-headed teen. The difference in our ages put us almost in different generations. And even though we did not move in the same circles and our paths did not cross, I used to hear about him from time to time from friends and acquaintances we had in common. He was a popular guy. Besides, Father seemed to know almost at all times the whereabouts of Uncle Pecko and his family and gave us bits and pieces of news concerning them.

Having lunch in one of the tripe-shops along Graf Ignatiev Street in the early sixties, I happened to notice a husky young man dressed in the working clothes of a construction laborer passing me by with a dour expression on his face. At once I was struck by his general looks. There was something uniquely familiar as well as completely alien about him.

The man came in the place alone, took a bowl from the serving counter, sat, and had his meal, utterly absorbed in himself, never throwing a glance around. He came in after me and left ahead of me. Throughout the whole time he was there, I kept looking in his direction, intrigued, wondering. It took me a long time to realize that the guy reminded me of Darcho, though he was much older-looking than he should have been. Also, there was something totally incongruous between this worn-out, shabby, antisocial man and the Darcho I knew, or imagined him to be.

At home I asked Father. "Where is Darcho right now? Is he in Sofia?"

"Yes. What makes you ask about him?"

"I think I saw him. Is it possible?" and I went on describing the circumstances and my impressions of the guy who looked like him, and yet was so different from him.

"Yes. Probably it was Darcho. He came back recently, and he is working as a laborer somewhere there."

End of conversation. This was as far as Father would go.

And I would never know where Darcho had returned from: camp, prison. or the uranium mines. This was the circle of hell where many people—born into the wrong class, left with families devastated by separation, displacement, and economic ruin, deprived of education—spent their youth, going round and round, moving from one death hole to another.

The young ones were usually called hooligans. The epithet was widely used to describe anybody who did not fit into the prescribed mold of an ideologically correct youth. Once branded as such, the detrimental characteristics of the accepted meaning of the word were automatically and freely applied. Miserable, disenfranchised people, decent people in normal circumstances, vented their frustrations against the world by eagerly agreeing with the authorities, pointing fingers at anybody young and spirited, probably motivated to an extent by the impotent envy of the growing old to the natural exuberance of youth. It was just another manifestation of the intolerant, mob mentality and uncivilized behavior that mark the retrogression of civilized societies subjected to oppressive totalitarian rule.

Once made an outcast, regardless of the categorization, it took a lot of courage, a lot of willpower, and, above all, a lot of toughness to survive. I don't know to which of the Internal Security's black lists Darcho was permanently affixed, but I had some indication of the kind of life he was enduring.

On the same occasion that Father related the story of his last meeting with Milcho and was reluctant to talk more about Darcho, after a moment of hesitation he said, "Darcho is bedridden, recuperating. He was detained in the militia headquarters and roughed up badly." And after a pause, his face lit up with pride and he added, "He is one hell of a tough guy. They will never break him!"

Artists and writers were courted and pampered by the Communist government. They were the ones who touched people's minds and hearts more effectively than any politician or lecturer could. In recognition of this importance, they were elevated to positions of great respect and privilege, as long as they were useful to the system. But their position was also a precarious one. If they veered off the prescribed path, their fall of grace was not enough of a punishment; the Party's wrath for the betrayal, in some cases, became merciless.

Since loyalty, rather than talent and creativity, became the prerequisite for success, this system of privileges brought mediocrity. It stifled free expression and originality and rewarded compliance and conformity with the Party line. Most of the arts were turning stale.

Especially coveted at that time were the few grand old actors left from the pre-Communist era. As long as they did not express an overtly anti-regime sentiment, they were left alone to play their *Volpones, School for Housewives, Government Inspectors, King Lears* and so forth to the applause of the public who filled the theatres. Konstantin Kissimov was, at one time, the most prominent of them, a dedicated, inspired, and decent human being who also happened to be an artist.

I must have been around ten years old when I first saw and heard "Bie Kosio," as he was affectionately called. Mother had taken me to one of his recitals, where he would invariably recite a few of the poems from Vazov's *Épopée of the Forgotten*. He was a small, almost fragile man, who grew in stature figuratively and visually when, stretching his hands forward and pulling himself up almost on his toes, he delivered those incredibly moving rhymes, as though reaching toward some lofty heights only he could see. He mesmerized audiences; he took people on an emotional journey that cleansed their souls.

My affection for Bie Kosio was well established before I met his youngest son, Georgi with the nickname of Choko. Choko was my boyfriend for most of my university years. He was a very charming guy, easygoing with a carefree disposition that was very appealing to me. Around him I could relax and forget all anxieties and problems I was facing. I felt like a traveler on an arduous journey who comes to a comfortable shelter and lingers there, weary of the distance left ahead; a distance I had to travel alone. I stuck to him for a very long time, at times, letting the relationship grow in importance out of proportion. He was a student in the Academy of Drama.

During those years, I came to know Bie Kosio as a person and, in some ways, as someone who had an effect on my life. His respect for the dignity of all human beings, his tolerance, in my eyes, acquired a symbolic meaning: an expression of the endurance of the human spirit.

Throughout my university years, I spent lots of time hanging about with a group of guys and girls, mostly students, whose favorite place was a small park at the corner of Rakovska and Moskovska Streets. At the very corner, on the sidewalk, stood a kiosk selling newspapers and cigarettes. Next to it, a cement pole covered with large placards advertised the latest movies, and, at the edge of the grass, a black cast-iron pole threw its light over a thicket of lilac trees. During the month of April, it illuminated the purple and white blossoms that filled the air with their sweet aroma till the middle of May. In the middle of the parkette, in the center of a water fountain, rose the statue of St. George slaying the dragon. And, to the east of it stood the ancient Byzantine church of St. Sofia.

The parkette was almost encircled by a row of benches at the edge of the grass. During the day, they were occupied by grandmothers, a few mothers with babies in prams parked next to them, and older men relaxing, chatting with each other and casually observing the goings-on. In the evening, though, the park belonged to us. From different directions, we drifted slowly toward it, one by one or in couples, some sitting, others standing, fidgeting, while waiting for the next person to appear. On the west side was the almost-empty square with a car occasionally passing through. At one of its corners stood the Soviet embassy, a single guard visible in front of the main entrance.

This was where we spent hours talking, laughing, even practicing rock and roll flips. This is also where, sometimes, late in the night after a performance, Bie Kosio would stop, take a seat on one of the benches to relax, and talk to those of us who were still lingering around. He talked about the stars and their constellations; he would look at the sky, pointing with a finger at a particular star and expand on his thoughts about the universe.

The park was our hangout, where we met after other activities, like going to the movies or to a pastry shop, or simply strolling along the drag. The drag was a stretch of Rakovska Street between Graf Ignatiev Street and Boulevard Rusky. Here, high school and university students, as well as a variety of characters with slightly dubious occupations, spent hours walking leisurely from one end to the other, looking for somebody or something, or just pretending to be. A few pastry shops and restaurants along the street served as stopovers. In addition, there was situated the Academy of Drama, a favorite place for young people to hang out, especially those with artistic aspirations. The same building housed the school theatre, where the drama students presented their productions during the school year. The National Theatre and the Theatre for Satire were in the same area. For the few of the guys and girls who were students at the Academy, as well as for the rest of us, occupied during the days with the study of our mundane subjects, the theatre was one of the most exciting and stimulating places to spend an evening.

Sometime at the end of the fifties, television appeared. It was black and white, sets were very expensive, and there were hardly any programs to see. The only existing station was on top of the university I attended, and it broadcast only for a couple of hours on a couple of days. Few people could afford to buy a set.

The ones who did immediately acquired a large number of friends, and the neighbors considered themselves lucky. On the night of a broadcast, a couple of hours before the scheduled time for the show, a stream of people carrying all kinds of chairs would head for the homes of the proud television owners. The small, cramped apartments were rearranged to make space for the rows of chairs.

The only show I watched was of a ballet performance, in a crowded room in an apartment I had no idea who lived in. A friend took me and my chair. Nobody inquired as to who I was; the people were excited, polite, and considerate.

We never bought a television set, nor did we feel deprived of one. The entertainment that we had and provided for ourselves was quite enough.

Speaking of entertainment, mention must be made of the music people listened to. The Party allowed most of the classical and supported and promoted the folk music. It was played over the radio continuously. The classical music lover could attend the performances of Sofia's Philharmonic Orchestra in the concert hall Bulgaria or go to the new opera house to see operas or ballets of his choice, and for a more intimate ambience one could go to the Marble Hall next to Hotel Bulgaria and listen to records played for a small audience.

But the music that made the adrenaline flow, that made us dream, that we loved to dance to, that we never had enough of, was the forbidden American music. It was circulated around Sofia on tapes of identical repertoire, comprised of an eclectic selection of rock and roll, spirituals, blues, jazz, even country. Elvis Presley, Ella Fitzgerald, Nat King Cole, Luis Prima, Louis Armstrong, Ray

Charles, Mahalia Jackson, The Platters—the list goes on—were loved, admired, even adored, regardless of the fact that most of us had never seen their faces on the jackets of the records smuggled from the West or of the fact that most of us did not understand a word of what they were singing. But that ignorance added to, rather than detracted from, the magic: each person could attach any meaning to the lyrics depending on the feelings the music evoked.

The same held true for the appearances of our idols.

The first time I saw what Elvis looked like was after I left the country and went to the West. What a great disappointment it was! I could never have imagined that this baby face, with the affected kink on his upper lip, belonged to the man whose voice had brought me to tears. His performances in what I felt were silly movies turned me off from watching him on film. So it was with relief that I saw him much later on television, performing in concerts—his personality shining, his performances bursting with intensity and genuine feelings. Though heavy and worn out, this was the man that I could have imagined listening to, enraptured, long ago, far away.

A crackdown on the influence of Western culture on the youth of Sofia was an ongoing event, but in January of 1958 it went beyond the usual—the usual like plucking up couples from the dancing floor in a restaurant by plainclothes agents for *immoral* dancing, et cetera. This time the target was anyone who dressed in a certain fashion, considered to be an expression of the corruption of the young people by the West (in this case, the ones wearing duffle coats and girls wearing their hair in ponytails). Anybody who did not conform in behavior or dress risked being branded a hooligan, and this was an accusation rather than a characterization.

Paddy wagons started patrolling the streets of Sofia, picking up anybody answering to the above description. All were taken to the militia stations where a checkup of their backgrounds was made. Some were let go after their parents were contacted; for the detained ones, a labor camp was a real possibility.

Panic set among most of the students. The month-long break between the fall and winter semesters was forthcoming.

It provided one with a great incentive to leave town.

Not too far away from the very summit of Rila Mountain, lay Borovets, formerly Chamckoria, a popular ski resort surrounded by a chain of lofty peaks, abode to eagles and hawks. The outlines of the majestic Musala could be spotted from nearby heights. A number of ski slopes, jumping platforms, and lifts covered the hills, while paths for cross-country skiing ran amid the tall pine trees. Every winter a small hockey rink was constructed at the onset of the cold weather for the training of the national hockey team, made up of a bunch of dedicated, though most of the time frustrated players, who compensated for their lack of skill and training with an extra dose of enthusiasm.

There were no private accommodations in the resort. All of the previously privately owned villas were nationalized and turned into government subsidized resting stations for workers. The fee for the vacationers was a small one. It entitled them to a bed and coupons for three meals a day in a cafeteria located in the central square of the village.

Now, in early 1958, the usually crowded resort was packed beyond its capacity. It was chaotic and noisy. It resembled a refugee camp. Students eager to escape from the city had risked coming without the necessary cards that were issued to the vacationers for identification purposes. Those who possessed tape recorders had brought them along, and the forbidden American music resounded everywhere.

Like any unprecedented situation, this one had its unforeseen problems—the task of housing and feeding the *illegals* was a most urgent one. A grass roots movement took on the challenge of solving it.

During the day students spent their time just hanging around the ski slope, cross-country skiing through the woods, or simply milling about the resort. But as the sun went down and dusk descended over the mountain peaks, the slopes were deserted. The crowds moved toward the canteen. Extra coupons were delivered to the ones without any, food was shared, and everybody had a meal. By word of mouth, certain villas were identified as spots where different groups were to congregate for brief meetings. Actually they were information sessions during which illegals were given the specifics of the sleeping accommodations for the night. The meetings were short and surreptitious. The interval between dinnertime and bedtime was spent in a pub, dancing, singing, and drinking grog. While for some, this was the fun part, for others, the adventure came later.

At midnight, everybody was supposed to be in bed. All the villas were inspected and locked. The village sank into silent darkness. Only here and there small, usually bathroom windows, were lighted and opened for a brief moment and soon after, dark shadows appeared under them. Pushing, pulling, and struggling, a few of them disappeared, head first, through the openings.

Early in the morning, before the villas were unlocked, the pantomime was repeated in reverse. And at the dawn of each new day, the same cycle started all over again.

I spent one week in Borovets legitimately, with a card that I obtained as a student, and a few days as an illegal. At the end of the vacation, the hordes of students boarded the busses and rode back to Sofia to find, with relief, that the crackdown had abated.

It was a memorable holiday.

The isolation we lived in was only heightening our curiosity of the outside world. It also made us naive. Many of the opinions and ideas we developed were just a product or an expression of the opposition to the propaganda and the brainwashing we were subjected to constantly. As a result of that, most of our beliefs were shaped by our emotions rather than by rational thinking.

We developed high survival skills for the environment we lived in but became so vulnerable once the danger was removed.

We could not function in a "normal" environment; we could not handle interaction with "normal" people.

Another characteristic of the state of the mass psyche was the preoccupation with our conditions of life and the belief (for some a conviction) that the whole world was interested in, or at least felt for us. It was especially so in regard to America.

My first contact with an American brought me only disappointment and anger. He was a reporter for a New York newspaper stationed in Belgrade. At least, this was what I had been told about his job and the reason for his interest in this part of the world.

Supposedly, he came to Sofia on assignment, but, as it happened, he arrived on Sunday, the only non-working day of the week. He had to wait till Monday. Meanwhile somebody had to take care of him—Western foreigners were not allowed to move around freely in the country without an escort.

A friend working at the Ministry of External Affairs was given the task of taking care of the American on the Sunday evening, of entertaining, and feeding him. The assignment came late and was unexpected; he decided to take the visitor to a restaurant called Kopito, perched on a rock in the shape of a hoof, high in the mountain skirts of Vitosha, overlooking Sofia. There was live entertainment and dancing. The usual food was served.

For company, he asked his brother and me to come along. I happened to be visiting when he got the call. To make the mix more balanced, he called a girl, the sister of his girlfriend, who spoke some English and was pretty and quite young.

I was overcome by surprise, curiosity, excitement, and expectation.

The American picked us up in his car. It was a Mercedes or BMW. Impressive. But we would not have expected anything less, anyway.

The view from the restaurant was marvelous, still unspoiled by the sprawl of gray, suburban high-rises that surround the city now, choking it in their concrete embrace. They were erected much later.

Inside, the band was playing, couples were dancing.

Dinner was served.

The restaurant had a reputation as one of the best, but that was due to its location, rather than to elegance, charm, ambiance, or good service; the latter attributes had no place in our society. The most appropriate description in this case was austere and dull.

None of these observations had crossed my mind until that evening. Suddenly I became aware of my rumpled, simple cotton dress, the soiled tablecloths, the plump singer on the stage sounding and looking rather vulgar.

The American seemed to enjoy himself, applauding the singer, smiling approvingly. Dressed in a business suit made of fine cloth, like the ones my father used to wear long ago, neat and relaxed, the man looked quite out of place, and yet he acted so naturally. A feeling of anger started to build up inside me.

"Patronizing phony," I thought. "He is amused!" His behavior was bewildering me.

There was hardly any conversation at the table. The friend in charge of the guest spoke very little English, and only the sister of his girlfriend, fresh from high school, knew enough of the language to carry on a small chat. And that seemed to be all that the American was interested in.

It never crossed my mind that he was on guard, that maybe he did not trust us.

We kept on dancing; he kept on observing.

We stayed till midnight.

Before leaving, the young girl presented the American with a single red rose. He was pleased, and I thought again, "He is amused!"

The trip back along the curvy mountain road was ordinarily a very pleasant one. But driving through the blackness of the lonely, unlit way down the slope in the middle of the night, feeling frustrated, humiliated and angry, was but an endless torture...

The moment the car stopped in front of our apartment building, I shot out of it as fast as I could, hardly able to keep back the tears any longer.

Looking back, I simply can't believe that I had failed even to mention in my diary Yuri Gagarin's flight into space in April of 1961. I remember passing by the Soviet embassy that day and noticing the open front door, inviting people to go inside and sign the commemorative book. I remember also the feelings most expressed—the enthusiasm of some and the indifference of others.

It was hard not to like Gagarin. He had such a nice, boyish, open face. The first cosmonaut was a man with an excellent poster face, perfect for the advertisement of the great achievements of the mighty Soviet Union. What stood in the way of giving in to the feeling of euphoria was that in the barrage of daily glorification of the Soviet successes, of their *unstoppable march toward a perfect future*, of their unquestionable superiority in everything, one more proof of it (and even if it happened to be a legitimate one) was bound, in the eyes of most, to be devaluated to just a good piece of propaganda. Furthermore, many of us were already suffering from a sort of victory fatigue inflicted by the constant drum of triumphal proclamations in attaining the supreme goal of the Cold War—winning the race between the two systems—East versus West.

Besides, there was no drama. We all knew that all news would reach us only if success was guaranteed, or after everything was over and things had gone according to plan. Nobody was worried about Yuri. Like all Soviet heroes, he was invincible, and all we did was smile and be glad that this one had a friendly, cute face.

Laika had gone in space before him and Valentina Tereshkova went there after him. She became the first female to fly in space, and I remember that made me feel good. In spite of the professed belief by the Party's ideologists in the equality of men and women, there were hardly any females occupying positions of power or importance in any of the Communist countries. It was a man's world exclusively, where, in the grand game of politics and government, women participated mainly in the role of cheerleaders who pushed along the agenda of the Party from the sidelines. Valentina Tereshkova did not turn out to be the pioneer one might have expected her to be, for there were no others to follow. I was still buoyed up, however, by her sharing the spotlight with the first.

Soon after coming to power, the Bulgarian Communist Party, in an effort to show its commitment to the idea of equality between men and women, elevated a few women to the exalted rank of heroes. Most prominent among them were Jordanka Chankova and Lilliana Dimitrova—both dead, having been killed during the time of the Partisan Movement. The most famous, though, was Tsola Dragoitcheva, a Party activist, sentenced to death by the previous regime but saved from execution while in prison because of her pregnancy, thus surviving till the Communists took power in September 1944.

She became a permanent fixture in the Party's organizational hierarchy, remaining there till old age, harmless and useless, encrusted like a fossil to the armor of a ship whose course was determined by an exclusively male crew. Her only role had been simply to keep a myth alive. Meanwhile she had acquired the unenviable fame of being the butt of many jokes as one of the two most favored subjects feeding the over-productive (in step with the times) political jokes' mill. And even in that role she had to take a backseat to the crude, inarticulate peasant, Dobri Tarpeshev, whose contributions to *the struggle* were much less known than hers, but who was able at times to put forward his point of views in a very effective, commonsensical, often vulgar way, which in its plain directness was refreshing, and that used to bring smiles of mirth to people's faces. The jokes were aimed at ridiculing the twosome by exposing their simplicity and utter lack of sophistication.

It was small revenge, the only one the people could muster against the system that oppressed them.

Before I leave the subject, I want to mention one thing that, in my view, goes to Tsola Dragoicheva's credit; she raised a son who created a name for himself as a respected and able medical specialist. And that was more than any of her colleagues were able to achieve.

Back on April 12, 1961, the simple joys and despairs of a daily life dominated by petty and overwhelming struggles would have easily eclipsed the mild feelings of excitement and human pride I must have felt on the occasion of the first cosmonaut's flight in space. On that day I failed to make a note of them too.

20

STARTING WORK. FINAL DISILLUSIONMENT

December 16, 1962

Sunday

Here I am again, pen in hand, trying to unburden myself, even just a bit, by sharing the pain with you. What else can I do? My very soul is rotting…

It has been seven months since I started work. The beginning was so hard; every passing day brought disillusionment. I could see my hopes fading away, another dream shattered…

I am boxed in for life!

My destiny seems to be a life without hope, one of meaningless existence and my future-unimaginable…

I am ending for now, will continue some other time…

I never did.
This was the last entry in my dairy.

Home now was a different apartment, a far cry from the depressing, dilapidated house we lived in for about three years.
It seemed we were forever in somebody's way. This time, though, it worked to our advantage.
The old house was to be demolished, and in its place a new apartment building, a cooperative, was to be erected for the employees of one of the government

establishments. In order for the project to proceed, all the tenants of the house had to be relocated. That was not a very difficult task for the powerful.

We ended up living in a location we could have only dreamed of had it not been for the necessity of expedience. My parents were presented with a list of available accommodations to choose from. The one they selected was right on the square of Alexander Nevsky, overlooking the cathedral. Every time the bells chimed, the sound drifted into the rooms through the windows. All Mother had to do now in order to enter the sanctuary of her favorite church was just to go across the street.

While in bloom, the linden trees surrounding the square sweetened the air with their aroma.

In front of the apartment building, behind the sidewalk across the street, in the middle of a small green grass patch, lay the grave of Ivan Vazov, the patriarch of Bulgarian literature. The gravestone was a large boulder brought down from Vitosha, from the moraine of the Golden Bridges, a favorite place of Vazov. It was the famed rock he used to sit on and write when visited by inspiration.

The apartment building was erected in the thirties. It was good-looking, with large windows, balconies, and the curved lines associated with the architecture of the period. The area was transformed after the establishment of the new regime. Most of the new occupants in our building were from the Communist elite. The old occupants were gone; some sent in exile. Many of the old owners from this and neighboring apartment buildings were affected by the nationalization of 1948. In their despair, after losing everything, a few jumped to their deaths from those same bright windows and elegant balconies.

There were a lot of pigeons in the neighborhood. They were everywhere, leisurely promenading about the square, heads moving constantly in all directions, searching for food, occupying every ledge protruding from the buildings and fences. Some practically lived on the windowsills of the two bedrooms we occupied.

In spring, Mother used to attach a cardboard box to one of the windows. The pigeons would nest there, and we would watch them tending their eggs, taking care of their small ones, and teaching them to fly.

Directly across from our windows, on a narrow side street, was the Students' Clinic. The chick's first lesson was usually to fly from their nest on the windowsill across the street and land, a couple of stories lower, on the clinic's roof. That was the easy part. After a brief rest, they had to fly back to the cardboard box, this time up two stories. Every time we watched them, we held our breaths and crossed our fingers, hoping that they would succeed. Four floors below was the hard, cobblestone pavement.

The Soviet Union was one of those places that never fired my imagination. As it happened, I ended up visiting Russia on a business trip and, in retrospect, regard myself as lucky to have had the opportunity to do so.

My job was that of project engineer in an Institute for Renovation and Design of manufacturing plants. We entered competitions for projects in Cuba, Indonesia, and, of course, got all the ones in Bulgaria. Needless to say, we never competed for projects in the West. The ones from Eastern Block countries were somewhat challenging: we had our pride after all, but the decisions to reward contracts were mainly based on political considerations.

Each of us had a dream to go on a business trip to one of the Third World countries.

I considered myself fortunate to be working on a project for Cuba, but when the time came to send the engineer on location, it was not me. The disappointment was big enough to give me the courage to go to the personnel department and inquire into the reasons for their rejection of me. By that time I had developed a notion that I would be treated as my own person, on the strength of my own achievements, rather than on my bourgeois background. That day I was told that I was not my own person, yet. My father was still the issue. I could not be trusted.

Late in the evening of the same day, I got home as usual after my parents' customary bedtime. I entered the room they were sleeping in, but, instead of crossing it and going to my bed in the adjacent room, stopped in front of Father's bed, looked at him for an instant—just long enough to overcome my hesitation—then, with swift movements, I bent over him and pulled the cover off his face. He opened his eyes and pulled himself up into a sitting position, staring at me, startled and confused.

"You are just a selfish man!"

I had not prepared a speech; a flood of words born in the spur of the moment started pouring from my mouth.

"Can't you budge a little? Can't you do just a small thing for me, just join the United? It is nothing. It means nothing. Everybody is in it! My life, my future is at stake!"

I could see Father's face in the pale light streaming through the windows; I could see his eyes, the hard, brimming with intensity look replacing the initial bewilderment. His voice was even, sharp, low, and controlled:

"What life? What future?" Disdain crept into his voice, "What are your expectations of life? Don't you have any principles, ideals? Travel, clothes, comfort? Is this your notion of the good life?"

At that moment, I knew that Mother must have told him about the business trip to Cuba.

"Yes, yes! This is the good life I want! Yes, I want to go and see places! Yes, I want to have a comfortable life! Yes, I want to…"

I don't remember everything I said, but I remember that I wanted to shock him as I screamed at him, shaking all over; I also knew that it was futile. Without waiting for the end of my tirade, Father moved his eyes away from me, dropped his head on the pillow, and pulled the cover over him.

During all this time Mother was lying quietly in her bed, never letting the slightest of sounds escape her lips. I could feel her gaze on my back; I was sure that she was listening, agitated and expectant.

I never learned the kind of thoughts and feelings this unforgettable exchange of words between Father and me evoked in her.

As I turned around, still trembling with agitation, angry with Father, myself, and the world, I could see them both, lying in their respective beds, in their accustomed sleeping positions, looking indifferent and remote.

At the time I could not fully appreciate the significance of the moment; still, it was imbedded in my memory forever. At the time, I felt only hurt and abandoned, overcome by self-pity. The message escaped me.

It took me a while to realize that I had to leave the cardboard box; I had to grow wings.

21

USSR, EAST GERMANY, CZECHOSLOVAKIA, HUNGARY, YUGOSLAVIA

The compensation prize for not letting me go to Cuba was a business trip to the Soviet Union. The trip was in regard to a plant we were designing for the manufacturing of spare parts for the Russian car Zaporozhets. As a member of the Sots Block, our economy was controlled by the Economic Council residing in East Berlin. It was the way the directions of all planned economies, of all satellite countries, were determined by. We were told what we could do and what we couldn't do—all for the sake of the common good.

A variety of spare electrical parts for the same car were already been manufactured in Kaluga, a town situated south of Moscow. The objective of the trip was to visit the plant there, as well as some other ones in Moscow with similar types of production.

The group of specialists I joined consisted of four people: two future employees of the plant in question and two from our institute. The other person from the institute (besides myself), was a man we all called "the hook." (slang word for secret service agent). He was the Party member assigned to keep an eye on us. He was also a colleague who was actually considered a nice man, exuding an attitude of resignation and acceptance, shrugging his shoulders every time he was put in an awkward situation exposing his position. He was never confrontational, but rather reasonable. His modus operandi was "You do your job; I do mine. Let us act like grown-ups." Thanks to his laid-back attitude, there was no tension in the group.

I benefited most from the situation. It gave me a certain amount of freedom in spending my spare time. For the after-work hours, we had an agenda full of prescribed activities that I really did not care for. So I skipped them and mostly did what I pleased. Of course we were all aware that the long leash we were kept on was not a testimony of the hook's trusting nature. In the first place, it was ridiculous to send a chaperone with a group on a business trip to the Soviet Union. There certainly could not have been any danger of anyone trying to defect. But as ludicrous as it sounded, that was the policy and policies had to be adhered to, on every level, without questioning. This was in accord with the prescribed rule for survival: "Keep silent; do not reason!"

It was April of 1964. The duration of the trip was two weeks, and the main destination was Moscow.

From the very first moment we arrived, Moscow overwhelmed me. It was an austere and bleak place, but also a unique one, therefore intriguing and exciting. The huge prospects, the splendid subway with marble-covered walls and crystal chandeliers, and, above all, the numerous onion dome churches, colorful and fantastic, interspersed among the cold, gray, and boring buildings of Stalin's architecture, surprised me. This mixture of symbols, rejected and deemed irrelevant to the present, reminded me of the Russian soul, of tales of bygone times, of the once-deep spirituality in this vast and mysterious land; the others, impenetrable and foreboding, bespoke to me of might, pride, and arrogance of the faithless. It was hard to figure out the people who lived in a city like that. We were told over and over that they were our brothers, our Slavic big brothers. It did not seem that way at all. I felt in a strange, foreign country, surrounded by foreign people, speaking a strange language. Russian was compulsory at school and I had studied it for many years, but, as it turned out, for the first week it was totally useless to me. By the time I began to understand and venture to say few words here and there, it was time to leave.

And there were throngs of people: on the sidewalks, in the subway, mobs pushing and shoving their way in front of the buses that came to a stop abruptly with a screech and just as abruptly took off, leaving angry and frustrated crowds behind. Some of the people were still groping for the handles, some had one foot on the steps—it did not matter. The driver hardly gave them a glance. There was no order, no consideration or niceties. On one of those bus rides, I almost lost my coat. After an enormous struggle to reach the exit, accompanied by pirouettes and arm wrestling, I disembarked, rather flew, out the door to discover that the button of my coat was gone together with part of the cloth, and the coat itself was off my shoulders, halfway down my arms and back.

Still, it was exciting. It was the biggest place I had ever seen; it was a different world, one I had never imagined. I felt like a wide-eyed provincialist coming to the city for the first time.

Thanks to a friend who was studying at the Gorky Institute of Cinematography, I saw the city, and, through his eyes and observations, I saw a side of the people one appreciates only if one shares one's life for a while. The friend's name was Vassil.

One of the items on our agenda was to attend a performance at the Bolshoi Theatre. Instead, Vassil took me to see a play in the Malii Theatre. He smuggled me in using the ID of a friend of his, a student in the institute he was attending. The students had free access to all performances in the theatre.

The play was Russian; the method, Stanislavski. The theatre was renowned for the high quality of its performances. The actors did not simply slip into their roles; they grew into them. All individual characters were perfectly defined and worked out; all details, to the smallest, were carefully polished for creating exactly the intended effect. It was rumored that rehearsals were so intense and prolonged that some went on for years. In the end, the performances were flawless. The stage atmosphere was so genuine and real—it captivated one's attention and evoked emotion so powerfully that one felt transported, transfixed by the play. It was magical!

The rest of my free time I spent visiting museums, galleries, the Kremlin. The Armoury Hall in the Kremlin fascinated me with its relics of former glories. It made me wonder how any nation could reject so completely the past embodied in the magnificent objects displayed there, though, thankfully, could preserve them. I also spent hours with Vassil, sitting on a bench, talking about "them" and "us," analyzing and comparing. But the most extraordinary experience for me was when he took me to the institute to see a projection of Eisenstein's movie *Ivan the Terrible*. The first part of the film had been seen everywhere, without provoking any controversy. It was appreciated for its artistic merits, as a creation of the revered master. It was just a historical film depicting the struggles of the tsar in establishing his rule. It ended on a triumphant, optimistic note. After Stalin's death, the film became a subject of interest again but for quite a different reason. It was rumored that the movie had more than one part, that the second part depicted the remaining years of Ivan the Terrible, his transformation from a popular hero to a despotic autocrat, obsessed with paranoia, who would not stop at anything, including murder, to hold onto power. The story was that the movie, originally commissioned by Stalin, was made for the purpose of drawing a parallel between the famous tsar and himself, on the positive side of history. It seems

Eisenstein went further than that. The widespread anecdotal account of Stalin's reaction to the film had quite an authentic ring to it: Upon seeing the first part of the finished work, Stalin was pleased, expressing his satisfaction with the words, "It is similar"; and that meant approval. On seeing the second part, though, he was supposed to have said, "It is too similar," and ordered all reels of that part to be destroyed. Risking his life, one of the cameramen hid a single reel and kept it. This was how the second part of the movie was preserved and eventually appeared much later. It was still not shown to the public at large, but it was shown to students in the institute as an example of Eisenstein's creativity. The avid interest, even admiration, of most people was due to the fact that the movie was viewed as an exposé of Stalin, as an act of defiance and unbelievable courage on the part of the cameraman responsible for the preservation of the reel. Was the story about the brave cameramen true? It didn't matter. For most of the people living in this reality of stark contrasts—seen through the distorting prism of an ideological dogma—the story was inspirational and uplifting. This is why I wanted to see the movie. And, without being a connoisseur of cinematography, I appreciated the originality and intensity of the film, if only for the fact that in the face and deeds of the raving, murderous Ivan the Terrible, one could feel, almost see, the cruelty and madness of Stalin.

The snow was gone; the winter was over. We were on our way to Kaluga, traveling in a big, black car along a road covered with potholes. A forest of white birch trees ran along the sides. There was no traffic; there were no signs of life anywhere. In vain I kept looking though the window, hoping to see a village. We did pass by a few spots where a score of log cabins stood by the road, but nowhere did we see a store, a tavern, a square. It was lonely, isolated, strangely empty. To alleviate the boredom of the long and monotonous ride, we started to sing and kept on singing almost till we reached Kaluga. The town was renowned for its vodka and as the birthplace of Tselikovski, the father of the Russian aviation, something I was totally unaware of until we were shown the monument erected in his honor.

Kaluga was a small, sleepy town, very much like the provincial towns I had imagined while reading Russian novels. At one point we saw on the side of the road the complete landscape covered by water, a vast lake, or a river swollen by the spring rains and melting snow, moving sluggishly in a direction hard to determine. And slowly, from nowhere, the lonely figure of a man standing in a boat appeared like a vision from a fairy tale. He was pushing his vessel along with a pole, which he kept swinging with measured, expansive movements, from one side to the other. His attire consisted of a pale blue "rubashka," a long shirt covering half of his pants, which were tucked in a pair of knee-high boots. The shirt was tied around his waist; on his head he wore a cap.

After a tour of the plant's manufacturing facilities, we were taken to the administrative area for the obligatory banquet. A long table, set with plenty of food and vodka, waited us. There were more than a dozen people: administrators and engineers. The atmosphere was warm, friendly. The director of the plant had visited Bulgaria a few years previously and had fond memories of Sofia, in particular, of a woman who lived in Kniajevo. As time passed and as more vodka was consumed, the conversations and the laughter grew louder, and the director's memory of his trip to Bulgaria grew more vivid. He kept asking me if I knew the woman from Kniajevo.

Toward the end of the meal, partly to escape the noise and stretch my legs, I left the room and started walking along the hallways. The whole area was quiet, not a soul around. Finally I ended up in the washroom. At first sight it also appeared empty, however, only a few moments later, the muffled noise of feet shuffling along the concrete floor drew my attention to an elderly lady moving behind me. She was wearing a uniform, which I perceived to be that of a cleaning lady. Her eyes were cast down at the floor; in her hands she was carrying a shovel and a broom. She seemed oblivious of me, absorbed in her work. Presently, a low, persistent mutter made me turn toward her, wondering who she was speaking to. An uneasy feeling came over me, and, even though she never looked away from her work, I knew that her words were meant for me. At first I couldn't understand anything. Slowly my brain started to process the words, their meaning penetrating my whole being and hitting me so hard that I began to feel physically ill. A weakness crept into my knees; my heart was palpitating and my breathing became shallow and laborious. I couldn't believe my ears. "Go home! Go away! Get out of our country! What are you doing here? My son, I lost my son in your country. Killed there, in your country! Go home!"

Her voice was hardly audible; the words came out as a hiss through her clenched teeth.

My initial reaction was to scream at her, telling her that her son could not have been killed in my country; that there was no fighting, no battles with the Red Army. That after they came, everything changed in my country. That they took our freedom! That they brought us misery and oppression!

Anger, mixed with compassion, was choking me. It was useless to try to say anything; my Russian failed me. The hatred in her voice was too strong, the bitterness too deep. I was a foreigner. And to the Russians, foreigners were the eternal enemy. So much for big and small *brothers*.

Somehow I dragged myself back to the banquet hall and took my place at the table. The rest of the time I spent struggling to keep my composure.

At the end of the visit, each one of us was given a package, a present. All were identical and very heavy. We were told that every package contained a set of spare parts for Zaporojets.

Back in Moscow, our work was almost done. There were only a couple of days remaining, and the most important thing on my mind was to get the shopping over with. One of the advantages of going on a business trip was the opportunity to buy items that were not available in Bulgaria. We had very accurate, current information of the supplies and shortages of goods in each of the Sots countries. The first helped planning the purchases, and the second helped solving the financial problem. If one did not have the guts or the inclination to get involved in some black marketing, the only way to end up with some rubles was by saving as much as one could from the expense fund given us in cash. We came prepared for that by bringing all the food we would need for the duration of the trip.

This meant going through most of the days without a meal. There were exceptions, though: once we went to a restaurant for lunch, just to be able to say that we had gone through the experience and, on a few occasions, were treated to lunch in the plants we were visiting.

In the evenings I would go to the guys' room carrying salami, cheese, or a jar of liutenitsa, a favorite puree made of red peppers—my contribution to the common meal. These get-togethers were more than just mealtimes. We talked about the state of affairs concerning the sale of the mohair skirts a couple of the guys had brought. There was a demand for them in most of the Sots countries. As soon as we arrived at the hostel, a number of women from the cleaning staff approached us surreptitiously, inquiring whether we had skirts to sell. The men, experienced in these sorts of activities, took their time in disposing of the goods, bargaining and biding their time till they got the best possible price.

I was able to save enough rubles for a Buran vacuum cleaner and a couple of pairs of pantyhose—one for Mother and one for Aunt Desha. After the purchase a little bit of money was left, so I decided to look around for a pair of cheap shoes for myself. The best place to shop was at GUM, the universal store located right in Red Square. Unfortunately there were no shoes in the price range I could afford. Without holding out much hope, I turned into one of the side streets, scanning for stores, then made another turn, and another one, until I realized that it was getting late, that there were hardly any stores anywhere, so I had better turn back and head toward Red Square, the point of reference for all my movements in the city. Suddenly, I bumped into a line of militiamen stopping and turning people away. In the distance I could see the Square, completely deserted. Some of the side streets had been closed too. For me this amounted almost to a calamity! How was I going to get back? What was going on?

The first of May was only a couple of days away. On that day the Soviet Union staged its biggest military parade, when, lined up on the tribune in Red Square, the members of the Politburo stood for hours saluting, waving at the marching Red Army, while a slew of invited foreign dignitaries, standing respectfully at attention, were sizing up the rockets, the tanks, and the rest of the menacing-looking military hardware noisily driving past Lenin's Mausoleum. It was too early, however, to close the area in preparation for the occasion. Then I heard, "Castro is coming."

The next day, we left Moscow.

About six months before my trip to the Soviet Union, in October of 1963, a group of young engineers, mainly from Machelectroproect, organized an excursion throughout some of the Sots block countries: Czechoslovakia, Hungary, GDR. It was supposed to be a sort of a professional development trip, and, to justify it, brief stops at a couple of plants in East Germany had been arranged. Some of the people who came along were not engineers. Friends and acquaintances of the Young Engineering Club members, an entity invented just for that trip, joined in. Inevitably, a couple of "hooks" were attached to the group to keep an eye on us.

The cities on the agenda were Dresden, Leipzig, Weimar, Erfurt, Prague, Budapest, and just a stopover for a couple of hours in Belgrade. We traveled mainly by train; though, when going on trips outside the cities where we had lodgings for a few days, the transportation was by bus. In Germany, we slept in hostels. For the rest of the countries, no arrangements for nightly accommodations had been made. During this stretch of the journey, we spent the nights dosing off on the train and the days walking in disorganized, uncharted attempts at sightseeing.

As it happened, our itinerary in GDR almost coincided with the schedule of a Hungarian group. It turned into a game of catch-up, and as soon as we arrived at a new destination we would start looking out for them in anticipation of their arrival. A sort of very brief friendship developed, and now their faces looking at me from photographs are an irritating challenge to my memory, for I can't recall any of their names.

In front of the international train at the Central Train Station of Sofia, the inevitable commotion and anxieties were short-lived, controlled. Boarding the train proceeded in a smooth and civilized manner. The compartments were comfortable, and everybody got a seat. At the border, passports were carefully checked; customs officials made their inquiries and inspection. The procedure was repeated on the Yugoslavian side.

Those of us who had never gone through the experience of crossing the border were completely bewildered at the mayhem that ensued at the first stop on the Yugoslavian side. The doors of the coaches were wide open, and a mob of people rushed in, including peasants pulling small farm animals, boarding without a moment's hesitation, chatty, pushy, totally unabashed. The corridor was packed; the air turned heavy with odors, and, at each stop, the same uncontrolled push-and-shove scene was repeated.

Actually, this was the mob scene we encountered daily while commuting by our overburdened, inadequate mass transit system. What was surprising in this case was that in Yugoslavia, the international train was used in the same fashion as any ordinary train. By contrast, in Sofia, and, as we happened to observe later in the rest of the countries we passed through, the international travelers were installed in separate coaches, where an atmosphere of strict control was created. And as illogical as it may seem, since Yugoslavia freed itself from the influence of Moscow and as consequence became a much freer society, even the slightest differences in the routines of our respective societies were interpreted in the light of the variance in the political situations of the countries. No wonder I looked at the whole incident—the disorder on their side in contrast to the order on ours—not as an objectionable intrusion or irritating uncivilized behavior, but as the normal hustle and bustle of a free society, unfettered by the austere discipline imposed on the oppressed.

As we crossed the border between Yugoslavia and Hungary, order returned, and the whole ride, till we reached Dresden, proceeded in the same manner.

The long, tiresome journey—cooped up for days, snatching few hours of sleep now and then in a sitting position, never able to get a real rest—finally ended at Dresden.

The city's train station, the first one of its kind I had seen then, as well as all the other remarkable sights we visited there, were overshadowed by the indelible impression of a ruined city. Eighteen years had passed since the savage bombing of Dresden by the Allies at the end of the Second World War. As a memorial to the event, a pile of ruble was left, and, in its midst, a jagged remnant of the exquisite facade of a once-splendid building stood precariously yet auspiciously—a testament of the endurance of harmony and beauty over the ugliness of destruction.

The next stop was Leipzig; a place drilled into our minds, connected forever with the trial of Georgy Dimitrov in 1933. As it happened, though, the only memory I have from the city—besides the shop in which I bought a scarf that I still keep in my closet—is of St. Thomas' Church.

Churches all over the Sots Block were regarded simply as historical, cultural monuments; that made it hard for a visitor to experience anything more than curiosity or admiration for the magnificent buildings. Yet, St. Thomas' Church was a special place—people who had prayed inside those stone walls were the first ones to have experienced the cleansing power of Bach's heavenly music. It was a house of God, not a museum. Only now, it was much easier to feel that special touch of the past by looking at the church from the outside, contemplating its architecture.

I still keep a black and white photo, the only group picture from this entire trip, taken in the square in front of the church. All are smiling.

My most vivid memories of this trip are from Weimar. Not long before the trip, I had finished reading a biographical novel about the life of Franz Liszt, and his connection with the city of Weimar had awakened my interest in the place even more. It was impossible to walk through the streets of Weimar without being awed by it. So many great people had lived and worked there, leaving cultural treasures so noble, so lofty, that made one feel like treading on a Holy Land of civilization. And only a few kilometers away from it, there was that horrifying monument of evil and human deprivation!

We traveled to Buchenwald by bus. Upon our arrival, we were taken to a reception area where we were given a brief lecture, a historical overview of the camp. There were more explanations and facts in front of a model of the building's set up, and finally we received a guided tour. I believe that first we viewed the area where the Polish prisoners were kept, segregated from the rest; many of them killed off by epidemics of cholera. The specially targeted victims, though, were the Jews.

We all knew about the fate of six million people, but it was one thing to read about a horror and another to be at, and see, the place where it happened.

The barbed wire surrounding the camp; the watchtower where the guards stood, machine guns ever at the ready; the kennels for the dogs the SS officers used for guarding the prisoners. All that was shocking, but the crematorium was the place where one suddenly felt overwhelmed and crushed by the starkness of this factory of death—a processing plant meticulously organized for efficiency in the business of elimination of human beings—with its pathology room for the sadistic scientists to carry on with their experiments, the shower cabins, the execution cellar with its wall hooks and a row of ovens...

We were told that this area had been damaged during its last days before the liberation of the camp in 1945 by the U.S. Army. When the time came for restoration of the site, the problem arose of finding somebody who could provide a description of the setup of the area before it was destroyed. There were no witnesses; nobody who had entered through those doors came out alive. A tradesman who had done some repairs while the camp was in operation helped with information.

The last stop of the tour was a visit to a room where some surviving artifacts and belongings of the victims had been collected, preserved, and exhibited for viewing.

Quietly I broke away from the group and went back to the reception area to wait for their return. I had seen enough; my knees had given out. I had to sit down.

In half an hour all were back. In silence, we boarded the bus, took our seats, and drove away, stunned and bewildered.

There was a considerable presence of Soviet solders in Weimar—moving around in rather large groups. Never did we see a lone solder walking the streets of the city. They were not liked here. Thanks to our shared Slavic background, the similarity in the languages and who knows what, we experienced the wroth of the German's resentment toward the occupational troops.

Supper in a nondescript restaurant. We were all seated at a long table for our evening meal. Occasionally somebody would get up and walk out of the main hall for a short trip to the washroom or to take a look at something of interest. Nothing out of the ordinary. Suddenly, one of our colleagues came in from the outside, all flushed and agitated. Right away a number of guys jumped up from their seats and followed him. Something was happening; a sort of excitement spread.

A few minutes later, in the grip of growing curiosity, the rest of us pushed away our chairs and rushed out into the entrance hall. A racket could be heard coming from downstairs. Hardly any speech, mostly the noises produced in fistfights: the swish of shuffling feet, the thud of punches. Sounded like a melee.

More guys went down, German as well as Bulgarian. The rest of our group remained standing in the entrance hall, worried but afraid to venture downstairs.

Eventually the noise ceased, and tired and confused guys emerged from downstairs. Surrounded by his buddies, with everyone's attention on him, Sasho, a colleague of ours, friend and classmate of mine, appeared. His face was bloodied; his clothes were in disarray. A pin of Hristo Botev, a Bulgarian poet and revolutionary hero of the National Rebirth era, had been pulled out of the lapel of his suit.

There had been a misunderstanding. A couple of Germans had mistaken Sasho for a Russian—which by itself was an annoyance to them—but became even more incensed by the pin depicting a man with plentiful dark hair and a bushy beard who they mistakenly identified as Karl Marks. The Germans went immediately into action, skipping the preliminary insults usually superseding most of fights. This was not an ordinary fight, and there was no need for an explanation.

Fortunately the misunderstanding was discovered, but there was a problem with the ensuing communications. Even though Russian was compulsory and was taught in the schools of all satellite countries, it never became a language that served as a unifying link. It was regarded as just another symbol of the subjugation we were forced under. It was no wonder we had problems. The Germans did not want to even try to speak Russian, and we were not too comfortable with it either. Most of us had never put in enough effort to learn it properly.

Somehow the situation was resolved. Apologies, and even good feelings, were professed. There was some dancing in the restaurant, and, at the end of the evening, a group of us ended up in a truly cozy pub frequented by students. All of this with the compliments of our new German friends.

Leaving Weimar en route to Erfurt, the bus we were riding in was forced by traffic to move slower for a while beside a group of Russian soldiers marching with frozen countenances on their faces. Probably, in light of our recently acquired understanding of the feelings of at least some of the population toward them, we felt a sudden surge of sympathy for these young men, so far away from their homes, so disliked. With a spontaneous enthusiasm we started waving at them, trying to attract their attention by shouting words in Russian, any words that came to mind, till we succeeded. And we were rewarded in kind. Their faces brightened, breaking into wide smiles that they beamed back at us.

I never forgot the trip to Buchenwald, the incident of the mistaken identity of Hristo Botev, the fight and reconciliation with the young Germans, the good time we had in the pub after the fight. I never forgot those unhappy Russian soldiers (or who knows what nationality they were), and I am glad we brought smiles to their faces. I don't remember any of the places we visited to pay homage to Goethe, Schiller, Liszt, Wagner, Mozart, and the rest of the luminaries connected one way or another to that city, which made it so special to most of us. On the other hand, the things that I remember about the time we spent in Weimar were exactly the things that we appreciate only in a state of a heightened awareness of our humanity. And that brings me back to Goethe, Schiller, Liszt, Mozart…

My memories of Erfurt are vague. Paradoxically, I think that it is a beautiful city without being able to defend my statement with facts or particular recollections. A church stands out in my mind, but a bit like a picture from a fairy tale. I think that we visited a factory there also, but I am not sure. Anyway, I am sure that I will always keep on stubbornly asserting that it is a beautiful place. There must have been something there, a mood, an ambiance, a soothing peacefulness, that had made me feel good.

The trip back was exhausting. It took us even longer to make it—spending the days walking around the cities left on our agenda, traveling the whole night through.

It was a bright, fresh morning when we first arrived in Prague—a city still associated in my memory with the smell of sausages and sauerkraut. It hit me right at the train station and followed me all day long throughout my wanderings up and down Vaclavske Namesti, the picturesque Staroe Mesto, and along all the long and short streets I happened to traverse, at times totally lost. Besides the problem of lack of sleep during that part of our journey, we all had the problem of extreme shortness of cash. The small amount of crones, the Czechoslovakian currency I was in possession of, was designated for a specific purchase that I left for last—to avoid the inconvenience of carrying the package all day long. At the end of the day, I went to a store someone had told me about and bought a few meters of brocade to take home as a souvenir of the trip. In time, we could use it for making new bed covers.

Without money to spare, none of us were able to visit any museums, galleries, historical buildings; on the other hand, though, we saw quite a bit of the city and its people.

On our arrival there, we broke into small groups, and at times I took off on the group in order to explore on my own. During the course of the day, we kept crossing each other's paths, exchanging information about places we had discovered, synchronizing our watches (figuratively speaking).

In late August of 1968, during Prague's Second Spring, watching on the television screen the tanks of the Warsaw Pact roll through the street of Vaclavske Namesti, the excited crowds accosting, shouting at, surrounding the foreign troops, I could identify the very spot shown through the lens of the video camera. It made me feel more like a participant in this event than like the remote sympathizer I had been to the events evolving in Budapest in 1956. The disappointment was not greater though; I never believed that Czechoslovakia had a chance.

The last place we visited was Budapest. The train arrived very early in the morning, so we had to spend a couple of hours in the train station waiting for the city to wake up.

At the time, in my circle of friends, there was an ongoing debate: which of the two, Prague or Budapest, was the better place? On the day I am writing about, my verdict was Budapest. It struck me as merrier, more romantic, more vibrant, and spacious. The couples seated on the banks of the Danube, the lively gypsy music wafting from restaurants, the Margarita Island, the towering crosses and statues sticking above the high fences surrounding Catholic cemeteries, all contributed to a uniqueness that I found quite appealing.

New massive buildings, with their boring symmetry and imposing Stalinist architecture, were taking over all the big cities in the Eastern European Sots Block countries. The disregard for history (the best was still to come!) and rejection of the past in general led to the destruction and neglect of many old landmarks, and that took much away from the charm of the picturesque and cozy cities with a more distant past. The architecture, the setting, became much less important in determining my like or dislike of a city. What left an impression on me was the spirit of the place, the people, the way of life, as I perceived it in that short visit.

Walking through the streets of Budapest, one could see the holes in the walls of buildings caused by shrapnel and bullets fired during the Revolution of 1956.

Repair and maintenance were not a high priority anywhere in Eastern Europe, yet I was surprised that no effort had been made by the ruling Communist regime to obliterate those scars, a bitter reminder of the fight for freedom they had crushed so brutally.

It had been a very long day. The train taking us on the last leg of our journey was leaving late in the night. Tired and hungry as we were, we kept looking with longing at coffee shops and restaurants. Most of us had no money left, but we had prepared ourselves just as the proverbial Bie Ganyo, the uncouth hero of Aleko Konstantinov's classic, had done before leaving on a trip to Europe at the turn of the twentieth century. He stuffed his saddlebags, in lieu of a suitcase, with vials of precious rose oil. Apparently things were not much different now. Only instead of oil we carried with us small vials of rose essence, which was very popular outside Bulgarian borders; in contrast to the rose oil, it was sold in stores and was not illegal to carry abroad. We gave the vials away as souvenirs to new and old friends. So when a few of us stopped in front of a grocery store admiring a display of large pears, perfectly shaped and ripe, we were surprised to find out that our vials of rose essence could be used in a profitable way—in bartering.

The proprietor of the store must have had a sharp eye out for hungry tourists. He stepped out and asked us point blank where we were from. Hungarian is one of the least popular languages and, as I mentioned before, Russian was not much of a help, so I have no idea how we managed to negotiate the transaction. As soon as he understood that we were Bulgarians, he inquired whether we had any rose essence on us. We did; he made us an offer we could not refuse—pears for vials of essence. On the matter of the rate of exchange, there was no bargaining whatsoever. It was accepted immediately; in fact, I could not believe our luck! With renewed energy we continued our endless and aimless, but thoroughly enjoyable, march through the streets of Budapest.

On our arrival in Sofia, after a train ride that had seemed to last forever, I felt dazed, exhausted, all my strength depleted, my ankles swollen, hardly able to stand on my feet.

Dragging myself home somehow, I collapsed in bed and in an instant fell into a deep slumber that lasted for eighteen hours.

On our return from Budapest, we had a brief stopover in Belgrade—only for a couple of hours, not long enough for a sight-seeing trip of the city. It was with a measure of regret that I boarded the train and kept on looking at the silhouettes of the buildings receding in the distance. I hoped that I would be back someday.

Yugoslavia was the only Eastern European country that had exerted, however small, a pull on me. The fact that its citizens were allowed to travel in the West meant they were free; the fact that almost all chose to return bespoke of their satisfaction with the system they lived in and of their confidence in the future of the country.

There must have been something good happening in Yugoslavia.

Tito was already the longest ruling dictator in the Balkans, ruling in the name of the Communist Party, while succeeding in convincing the world that he was a different tyrant, one with a soft touch, who took good care of his people. And in return most of them loved him, or at least professed to. The West pampered him—great men called him a friend.

Yugoslavia looked like the brightest spot in the vast lands east of the impenetrable curtain that threw a deep shadow over it. This is how it looked to me then. Little had I known about the dark side of this former satellite, the duplicity in Tito's foreign policy, the thin line he was walking between carrying on with his ruthless Communist agenda while playing the role of the independent, reasonable leader.

Only a couple of years later I heard the saga of a thirteen-year-old child whose whole family had taken the risk of crossing the border in the belief that behind it, in Yugoslavia, they would find a safe haven from the brutal policies of collectivization in Bulgaria. Instead, they were thrown into the dungeons of the prison in Nish, crowded with local political prisoners as well as refugees from the neighboring countries. The howls and screams extracted from a tortured Bulgarian interrogated nightly horrified them.

For over a year they were treated like criminals, outcasts: kept in a state of suspense, never told what would come next, moved around the country to destinations unknown, transported like cattle in freight trains, always surrounded by armed state security troops, the dreaded "udba." Mistrusted, mistreated, used as cheap labor—men, women, and children. Their destinies hung in the balance, used merely as currency in Tito's foreign policy in playing East against West for the benefit of his Communist State. Never could they be sure that would not be sent back across the border, straight into the bullets of the waiting guards. Many were, and some died—hit in the back—before reaching the other side. Or would they finally be herded together with Hungarian and Romanian refugees, brought to a spot along the southern border across Trieste, where, after asking them to

hand over their money and watches, the guards would point toward a direction and shout, "Here is the border. Off you go."
And that was the salvation they were praying for...

One summer night in 1950, a group of about one hundred and fifty Bulgarians and Hungarians were brought close to the Italian border, at the edge of a forest, next to a small village on the Yugoslavian side of the divide called Sezana. Broken into groups of twelve, deprived by the guards of their meager savings—there were no watches to be taken—they started on a three-hour trudge toward the other side, to the American soldiers waiting for them, ready to transport them to the closest refugee camp in the vicinities of Trieste.

Men, women, and children rushed forward, petrified with fear and anxiety. They had heard that of the previous group brought to that same crossing, fourteen Bulgarians had been killed by the guards.

One of the hundred and fifty refugees that made it that night was the thirteen-year-old boy, my future husband. This is his story.

There is much more to it, but it is for him to tell all. For my part, I could not leave it completely out of mine, because from the moment I heard it, the memory of my trip to Belgrade became tarnished forever.

So, early in January of 1964, with a considerable sense of anticipation, Liudmila, Annie, and I were on our way to Belgrade. The three of us were working at the institute. Liudmila had also been a classmate of mine in the university; besides that, we were friends. On her father's side, she descended from a distinguished Macedonian family, and she was quite proud of it. On account of that, or simply because of her outgoing and sociable nature, she befriended a Yugoslavian couple: Dragomir, a Macedonian, and his wife Dushitsa, a Slovenian. She met them in a train while traveling to, or from, somewhere. They lived in Belgrade and Liudi, as we called her, had a standing invitation to visit them.

Annie was married to one of the stars of the Bulgarian National Basketball Team. He belonged to a sports club affiliated with the security services within the Ministry of External Affairs. With his help we were able to acquire visas for Yugoslavia, and thanks to Liudi we had a place to stay in Belgrade. I was just tagging along.

Christmas was celebrated on the seventh of January in Bulgaria as well as in Yugoslavia in accordance to the Julian calendar; Bulgaria later switched to the Gregorian calendar. A unique cultural characteristic of the Serbian people was that their big New Year's celebration was held on January the fourteenth, the feast of St. Basil. Those were religious holidays, therefore not listed on our official civic calendars, but they were celebrated in a big way in our Western neighbor. It was an exciting proposition to go to Belgrade and join in the festivities.

Dragomir and Dushitsa turned out to be a genuinely warm and hospitable couple—beyond our expectations. They had a small child and another on the way. Suddenly, we found ourselves embraced by the family, their friends, and relatives. Prompted by a desire to demonstrate our gratitude for their kindness, we did something that was a bit odd in the eyes of some tenants living in the apartment building: armed with pails of water and washing rags, we took on the task of cleaning the mosaic-covered staircase running up the few flights of stairs. People going up and down looked at us in surprise while walking gingerly around the pails, mindful of the freshly cleaned, still wet, spots.

We spent most of the time going for walks along Terazia, admiring the new modern buildings done in an architectural style I perceived to be Western. Belgrade was a much more attractive city than Sofia at that time. The people seemed much more easygoing, though at times it was difficult to interpret their behavior: their brash comments, their unabashed stares. In fact, some were rather vulgar; the remarks sent in our direction sounded more insulting than anything we were used to hearing. Back with Dragomir and Dushitsa we asked what we were doing to provoke their rudeness. The explanation we got went something like this: "Oh, no. You are misunderstanding. They are not swearing at you; on the contrary, they are expressing their approval of you, of your looks. Don't be insulted; rather, feel flattered."

I don't think we ever felt insulted, only embarrassed. To say that swearing was common is an understatement; *accepted* would be a more appropriate word to apply in this case. Very quickly we adjusted our behavior accordingly.

The greatest surprise, though, was the discovery of a lingering sentiment that had flared up for a short while years before, when the relationship between the two Balkan countries was at its best but had been completely buried by the loyal Communist regime in Bulgaria after Tito's rejection of the domination of the Soviet Union. It was the idea of the creation of a federation between Yugoslavia and Bulgaria. The reference to this sentiment came about in a most unusual way.

Belgrade had the reputation of a city with a lively nightlife. This was attributed to the temperament of the people, as well as to the fact that they were more prosperous than any of the other Eastern European countries. The free expression of their natural exuberance and joie de vivre gave a color to their daily lives and nightly entertainment. One could really experience it, feel it, in the numerous taverns scattered over Belgrade. Once we did visit a restaurant where the atmosphere was as subdued and the food as bland as it was forgettable; but an evening spent in a tavern was hard to forget.

The tavern where we spent the evening was a cozy place with live entertainment, which consisted of a few musicians and a singer. There could have been more than one singer; however, I distinctly remember the performance of the female singer who sang "White Hollyhocks," our request. She announced the song, and she introduced us as Bulgarians who were visiting Belgrade. A noisy welcome followed: greetings were shouted from the farthest corners of the room. It was easy to spot us as we were seated at a table on an elevated area close to the center of the room. Dragomir, Dushitsa, and a few of their friends were smiling, gesturing at us.

The music started, the singer fixed her gaze on us and, in a pleasant, rich voice, started to sing. The melodious, moving sound of the beloved song, the heartfelt performance touched and excited everybody so much that at the end of the song, along with the applause and shouts of *bravo*, a chant *to the federation* erupted, growing louder and louder, drowning out all other sounds and noises.

It was startling. I don't know where this spontaneous cry came from; whether the idea of a federation with Bulgaria was still appealing to the people of Yugoslavia or it was simply an expression of the feeling of brotherhood stirred up by a simple song we all loved, by the melancholy beauty of the music of the Balkan countries that speaks to our very souls.

Many stood up and raised their glasses to us. One man motioned to a waitress and demanded that an empty wine goblet be brought to him. She scurried back and handed it to him. The man took it, raised it close to his eyes, and after examining it in a glance, in a booming voice, yelled, "Bring me another. This one is dirty."

As soon as the waitress fulfilled the command, he raised his arm, glass firmly in hand and, with an expansive swing, threw the glass against the hardwood floor. The gesture was met with a roar of approval. The sound of shattered glass filled the room.

This was a sight I had never witnessed. At the moment, for me, the most baffling thing was the request by the guy for a clean glass—after all he was going to break it. On making the comment, I was told, "She should have brought a clean one in the first place. There is a fancy restaurant where they serve crystal glasses for breaking. Of course, that is too expensive for this one."

The evening was full of surprises; the emotions I felt brought tears to my eyes—from exhilaration to embarrassment. Just when we thought that things were settling down, a request from all around came to us to follow the ritual we had just witnessed. Everybody wanted us to break a glass. The more we hesitated the more insistent the invitation became.

I don't remember how Annie and Liudi came through that. For myself, it was a moment of truly supreme discomfort: I felt frozen; my only salvation was to become invisible. It was not that I abhorred the gesture itself; it was the attention, the spotlight we were under, which I could not handle. I could not even raise my arm to throw the glass; I just kept on tightening the grip around it, until a sharp pain in my palm made me release it in an instant. The broken pieces slid noiselessly from my hand. Drops of blood spurted from a few superficial cuts. I felt fine, however.

The rest of the evening passed in the same excited, though relaxed, happy mood. In my memory, the evening has stuck as the highlight of the trip.

The personnel department was located on the floor below the Technology Department, the one I was working for. The office consisted of a single, large room overlooking Vazov Street. The director, actually the only person occupying the office, was a woman, a polite, aloof, enigmatic figure seldom seen in the hallways of the institute, dashing from door to door. She put me on guard every time I came in—even only accidental—contact with her.

She had sent a message upstairs that she wanted to see me in her office. It was urgent. With trepidation, I descended the one flight of stairs and knocked on her door. Before long, the door opened, and the director emerged, her figure outlined by the brightness streaming from behind her. The large office seemed empty, and, when two tall, dour men, clad in long gabardine coats appeared next to me, I was startled. In a soft voice, the personnel director presented me to the two men and immediately retreated behind her desk, assuming the attitude of a spectator. The men did not introduce or identify themselves. It really did not matter; it was obvious that they were officers from the state security.

With sweating palms and racing heart I waited for the questions that followed. Only one was doing the talking: Where do I live? We share the apartment with another family, don't we? Which rooms do we occupy? Do I know the rest of the tenants in the apartment building? Do I know who lives on the floor above us?

Something clicked. The apartment above us was occupied by the family of the chauffeur of the French embassy. We did not know them; we knew only their two small children. We had often met them in the entrance foyer, accompanied by their governess, usually going out for a walk. We had the feeling that she was Bulgarian.

The questions concentrated on the French family. My answers became quite redundant. I did not know anything about our foreign neighbors. We did have an issue with the family, in particular with the two kids, but it was not something to discuss with secret agents. Sometimes the racket created by these two tiny creatures was so disturbing that Mother would fetch the long rolling pin from the cupboard and start banging on the ceiling, the signal that they had crossed the limit of her patience. It seldom helped.

Then, they came to the point. No more questions, rather a statement. "We would like to spend some time in your rooms in the apartment. On our own. We need your cooperation. It is very important." This was the other man talking; the one who had kept silent till now.

I could not believe my ears. "I do not live alone. I live with my parents, and anything that relates to our home is my Father's responsibility. He is the head of our family."

This was the best I could do to manage the situation.

A moment of tense silence followed. Then the personnel director left her spot from behind the desk, approached the door, and let me out of the office. Meanwhile the two agents had already retreated to a corner of the room, hidden from outside view.

A couple of weeks later, Mother met me at home with a sort of triumphant smirk on her face. "Two agents came today. Must be the same ones who talked to you. Your father met them."

"What happened?"

"They came inside and started snooping. Looked around the windows. They told your father that they would need to spend a day or two in the rooms, by themselves; and then would be coming at intervals to do some work. We would have to leave the apartment at those times."

"What did Dad say?"

"He told them that he can't let them do that."

"He told them just that?"

"Yes. He told them that, and he gave them his reasons."

"Reasons? He told them his reasons?"

"Yes. He said that he could not allow strapping, young men going in and out of the apartment on a more or less regular basis. What will the neighbors think? What are we doing? Are we running a bordello?"

"A bordello!" I had never heard Father ever use that word. This did not sound at all like my father talking! His concern about the neighbor's opinion had a false ring to it also. He never paid attention to the opinions of strangers, and, since he never made any effort to get to know any of the residents in the building, they fell into that category.

"Oh, there was more. They would not leave and kept pressuring him. He told them also that he had to protect your reputation. You are young, unmarried."

It was hilarious; it sounded like a farce. It really did not sound like Father at all. It was a performance, but I never thought of him as a ham.

"And it worked? Did it, Mother?"

"They left, and they are not coming back. Something must have worked."

"Do you think they went to the neighbors?"

Mother's face darkened. Her lips tightened. With a shrug of her shoulder she said, "Who knows? I don't care."

22

DESPAIR. "GOOD-BYE" FOREVER

Since the spring of 1959, the entries in my dairy started to shrink to fewer and fewer while the intervals between them grew longer and longer. When I wrote, I filled the pages with long, rambling accounts of insignificant happenings, crowding them with names of people and events that I can't recollect now. Or, perhaps, I have blocked them from my mind too well.

But there are a few bright and clear memories that bridge the gap and run like a lifeline through the emptiness between "before" and "after." One of them is an event, which turned into a tradition in my family life in Toronto; a happening that had its beginning at the turn of the sixties. For me, it was a time when I felt serene, that I belonged, rather than feeling lost and disconnected.

The motto of the atheistic society we lived in was "Religion is the opium of the masses," while, in the spirit of the double standard that reigned during that era, the constitution of the country was proclaiming freedom of all religions. In fact, all religious practices were effectively forbidden, for a high price was to be paid by those who chose to ignore the motto that ruled the state.

Students were expelled for attending places of worship; working people were threatened with losing their jobs for getting married in a religious ceremony or for baptizing their children.

Alternative civil ceremonies for weddings and funerals were introduced. Many of the new rituals incorporated elements of the religious ones. In time, that made them quite acceptable.

New civic holidays were created to replace the religious ones: New Year's celebrations replaced Christmas; the Day of the Shepherd was created to replace St. George's Day. People baked Easter bread and dyed eggs, slaughtered lambs, exchanged presents, prepared traditional foods—all the activities done for the new holidays, performed only for the sake of tradition, completely apart from any religious sentiments.

In this environment, belief in superstitions and psychics flourished. Fortune-tellers were treated like gurus endowed with an almost-scientific authority.

People were looking for miracles. In this ancient land it felt quite easy to believe in the supernatural, in cosmic powers; paganism had never been completely forgotten.

Nevertheless, religion still exerted its pull. Most of the time the priests conducted their services and read their sermons in almost-empty churches to a congregation of a few old grandmothers. On Palm Sunday and Easter, though, people came in increased numbers, and, suddenly, about the time I am describing, on Saturday nights before Easter Sunday every year, a dramatic occurrence took place in Sofia. Crowds of people began flocking to Alexander Nevsky, St. George, and the other churches, filling up the interiors and spilling over into the squares and gardens surrounding them. It looked as though, for a night at least, the population of Sofia was going through a Christian revival. It was not a rowdy, unruly gathering. Old and young stood next to each other, a thin yellow wax candle in one hand, a red painted egg in the other, talking quietly, waiting patiently for that magic moment when the bells would start their mighty and triumphant peal.

"Christ has risen!"

"Indeed, He has risen!"

Smiles, hugs, clicks of egg shells coming in contact with each other. The sounds of Easter. Slowly, as the bells went silent, the spell was broken; the multitude would start drifting away from the square, leaving it completely empty, abandoned—left only to the droves of pigeons descending from the trees, picking at the broken red egg shells strewn all over the pavement.

Mother never left with the crowd. She would arrive early and remain inside the cathedral till the end of the midnight service that lasted for a couple of hours. She would be back home at around three o'clock in the morning.

I did not have to rush home either. This was the only time I could stay out as late as I wanted—no questions asked. We were already living on Moskovska, and the crowds in front of Alexander Nevsky on that night almost reached the door of our apartment building.

Being there that evening, standing among all those people and so close to home, with friends or alone, I felt content and happy. One year, a rumor spread that after midnight, at the church of St. George, a flock of white doves would be released. I remember how, as soon as the bells of Alexander Nevsky went quiet, I dashed through the streets, hoping to see them flying away.

The celebration was over only after Mother got back from church and the three of us had finished our small supper. Father would have spent the evening at home, waiting, celebrating in his own way, never joining in anything. As the three of us would gather around the small table, he would pour red wine into three glasses; Mother would bring the Easter bread that she had made and the painted eggs that we both had decorated. Then we would eat the bread, drink the wine, and knock our eggs until the strongest one was left unbroken.

And we felt like a family again. For one magical night of the year.

I was moving in a dark and gloomy world surrounded by walls, and the walls were closing in on me. A feeling of claustrophobia kept me in a state of almost-constant anxiety.

Despair weighed me down constantly like a burden. It kept pushing me closer and closer to the ground. It exhausted me and even changed my appearance. I began to avoid looking in the mirror, for the face in there looked back at me with haunted, sad eyes. It was the face of someone crushed and weak, hopeless and helpless.

Finally, I had to face the world. I had tried to postpone that moment for a long time. My parents had their memories and dashed hopes to ponder. I had none of that. My memories and hopes were secondhand; I had lived with theirs—and I was not ready to sacrifice my life yet. It was time to become me. I was unprepared, however, for the world around me. I could survive in it as long as somebody took care of me, protected me, and filled me with false hopes and expectations. But on my own, I could not survive in this gray, bleak, oppressive and lonely place. And it was so lonely…

A day, 1964

> During the day it is easier. There is work. At work there are people, and that brings distraction. Though I feel detached, my mind is occupied; the void is not complete.
>
> At the end of work, I head toward the apartment, walking slowly along the streets. Still, the distance I have to travel is short and it takes me only minutes to get home.

Mother is there. Her face is bloodless, her lips have a bluish tinge, her soft, doe eyes have the same look as mine. The air is heavy with feelings of depression, recrimination, and a sense of guilt; somebody must be guilty for all that.

We all feel it and look for it. For the guilt.

Mother's first words are the same as always: "Have something to eat."

The answer is also the same as always: "I am not hungry."

I am never hungry, and I feel guilty about it. Mother is worried that I will get sick.

After a while, I start for the door. Can't stay in the apartment for long, especially in the evenings. Will simply burst if I stay inside any longer.

Outside twilight is descending. I look around the street making up my mind which direction to take. And I start walking, avoiding the places frequented by people who know me.

At least the streets are safe.

I am walking fast, eyes downcast, hands thrust deep in my pockets, head empty of organized thoughts, hurriedly crossing from one side of the street to the other, turning arbitrarily at corners in pursuit of a new direction, walking and walking for hours.

Never stopping, never resting.

Time is passing. I am alone, absolutely alone in the whole universe.

Organized thoughts start to take shape in my mind, rhymes start rushing in, I am composing a poem…

Finally, it is time to turn back. Absorbed in my thoughts, repeating them over and over, trying to remember so I can put them on paper once I get back home, I have been walking staring at the sharp toes of my shoes, oblivious of all surroundings. I have lost my way. Stopping for a while, figuring out the location, checking the time; luckily, now I have a watch—calculating the return time, I conclude: should be home no earlier than 11:30.

The way back is almost pleasant; it is good to have a destination.

Here is the apartment. I open the entrance door and climb the few steps to the elevator. The stairs curve around it. The elevator looks like a metal cage, open on all sides. It takes a coin to start it.

The staircase is always lit. On the second floor landing, in front of the door of one of the apartments, stands a militiaman. The apartment is the home of a very important member of the Central Committee. It is guarded twenty-four hours a day.

The guards get bored, and some of them try to strike up a conversation with tenants going up or down the staircase. Sometimes they even tell jokes, but the response is usually an ambiguous smile. One never knows if it is safe to laugh. Once Mother was asked by one of the militiaman: "What are you going to do in case of a nuclear raid?" This was a popular politically loaded joke and everybody knew the answer. Mother faked ignorance: "I don't know," she said. And the guard proceeded with the rest of the joke.

Taking the elevator up is much better, no time for jokes.

The elevator stops on the landing of the fourth floor. In front are the two doors of the apartment we share with an elderly couple and an old lady. The apartment belonged to the old lady's niece before it was confiscated by the government. The niece lives in Vienna.

The door on the left is used by us, and the door on the right by the others.

I unlock our door and quietly move through a long corridor, then turn right and enter the big room where Mother and Father sleep in separate beds, along two different walls. I walk across the room, tip-toeing in the dark. I know that Mother is awake; she always waits for me; Father is asleep, his cover pulled over his head, his feet sticking out, uncovered. I feel my mother's eyes following me through the darkness. I feel guilty. I feel the accusing look burning on my back.

My bed is in the small room, adjacent to the big one. There is a glass portal door between this and yet another room, but the door is locked, covered with a heavy curtain and blocked by a buffet in front of it. A similar door in the large room is also locked, curtained and blocked by a piece of furniture. Behind these doors lie rooms occupied by the other tenants.

I start undressing in the dark. The bed is in a corner, next to a chesterfield. Carefully I lay my clothes on it. The clothes are the same ones I am going to wear tomorrow. I put my shoes at the foot of the chesterfield. They are the only shoes I have, and I will be wearing them also tomorrow. And tomorrow is going to be exactly the same as today.

> Quietly I slip between the sheets. After a while, I reach under the pillow, searching for the pen and paper I keep there, and, feeling the paper in the dark, start scratching the poem I have been composing while walking along the streets—as softly as possible…

The security guard at the entrance to the institute had sent a message that someone was looking for me downstairs. It was Mother. She was waiting outside, standing on the sidewalk in front of the building, looking impatient, excited. As soon as she saw me, she reached inside her handbag, pulled out a long, blue envelope, and handed it to me. It was a letter. The sender was Andrei Yakimov, and it was posted from the United States. It was addressed to me. Mother told me that she had just found it in the mailbox and immediately had rushed to the institute; her curiosity was aroused to such an extent that she could not wait till I got back from work. We did not know anybody living in America, and, even though the family name rang a bell, the person and the address were completely unfamiliar.

The first thing that grabbed my attention as I ripped the envelope open was a small black and white picture of two guys sitting at the opposite sides of a table. Both were leaning forward, supporting themselves on their arms and looking at each other like people engaged in a conversation. One was a fair fellow with light eyes wearing a white shirt with sleeves rolled up to his elbows; the other was dark and had a less casual appearance.

The letter was a couple of pages long. It explained that the sender was the youngest son of Simo Yakimov, a cousin of Grandfather Vassil. Mother's face lighted up. She knew about Uncle Simo and his wife, Nadejda, though she did not know anything about their children. Andrei went on telling me that he was a student of Economics in the University of Montana in Missoula. He was a child in 1949 when his family ran across the border in Yugoslavia and eventually ended up in Canada. In Bulgaria, he had completed four years of schooling in his native village of Zavala. He was writing to me basically to ask if I would like to be his pen pal. The letter was written in Bulgarian; he was anxious to know how well he had managed the task. He also mentioned that the picture was of himself and his friend Sami, a Kurd, but omitted identifying himself on the photo. For a while, Mother and I kept looking at the picture and wondered. Finally, after reading the letter a couple of times more, we came to the conclusion that Andrei was the one with the rolled-up sleeves.

The letter was unanticipated, but was not a complete surprise. A few months before, Mother and Mrs. Nikiforova had gone to a small provincial town to visit Uncle Simo's sister, Parvanka. It was unusual for her to undertake the trip; she did not know many of her numerous relatives and her contact with them was sporadic. On the other hand, Aunt Nina knew and kept in touch with many of them. In those last couple of years, though, Mother had started to take short therapeutic trips to the countryside, or, as she called them, excursions, accompanied by one friend or another. This is when she rediscovered some of her relatives living outside Sofia, whose addresses she usually got from her sister.

This particular trip had been prompted partially by her interest in an old story, the story of the daring escape of a large, organized, armed group of people decades ago, part of whom was Uncle Simo's family. It was not a tale talked about openly; it was still told in a whisper, as if it were a rumor rather than a real event. It was a fascinating one and hard to forget.

On her visit Mother was told that Uncle Simo and Aunt Nadejda were living in Calgary. She saw pictures of them both and of people she never knew existed. She left the place impressed with the kindness of Aunt Parvanka and with Uncle Simo's address in Canada.

Correspondence with the West was a risky business, but by then Mother had become quite reckless; she had reached a state of mind when she felt that there was nothing more to lose. Without mentioning it at home, she wrote a letter to the relatives in Calgary. Grandfather Vassil and Uncle Simo were not just cousins, there was a bond between them based on more than blood; they belonged to the same political party and had an affectionate personal friendship. That relationship did not, however, extend to their families. This is why in her letter Mother had to explain who she was first of all; furthermore, she sent pictures of herself and me. Then she wrote about Grandfather's life in the last few years, and about his passing away. She did not bother telling me all that until we received the letter from Andrei.

In the next couple of months, I received another letter and an open postcard; I answered all of them. Sometime toward the end of 1964, however, Mother told me that I should discontinue the correspondence. It was too risky; besides, she was on something that required extra vigilance. Hopefully, I would be able to explain everything to Andrei, someday.

I did what she asked me to do.

For most of us, the place we were born in, the country we loved, had been turned into a prison. Instead of walls, we were surrounded by an Iron Curtain. Like all prisoners condemned to life, we dreamed of freedom. The dream was as bright and unreachable as the stars in the skies. To me it meant, most of all, normalcy.

Freedom was always associated with the West. Speaking, even thinking, about the one brought the other to mind. The pull of the West had little to do with riches or even happiness. It was a matter of survival. As a generation that grew up in times of material deprivation, our demands were modest. We were the children of the professionals and the intelligentsia, now branded as bourgeoisie. The children of the kulaks, another branded and persecuted segment of society, were not faring better. The values instilled in us were based on the traditional morality reflected in the once-cherished reputation of Bulgarians as hardworking, honest, and hospitable. By this time, the fabric of our lives was in tatters. We had no future. The future belonged to the new, red bourgeoisie, a class created for the children of the proletariat and the peasants, a landless, nonexistent identity in its traditional sense by now. Instead of moving forward, the society had moved backward.

We were ignorant and naive in our perceptions of the West, but we had confidence. To a degree it came from the education we had. With no prospects in any other direction, the focus on education became foremost. All explanations aside, the readiness and the optimism with which we were looking forward to a new life in the West was remarkable.

The road to freedom was blocked by the all-encompassing Iron Curtain. There were two ways of escape: one by bursting through it, running across the border to Yugoslavia, Greece, or Turkey and risking your life; and the other, by lifting it and sneaking out as a tourist who never comes back. Lifting the Curtain was also very hard. But it was the preferred way.

I have never been told how my parents succeeded in achieving this; and now I will never know. The initiative must have come from Mother; she was the more practical and enterprising of the two. We never discussed whether I wanted to go away; it was assumed that this was the only opportunity for me to have a normal life.

Without the right connections, meaning people in powerful positions, the only way to get things done was through bribery. In spite of the high-minded slogans of worker's pride and selfless dedication, corruption existed and in many aspects of life was accepted as a part of it. The problem was finding the right person and having the means.

At the moment we had some means. After Grandfather Vassil passed away, Mother came into some money from the sale of his house in Sofia. It took years to settle things, but eventually the house was sold and the proceeds split four ways among Grandmother Lia, Mother, Aunt Nina, and Uncle Manol. We never saw Mother's share; it just exchanged hands.

In February, I got the external passport. Throughout the process of getting permission and the documents, I was kept in the dark. Mother attended to everything and that was fine with me; the less I knew, the better I could keep my emotions under control. Finally, though, I had to go through the last formality, an interview with an officer from Internal Security. It was the last opportunity for brainwashing before allowing anyone to travel to the West, consisting of mini-indoctrination, instilling fear, and nationalistic pep talks. There was nothing new in the whole tirade delivered by the officer; I had heard it all, bits and pieces of it, as part of the daily propaganda, over and over…It is doubtful that it had ever had any of the desired effect on anybody who had gone through it; it felt like an endurance test. During the interview I was told how to behave once in the West, that the West was a very dangerous place where one had to be most vigilant; to especially make sure to stay away from any Bulgarian émigrés; they were traitors and foreign agents. And I should never forget who I am, a Bulgarian.

The words sounded hollow. The traitors were not away, they were right here, busy betraying their own country, their own people, their own humanity. It was hard to listen…

March, 1965

The day was gray and gloomy, with an overcast sky. It was March, but there weren't any of the signs of spring. The three of us were standing on the platform at the Central Train Station. The express from Istanbul was due to arrive soon, and I was to travel on it. There weren't the usual crowds; very few people boarded the international train from here. A sense of desolation permeated the air.

Everything is etched in my memory: the small, yellow suitcase made of heavy pigskin covered with stickers of places I had never been to, the seven-eighths-length olive-colored coat, the high-heeled beige and brown Swiss model shoes…

A locomotive appeared in the distance—a small black dot that kept growing as the clicked and clicks of the wheels grew louder. Time was flying; we had to say our good-byes. Mother hugged and kissed me; Father just stood and looked at me, reserved as always, never demonstrative with his feelings. I was waiting for him to do something.

The train had come to a stop in front of us; the doors of the coaches were wide open. Few people were getting off, carrying their luggage.

Mother broke the silence. "Kiss her."

For the first time I could remember, Father kissed me on the cheek, shyly and awkwardly.

Then, I got on the train, followed by him carrying the suitcase. A briskly walking conductor was passing through the hallway when I heard Father's words: "Take care of her."

"Who is that?"

"An old client."

That did not surprise me; sometimes I thought that everybody knew him and he knew everybody. Sofia was a small city when he had been born, and, in some ways, it still was.

The train started pulling away from the station. I looked through the window; there they were, standing, Mother on the left, Father on the right. Snow had started falling and covering their bare heads. We did not wave at each other; they just kept looking in my direction. I thought: "Here they are. I will never see them again…" I kept turning in my mind their last words before we left the apartment: "Go and never come back. Don't worry about us. We will be all right. Save yourself. Remember there is no life for you here. An opportunity like that comes only once."

They were getting smaller and smaller, receding into the city's background like a pantomime frozen in time: heads turned in the direction of the vanishing train that was taking me away, from them, from everything I had ever known.

A strange sensation overtook me; all emotions were draining out of my being, it was as though life was seeping away from my body and only the instincts remained—to keep me existing until I could find something to cling to in order to start living again.

A few times I slipped my hand in the pockets of my coat, feeling the letters that Dad had given me to take to people he had known once, in case I came across them in my wanderings in the foreign land and needed help. One was for someone in Torino, the other for somebody in Vienna.

I felt tired; did not even want to think any more. I slumbered in an empty seat by the window and closed my eyes.

PART TWO

EPILOGUE

The house is almost ready, and we are leaving in a couple of days. I am going all over the place—organizing drawers, putting wardrobes in order, taking inventory. It isn't of much use, I know, but it helps me regain some sense of order and control—in a way, to put things in perspective. Since the break-in, every time we start looking for missing items we can never figure out if they were stolen or simply misplaced. During the time the construction work was going on, things also kept disappearing: small, useful things that we had brought all the way from home or spent much time and effort in searching for in Sofia. And that brought constant feelings of aggravation and frustration—especially upon discovering that they were gone the day after we left them out in the open. It seems we never remember to hide things—we had never acquired the habit, and to start hiding things now would be too burdensome. It would also mean giving in to a mentality of mistrust, and surely this would not make our stays here less stressful.

Besides, there is nothing else that I could do at the moment. I can't wash, cook, or even listen to the radio. During the summer months there is a water regimen. For some reason, water is free, and even though there are water meters, nobody is coming around to read them. That takes away any incentive to preserve water supplies. People are drowning their vegetable gardens morning and evening, sometimes leaving the hoses on full blast all night long. On the other hand, the village mayor has complete control over the schedule. She turns the water on and off at her discretion and when, from time to time, surprised villagers find the taps running during the day, the men start whispering with a smirk, "The mayor is taking a bath." Today, there is no electricity either. Somebody with connections succeeded in getting a new concrete electric post and even new wiring for a three-phase electric current. Never mind that we don't have any post, even a wooden one, and are forced to get electricity by stretching wires from Tommy's house—Aunt Nina's older son. The younger one, Vasko, also has a house, attached to Tommy's. Both stand on the lot where Grandmother Lia's house used to be. Now the whole village is without electricity for days, even weeks; the pace of work is quite leisurely. But nobody complains; it is not neighborly. At least, this is how they explain their silent acceptance of the situation to us. Hearing the statement, I begin to wonder how the constant stealing so many complain about, though mostly in private, has not already eroded their neighborly bonds.

It would have been nice to have some background music in the house while I am going through the monotonous daily chores. But with the electricity off, one can't even create an ambiance to raise one's spirit or simply help one drift away for a while and unwind.

We have no television here—we don't like to watch old American programs and movies dubbed in Bulgarian. I find it disturbing; the spoken words do not seem to have anything to do with the action on the screen—they clash somehow. We have a cassette deck though; we play the tapes we brought from home and the few others we bought in Sofia over and over. As for the radio, this is no good either. There is not much of a choice and the reception is poor; it must be the terrain. I miss my twenty-four-hour classical music station of Toronto, which we use to keep on all day in the house and in my car; the music helps me put order into my thoughts and sort out my emotions. Here, the Serbian, Bulgarian, and Gypsy folk, as well as the latest American pop music, rule the air waves.

Fundamentally, things have not changed much from the old times. The role of the media is still seen as more than providing entertainment and information. The radio news lasts from half an hour to over an hour, a few times a day. There are interviews, opinions, discussions going on all the time. The news is delivered in a solemn, dour tone, in fast staccato. They all seem to breathe an attitude: pomposity and conceit. The programs reflect preoccupation with culture and the opinions of the intelligentsia—the undisputed, know-it-all gurus bred and educated in totalitarian times. The approach is patronizing, one that evokes wariness. To me, it all sounds like propaganda and indoctrination.

I am tired and disappointed. I want to go home.

◆ ◆ ◆

The return journey leading to this moment was long—filled with anxieties, happiness, anguish, joy, incredible surprises, and sorrows.

My trip in March of 1965 ended in West Berlin. West Berlin was the first place I saw behind the Iron Curtain. It was everything I expected and more. It was a shiny island surrounded by a sea of drab and gloom. I wrote to Andrei that now I am in the free world and I have no intention of ever going back. He wrote back, advising me to try to avoid going to a refugee camp; he had bad memories from the years he had spent in a Yugoslavian prison and refugee camps in Trieste. He also indicated that he had been planning to come to West Germany as soon as he finished writing his thesis. He proposed that we meet.

We met in early May in the city of Cologne. At the time a crisis was looming over East-West relations—the hot spot was West Berlin. The West German government had decided to hold its Bundestag's meetings in the free zone; the East objected. Low-flying planes over the city shook the buildings, creating tension and uneasiness. Andrei wrote from Cologne that he did not want to come to West Berlin in the present circumstances; it was up to me to go to Cologne and meet him. I did.

As things turned out, I did not have to worry about going to a refugee camp. I had never met a guy like Andrei. From the moment we saw each other and I got over my neurotic fits of laughter and he, over his jet lag, we could not stop talking. His Bulgarian was limited and my English nonexistent; still we went through a marathon of discussions and even managed to have an argument and reconciliation.

On May 25, we got married in Baden-Baden. Three days later, we landed at the Toronto Airport and my life in Canada began.

Andrei was elated by the adoption of the new Canadian flag. He had almost finished his studies in the States. The future belonged to Canada. And we were going to be there. To me, it did not matter one way or another: the States or north of it, it was all the same as far as I was concerned. Wherever we ended up living, the challenges were the same: to learn English and adapt to a new place. Besides, what was the difference?

The sun started to shine on my life, but the shadows did not disappear or retreat into the background for long. In a few years new nightmares began haunting my sleep.

I never experienced the nostalgia so many emigrants suffer from. The finality of the separation from my homeland was unquestionable. The odds of ever going back were as infinitesimal as the odds a Martian, stranded on Earth, had of getting back on his Red Planet. The "red place" I had come from was just as remote from me as Mars. I did not miss it. But I missed my parents. And they missed me. Even though we knew how unreasonable our hopes were, we never stopped dreaming of, or trying, to be together again. The lifeline between us was the letters, two or three per week, year after year. Now, packed in a few cardboard boxes, they remain hidden in the basement of our house: out of sight, out of mind. The agony and anguish, the longing and love they are full of, make it impossible for me to read them now, but I can't imagine destroying them. I can't make up my mind what to do about them, so I think I shall just leave it to Audrey to deal with them some day.

Audrey, our daughter, was born three years after we got married. Meanwhile we lived in Calgary for a year, where Andrei was teaching at the University of Calgary, and in August of the following year, moved to Toronto, where he enrolled in the PhD program at the University of Toronto. During this time I was busy learning English on my own, preparing for a new career in Canada. There were plenty of engineering jobs at the time, but it did not take long to realize that a woman in engineering was almost an exotic notion here. There were going to be unexpected challenges, new battles to be fought. But that is another story…On with this one.

My first job was at the library of the University of Toronto. It was one place where many of the American draft dodgers found employment. It was impossible for me to remain neutral to them, or to ignore them, as most people seemed to. Though doubtful about the sincerity of their motives, I found them interesting to talk to. Most of them struck me as naive and misinformed, but they displayed a political passion that was something rare here, something that I had grown up with and could never shake off, not that I tried. Even though our views, sympathies and opinions were contradictory as far as the war was concerned, the fact that we could have discussions or simply conversations on the topic made me appreciate them. No expressions of any kind of convictions could upset me as much as the lack of any or apathy.

In November of 1976, when our hopes of ever seeing my parents had all but faded away, Mother was allowed to come for a visit. She was one of the many given permission to travel abroad for the purpose of reunification of families—mostly parents with children living in the West. The credit for this humanitarian act of compassion goes to the adoption of the Helsinki Final Act at the conclusion of the Conference on Security and Cooperation held in Finland in 1975. By then we had sent numerous joint and separate invitations, accompanied by declarations, promising to undertake all expenses for travel and support of Mother, or Father, or for both of them. Provided with this documentation they had been applying—mostly on Mother's behalf—hoping that if Father had to remain, as sort of a hostage, there could be a chance of letting her come. By the time she was allowed to travel to Canada, she had received twenty-six rejections.

We met her at the airport. Andrei and Audrey knew her only from pictures, and the last image of her I carried in my memories was of a fifty-one-year-old, middle-aged woman. As she finally emerged from the crowd pouring out of the gates, my heart sank; there she was: an old lady, weathered, worn out far beyond her years. My first reaction was that I would never let her go back. I could not imagine going through another separation, or for that matter, through another reunification.

Mother did recuperate, and on the photos taken during that Christmas, the only one she spent with us, she even looks radiant. We believed that by sponsoring her there would be no problem in her getting a permanent residence in Canada. After all, she had gotten over the greatest hurdle: she had broken through the Iron Curtain. Surely she would not be sent back; she would be allowed to stay with us so we could take care of her. Meanwhile Father would be awaiting his turn...

Neither of my parents wore a wedding band; I don't think they ever had one. At their belated marriage ceremony, they must have used borrowed ones. Instead, there was a ring that Mother always wore on the appropriate finger: a large, gold man's ring with a large blue letter K inlaid on its flat top. It was originally Father's, one of the rings Grandfather Mirko had made for all his children. When they met, Father had given it to her, and she had never taken it off. Now the gold on the inside was worn out, making the band look disproportionately thin for its solid upper half, a testament to their long life together. Also, this was the only jewelry she ever wore. One of the first things Mother did when she came to Canada was to take off the ring and put it away. Now she belonged to us.

Soon after her arrival, she applied for permanent residence. Interviews followed, and, at the end of each one, our hearts grew heavier.

The Canadian emigration laws for refugees at that time were not remotely as generous as the contemporary ones. The emigration officers did not have any knowledge or understanding of the situation in Bulgaria; they were patronizing and insensitive. Begging for sympathy in any circumstances strips victimized people of their dignity, but, when the laws made to protect them are deficient and the policies unenlightened, the pressure to gain the understanding of skeptical, often disinterested officials becomes so overwhelming that it can bring the anguish of an already-mistreated soul to the point of saturation. This is what happened to Mother. In the end, she simply could not take it any more. The mistrust underlying the treatment she was subjected to spilled over on us, making me feel rejected by my new country, filling me with shock and anger. The request for granting her permanent residence was based on humanitarian grounds, but the thrust of the inquiries was in a different direction; the point of bringing a family together never seemed to be the central issue. At one of the interviews, Mother was told by the emigration officer, more or less, "There is nothing wrong with Bulgaria. Go back and be happy." I had to interpret his words for her.

The months were rolling by without any resolution of the question. But there was much more going on in our lives. Mother was struggling with the task of learning English. It was a long-term goal, a concern for the future. The communication between her and Audrey, though, had its immediate requirements. The end result was amazing: in less than six months Audrey learned to speak Bulgarian. The relationship between the two of them was also quite remarkable. The similarities in their characters were many and surprising. Laughing, singing, and sulking were parts of their daily routine.

Some of the best times we had together were on the few long trips we took by car; once to Quebec city and Montreal, and the other to Hudson, Ohio. The destinations of both trips were determined by Mother's desire to visit friends she had made while trying to get permission to come here, other mothers in her situation, who had finally been allowed to go visit their children. They kept in touch and were eager to meet here, on this continent, to present their offspring to each other.

Throughout the long hours on the road, cooped up in the car, we managed to have a great time. And it was Mother and Audrey, sitting in the backseat, singing and laughing, who provided the entertainment. Mother still had a very good voice and loved to sing. I would join in and even Andrei, on occasion, would start humming along. The melodies and songs were potpourris from the popular operettas, operas, and city songs I grew up with that I never have had the time, nor the inclination, to sing to Audrey, and now she was learning them enthusiastically.

Other cherished memories of those times are the conversations we had around the dining table, when after the evening meal, we would linger over a bottle of good French wine and spend hours talking and reminiscing. The latter was most remarkable when Mother and Andrei would start sharing memories of their childhood years. Coincidentally both have spent the same number of years in similar village environments. They talked about the domestic animals they loved, about frightening experiences, and we all laughed hard at their escapades with vicious dogs, crazed cows, temperamental horses, or combative goats. Some of the stories were hilarious, some were touching, like the attachment Andrei developed toward a small kid that eventually ended up on the dinner table. They talked about the games they played, and, surprisingly, one was a crude type of golf, played with wooden sticks and wooden pegs instead of clubs and balls, but to the same effect. In their constant contact with nature, they had also learned a lot about the vegetation and the fruits of the land and had developed a taste for strange foods that grow in the ground, which nobody would even think of eating now. They kept exalting over some plant called "sheremetka," that eventually, years later, we discovered growing in the foothills of Liubash and stubbornly collected and forced ourselves to eat, just for the sake of old times.

Some of the conversations would stray in a different direction and brought me to a new understanding of Mother. We asked each other questions like, "If you had a choice to be born again, when, where, and who would you like to be?" Mother's choice was to be born at the end of the nineteenth century in Vienna and simply dance her life away; Andrei chose to be born at the dawn of Christianity in the person of the Apostle Peter, the fisherman; and my choice was to be born in ancient Greece as a free person, only I was not quite sure if it was a good idea to be a woman then and there. We tried to be as truthful as possible and had a great time discussing our choices. Mother's answer to the query, "What would you do if you won the big jackpot of the lottery?" was more indicative of her state of mind; she was going to give all of it to the poor people of Calcutta. Sometime in the fifties we had seen a few Indian movies with the actor Raj Kapoor, who had become very popular with a movie called *Brodiaga(Awaara)*. It depicted the life of a poor Indian boy. The music became very popular, and many gypsies capitalized on the sympathetic mood it created toward the Indians by identifying with the hero and making money by singing and dancing the catchy melodies from the film. There were other heart-wrenching movies with the same actor on the same theme of the hard conditions of life in the subcontinent; they seemed to have touched Mother so deeply that she never forgot them. As far as our answer to the same question, we were not so noble and compassionate; we were going to keep most of it, only we could not settle our priorities.

From bits and pieces, from stories Mother related in our endless conversations, a new picture of Father and a somewhat-changed, different relationship between them started to emerge. Some just amazed me and some shocked me.

Father did not write often. I missed his laconic, low-key letters, and I must have mentioned that one too many times, enough to provoke Mother into breaking the pact of silence that, as it turned out, had kept us ignorant in one respect of Father's health for years—as usual, in the name of sparing our feelings. We were sitting at the kitchen table, facing each other, when she fixed her eyes on me in a determined, hard look, portentous with disturbing news, almost like a warning.

"Your father went blind. Years ago."

The statement sounded so preposterous that it was almost meaningless.

"What do you mean?"

In her letters there had never been even a hint of an accident, illness, of anything remotely connected with consequences of that kind. She told me that it was caused by glaucoma, a hereditary disease that had afflicted him and most of his siblings. For so many years, we had been receiving pictures showing him looking back at us with the same stern, intelligent eyes. The sight was gone, but the eyes had remained unchanged.

There was another, this time visible, change in his appearance in a most unexpected fashion, hard for me to read—he had let his thick, curly, now almost completely white hair grow long. This had the greatest effect on Mother. In her words, he was growing more attractive as he became older; he was looking very distinguished with his new, white mane; he carried himself well. Then she told us a story that was so touching to me, but to her there was nothing teary about it. It was a small adventure full of mirth and excitement.

Apparently Father did not let the loss of sight alter his daily routine. He met this new adversity in the same way he reacted to his disbarment: he just continued to carry on with his life as before, as always. He still went out every day, did some consulting with old clients and refused to carry a white cane. The route he took was along the same pavement he has been beating for a long time. So he managed. The only problems were the couple of intersections where he had to cross the streetcar rails. Sometimes he asked people, complete strangers, to help him across. On one occasion, Mother, walking toward the apartment building they lived in, saw him ahead of her, standing at the curb of one of these intersections, listening for noises, waiting for a suitable moment to cross. Quietly, she approached him from behind and gently slipped her hand under his arm. Without saying a word, she pulled him forward, leading him to the opposite side. Surprised and intrigued, Father asked her name, was she someone he knew, etc., but Mother kept her silence. As soon as they reached the sidewalk, she pulled her hand away and hurried ahead, leaving him standing in wonderment.

The apartment they lived in now was different from the one I knew. After I left, they were moved to another place, on the top floor of a building not far from the old one. There was no elevator. The climb up the five stories above the stores at street level was an arduous task for Mother. It took her a long time to reach their front door, stopping for a rest on each of the platforms, breathless and tired. Father had no problems of that kind; he was agile and fit. When they met upstairs, after the brief interlude on the corner, Father could not wait to tell her about his adventure. He was excited and in high spirits; a mysterious lady had come from nowhere and helped him. She never said a word, but he felt that she was very nice and gentle. He wanted to thank her, only, had not had the chance. He wondered if this was the friendly young woman who lived in the attic above them. Could Mother find out if this was she? No, Mother said, she would not inquire; it was for him to do that, and she went on asking him about this young, kind, wonderful lady. Mother was never a jealous wife, and that must be why he never made anything out of her exaggerated interest. If he could only have seen the glow on her face listening to him retelling the story, piling praises on the unknown woman, he would have immediately discovered her identity.

Eleven months after she arrived, Mother had to pack her bags and go through another heartache. She had already put the ring back on her finger, months ago, when it had become obvious that her symbolic gesture belonged to a world of shattered illusions. The world she was going back to had disillusioned her long ago; this one could be hard-hearted as well. Moreover, she had seen the land of plenty now, and it had an unexpected effect on her.

The first time we took her shopping for groceries, she kept walking along the isles, hands in pockets, just staring at the shelves packed with goods, refusing to choose any. On our return home, she disappeared somewhere in the house. After a while, noticing her prolonged absence and getting worried that something was wrong, we started looking for her. We found her in the family room, huddled in one of the corners of the chesterfield, arms and legs tightly crossed in an almost defensive attitude, tears streaming from her eyes and down her cheeks, looking pale, distraught. Bewildered, we asked her what was wrong. Her answer took us by surprise. "You kept telling me to pick what I want, to choose a brand! What do I know about brands? If only I could pick the whole store and take it to my hungry friends in Sofia…All that food to choose from here, and people standing in lines for scraps there…"

She was inconsolable. We just left the room; she wanted to be alone.

Before her departure, we did the best we could. We bought her presents, things for her, Father, relatives, and friends—to give away. This would dull the edge of the pain for a while.

Twenty years have passed since I saw Father for the last time. It has been thirty-six years since Andrei had left Zavala. His parents had passed away here in Toronto, had never been back, had never even contemplated it.

For years, Father was adamant that we should not venture a trip to Bulgaria, but lately his resolve seemed to waver. Things were changing—people had gone and come back. What seemed unthinkable for so long was slowly turning into a possibility. Buoyed by a newfound hope, we begun contemplating the idea of crossing the divide again—this time, in the opposite direction. There was a catch though—the matter of the entrance visas, for these were regarded as more than permissions to enter the country, but as guarantees of safety. For the less trusting, like ourselves, they provided a measure of comfort against the worries and fears we had nurtured for many years.

So we applied for visas, for the three of us, and got them. Still, we did not feel quite at ease going straight to Bulgaria; instead, we opted for an alternative scheme: travel to London and join English tourist group going to the Golden Sands resort by the Black Sea.

The chartered plane took us to Varna, where we left the group and flew to Sofia. We had made arrangements to return in four weeks, and, after spending a week at the Golden Sands with a different group, fly to London.

At the airport in Sofia we were met by Mother and Father. We saw them from far away, standing next to each other, very much in the same postures as I had left them on the platform of the Central Train Station more than twenty years ago. They did not look changed much, just faded. This time Mother was standing close to him, her left hand under Father's right arm. Their eyes were fixed in our direction, their feet rooted to the spot, waiting for us…Father had mellowed. We all hugged and kissed, and he never pulled away, accepting our shows of affection with an agreeableness I had never seen in him.

Our reunion was joyous. Andrei and Audrey immediately took to him. Andrei started shaving him; an act of such intimacy accepted by him that surprised me. Father was relaxed and seemed happy. We talked, laughed, and listened to tapes we brought of Audrey playing the piano, and he praised her lavishly, exactly the way he used to praise me.

Mother, on the other hand, was moody and tense. To her, this brief reunion was unsettling. She lived for the day when, somehow, we would be reunited once and for all, the day when this emotional tug-of-war would end. She lived in a state of limbo; there were no permanent solutions she could envision. For too long we had believed that the moment she could come to us, all would be all right—destiny had proven us wrong. Her faith in everything but God was completely shaken. She hung in and around Alexander Nevsky, crestfallen and despondent. From the moment we hugged and kissed her hello, she started thinking about the inevitable good-bye.

We took some photos—the five of us: Mother, Father, Audrey, Andrei, and me—all around the cathedral.

Andrei got to know Sofia. He knew very little about Bulgaria, apart from the village of his birth. The farthest place he had traveled before he left had been no more than fifteen kilometers away from Zavala. Now he walked all over Sofia, volunteering to do any errand, curious to discover the place and its people. He became very good at finding all kinds of goods that were in short supply. After one searching expedition for toilet paper, he came home carrying a bunch of rolls, brimming with satisfaction; he had been able not only to find and buy the stuff but had directed a slew of people to the place. They had thanked him; he had in a way bonded with them, and that was very rewarding. His friendliness and easy manner set him apart, made him different. People kept stopping him and asking him to change dollars for levs, a forbidden activity we were very wary about. I, on the other hand, right away fell in step with the common mode of behavior and blended with the rest.

The few trips we took were short, daily excursions to Tarnovo and Plovdiv.

We visited Zavala also. The trepidation and apprehension we felt on the way melted as soon as we got there; nearly the whole village turned out to see Andrei and his family. Andrei had left almost as a child and came back a bearded adult; in spite of that, many said they recognized him immediately. It was doubtful, nevertheless, heartwarming. Everybody had a good cry—including Audrey, me, and Mother, even though we had no idea who these people were. Andrei hardly knew them either. He kept answering their question, "Do you recognize me?" sincerely with no, but it did not offend them at all; it just made us all cry harder.

We went to take a look at the house that used to be his home, confiscated and sold after they had run away. The people living there now invited us to go in and see the place. Andrei and Audrey went in; Mother and I remained in the yard.

There were more tears…

As planned, before leaving for London, we spent a week at the Golden Sands. We tried to take Mother with us but could not do it; the hotels there were exclusively for foreigners, Bulgarians were not allowed.

Upon our return to Toronto, we became aware of an unexpected benefit from our trip to Bulgaria. Long ago we had found out that many of the emigrants had been having recurring dreams or rather, nightmares, always recalling in some way the traumatic events or feelings experienced during their escape or separations. Sometimes lightheartedly, we shared them with each other, glad that they were only dreams and not reality.

In his dream Andrei relived a scary moment from the night-run across the border, when he fell into one of the trenches along it. With a heavy backpack on his shoulders, he had fallen into a hole, unable to pull himself up. Instructed to be quiet, no matter what, he could do nothing but just wait, whatever might come. Fortunately, his sister, Vasilka, kept an eye on him and, noticing he had disappeared, returned, found, and pulled him out. The incident could not have lasted much longer than a couple of minutes, but for Andrei it must have felt like an eternity, an everlasting instant frozen in his mind that kept coming back in his dreams for years.

In my dream, I was back in Sofia looking for my parents, confused and anxious, wandering through the streets, unable to recognize the new apartment they were living in—a building I could not find in my memory even in my waking hours. While running up and down nonexistent paths, I would see Andrei and Audrey appearing from somewhere, but soon they would be on their way back to Canada, and I could not join them. In a panic, I would start walking and walking, sometimes reaching the ocean, searching for a ship to take me across. This is where the dream usually ended and I woke up.

After our trip to Bulgaria, the nightmarish dreams were no more. They vanished…It was a sort of liberation.

Nineteen eighty-seven was a dark year. I would rather not remember it.

In February, Mother's fragile health deteriorated drastically. The year before she had applied for an exit visa to visit us again but had been rejected. She had reapplied and was waiting for the decision when she became very ill. She had been admitted and than released from a hospital. We were worried enough to apply for entrance visas for Andrei and me, in order to be able to go to her. Three months went by and there was no reply from Bulgaria. Finally, we were told by the Bulgarian consulate in Toronto that the visas had been refused. No explanation. The Consul himself was sympathetic; however, he said he could not be of any help. He had promised that in June, when he would go to Bulgaria, he would try to do something about it. It was May; we applied again.

In June, Father had a stroke. Late in the same month we received visas—valid just for a month.

We flew to Sofia on the first of July, Canada Day.

On the twenty-eighth of July, we had to leave Bulgaria.

Left Mother and Father in two separate hospitals; took our good-byes—with each one in a different place—till the next time.

Made some promises.

Eight days later, Mother died.

The following year, in September, Father died.

There was no next time…

The radio was on. Andrei was behind the wheel, driving to the college we were both working at now. We were not going to work, however, but to take up our striking duties. The faculties of Ontario's colleges were on strike.

For me, leaving industry to go teaching was something of a cop-out; nonetheless, it also meant giving up a fight I had already grown weary of—tired of proving a point, of swimming against the flow. This new profession seemed to suit me fine; besides, I was glad to be working in the same place with Andrei. In the rare situation created by a strike, the drawback of the loss of two incomes was recompensed to a degree by the comfort derived from keeping each other company while beating the path along the picket line.

On that particular day, the eleventh of November, less than a mile from the college, listening to the news, we could not believe our ears. Todor Zivkov had fallen from power! Communist rule was no more in Bulgaria!

It was unbelievable!

Fantastic!

I was sobbing, caught in a wave of shock, joy, and anguish. If only Father and Mother had lived a little longer to see it happen…Andrei kept assuring me, "They know; they do!"

By the time we reached the picket line, we were euphoric. I hugged some of my colleagues, who gave us bewildered and smiling looks. One asked me if we were going back. That gave me a jolt.

"Go? Where?"

"Back to Bulgaria."

"But why? My home is here. I have nobody there anymore."

It crossed my mind that it must be difficult for most people to understand our overemotional reactions to events happening in faraway places and still insist that our home is here. Sometimes I was not sure if I understood it either. The only explanation was that I could not, would not, and now did not have to live as though my life ended when I left the country of my birth; or that I did not belong here, and my life in my new homeland was a waste—just a bridge to the next generation. I was not torn between two places; my life had been broken in two for sure, but now, that split could be mended—into one life in two countries.

It was time for healing, time for pilgrimages, time for new beginnings. The world had become one again.

The following summer we rented a car in Germany and went on a long trip across Europe toward a final destination, Bulgaria. On the way we stopped to visit my classmates Valia who was living in Dortmund, and Gina, living in Milan. We also visited Baden-Baden to celebrate our twenty-fifth wedding anniversary. Before continuing along the Adriatic coast, we decided to go to Trieste and look up a place called San Sabbo where Andrei lived with his family as a refugee after running across the Yugoslavian border to Italy. It seemed an appropriate thing to do now.

It took us a long time to locate the former refugee camp. We drove around and around, asking people to direct us, but nobody remembered the place. In the end, it was Andrei who found his bearings and spotted an old, abandoned prison. That was San Sabbo.

The day was sunny and warm—it was midday, the streets were deserted. After circling the building a few times around, Andrei began to recognize a corner, a door, a stairway. We entered the courtyard surrounded by walls and the building along one of its sides. Inside, the red brick prison had been completely gutted; there were no longer any interior walls. Still, Andrei was able to identify the area where they had lived, crammed in a suffocatingly small room, behind flimsy partitions dividing the floor into living quarters for each family. The camp was only for families.

The light was streaming in through the rows of gaping holes that once used to be windows, but nothing could dispel the macabre sense of doom in this dilapidated, lonely place.

Unexpectedly, the quiet was broken by the sounds of footsteps and hushed voices coming from the courtyard. Bunched together, a group of tourists were following an animated guide pointing here and there. We rushed outside to join the small crowd when they disappeared inside another part of the building, never seen by Andrei. It used to be an area restricted to the refugees. As we caught up with the group, we realized that the guide was speaking in a language we did not understand, so we waited till he took a break to ask in English about the history of the place. Obligingly he told us that this was a prison notorious for the incarceration, torture, and execution of Communists. Some of the cells they were kept in still stood intact inside the dark smelly ground floor. This was news to Andrei. We wanted to know more. "What about after the war? It used to be a refugee camp. When was it closed?" The guard was taken aback, and, when we told him that as a child Andrei spent time in the camp, he turned hostile. He did not know anything about the existence of any refugee camp; he did not want to hear or talk about it.

In this place, it was so easy for anyone to see the vicious circle of history; how the victims of the past had become the oppressors of the future. But nobody was the wiser for it.

Just around the corner, brewing and waiting, was more to come…

The drive along the Adriatic coastline was exhilarating, and, at times, dangerous. The road, cut high in the side of a mountain, was curving along deep precipices at the bottom of which one could see straight down, the clear, blue, calm waters. There was nothing to detract of or obscure the breathtakingly beautiful, sparkling, sunlit sea panorama. For long stretches of travel, one could imagine that this was just the way it looked thousands of years ago, and one was tempted to search the horizon for Ulysses' ship to appear from behind an island or from a hidden lagoon.

Dubrovnik enchanted us.

We decided to spend a day there, and after a long walk up and down the narrow steep streets, climbed to the terrace on top of the house we were spending the night in, remaining there for a long time, just feasting our eyes on this jewel of a city.

After Budva, we cut through the mountains of Montenegro. More terrible beauty, more treacherous roads…

Finally we reached Kosovo. The magic was over. For our overnight stop, we chose a five-star hotel in a town we had never heard of, Pristina. The hotel was run down and dirty; its vandalized rooms were in dire need of repair. Once, it might have been a decent place; now, only the price was in keeping with its high rating.

There was something in the air, a feeling of tension and uneasiness. Hardly able to get any sleep during the night, we left the hotel at the break of dawn. As the sun came up and people came out, we were surprised to be greeted by numerous smiling children walking along the road, showing us the victory sign. Slightly perplexed and wondering what they meant, we waved back.

Pushing hard ahead, we made it to Sofia the same day.

The first thing we noticed there was a big change in the people: they were smiling! Bearded men of all ages were everywhere. The mood was hopeful, exciting; there, also, was something unpredictable and chaotic.

In the square, in front of the former palace, a city of tents had sprung up. People called it the City of Truth. It was hard for us to understand what it was that the inhabitants wanted to accomplish with this demonstrative action, but it was wonderful to see that people could now express themselves, proclaim their beliefs, and set their demands freely. Some had hung cardboard signs outside their tents with their names written on them—sort of an address. An energetic priest was walking among the tents, busy and engaged, clearly an inspiring force.

Everywhere we went we could see young people challenging their parents, at dinner tables or in less formal circumstances. They were spirited and confident, critical of the old, standing up for the new. Their expectations were high and that seemed only natural.

We stayed with Margarita Nikiforova and her family. I felt at home in their place. They were living in a new apartment, but most of the furniture was from the old one, the one I knew. Margarita had not changed much either. When we were together, I felt like we had traveled back in time, half-expectant that our mothers would walk in at any moment.

Several times we went to Alexander Nevsky to attend a service, to listen to the choir, or simply to spend time in cleansing reverie.

When, at the end of our stay, we left Sofia, we were in high spirits, convinced that the future of the people of this country was bright.

Three years later we were back. This time, it was the three of us. It was another hot summer. The climate in Sofia had changed;—on all of our visits there, we had experienced weather much warmer than I remembered.

The place was different from the place we had seen three years before. I felt a bit like a stranger now. People had stopped smiling. They had lost their direction; their high expectations had not materialized. Many were disappointed. Embittered people often become callous and cynical, and we kept running into them in the most unexpected places and circumstances.

Audrey and Andrei got sick. It was in part the heat and in part the tension. One way to escape both was to go to Lialintsi.

Lialintsi was not the same village where I used to visit Grandmother Lia. Many of the traditional, old, ramshackle houses had been replaced by villas in the attractive Alpine style, whitewashed and red tiled, and many new ones had sprang up, creeping up the hills, overlooking lovely panoramas or hidden among the trees. For many years, the region had been neglected, left to linger in an economic stagnation; however this ill fortune had brought an unforeseen benefit: it remained free of the modern evils of pollution and noise. As far as one could see, there was not a single chimney blowing smog, and there was hardly any traffic, even along the main road far below the village, to disturb nature's serene peacefulness. We loved it.

Tommy was building a villa there, attached to Vasko's, which had been built a few years before. Vasko's villa had a large verandah facing Liubash. From there, Tommy and I watched Andrei and Audrey as they went on an adventure, climbing to the top of the mountain peak.

On our first visit in 1985, the two had done it, impressing everybody. In a symbolic gesture, they took Grandfather Vassil's walking stick, which we found lying about in one of the houses, put on their heavy shoes and took off...When they came back, hours later, they told us about a spring they had found on the way up, about the marvelous view from the summit. Most regretfully, they had forgotten to take the camera, but made a promise to return and take some pictures. Now was the time to fulfill that promise. Meanwhile Grandfather's stick was nowhere to be found, so Andrei crafted a couple of new staffs, and here they were on their way up again, to conquer Liubash.

Tommy and I watched their progress with the help of a set of powerful military binoculars belonging to a man working on the villa—an old soldier. Halfway up the mountain, we lost sight of them.

The villagers, born and bred there, treated Liubash as a mysterious place. Some of them had never gone to the summit. Maybe, wisely, they preferred the legends.

On their return, Andrei and Audrey were just as enthusiastic about the experience as they had been coming back from their first trip up there. And just as before, they had forgotten to take the camera. And the legend about ancient ruins could go undisputed, at least in the minds of a few of the old and respected citizens of Lialintsi, who knew best.

Relaxed and happy, on the spur of the moment, I remarked how lovely that place was, how much I enjoyed just sitting on the verandah, looking at the ever-changing sky over Liubash.

"Why don't you build yourselves a villa down there? This is your lot, isn't it?"

Tommy was right. The lot below the low road was Mother's share from the inheritance, and now it was ours. Her wish was that it go to Audrey, as a tangible link to a reminder of her heritage.

"Yes! Why not! It is a great idea! Audrey, what do you think?"

"Yes!"

The approval was unanimous.

And this was how it happened: the idea of building a villa in Lialintsi, facing the mountain, surrounded by tall, leafy trees, where in May, all the nightingales come to nest, and their songs go on all night and day. They are the last sound we hear before falling to sleep and the first one we hear as we wake up. During this time of the year, the fields are red with poppies trembling in the wind.

It took us a while to get used to the rest of the sounds of nature. A couple of times in a row, a strange knock woke us up in the middle of the night. Half asleep, Andrei got out of bed and went downstairs to check who was at the door. I could hear his footsteps inside and then outside in the dark, when I realized that the noise was coming from the wall behind our heads. Eventually, Andrei came back without finding anyone around the house. It took some real detective thinking to discover that a woodpecker was busy pecking at the trunk of a tree, right behind the wall. We thought it was an amusing nocturnal incident and, after a good laugh, went to sleep. The next night the same knock woke us up, and again, half asleep, Andrei went downstairs, and…This time we did not wonder and it was not as amusing.

The saga of building our villa went on for years. Every summer we would go there, determined, but lost—our enthusiasm turning into stubbornness and our frustrations, into anguish.

It took us six years to get a title to the land that already belonged to us. Even though the law was on our side, all kinds of obstacles were raised from everywhere. Meanwhile, the shoddy workmanship on the construction required everything to be done at least twice: walls had been erected where they were not supposed to be, staircases had been built leading to the strangest spots, floor tiles had been mixed up, the roof tiles had started to break and the roof had started to leak soon after we moved in, supporting walls had to be built at several places along the original supporting wall to stop it from breaking. The list goes on and on…

And, still, something kept us going. The remoteness of the place, the beauty of the mountains, the mystique of the forgotten past embodied in the old, small church—even though now completely useless, its icons stolen and its frescoes destroyed—all of that had a pull that was hard to resist. And the ruins of a monastery we found in the middle of a forest...

What an unforgettable day it was when we discovered the old monastery on the other side of Liubash. I remember Mother mentioning it, but was never sure of its exact location.

On a lazy afternoon, when everybody had gone inside for a siesta and only Tommy, Andrei, and I had kept hanging outside, wondering how to spend the time, Tommy had a proposition for us. A couple of days before, he had had a conversation with a local about the monastery and had developed a vague idea as to how it could be found. How about going on an expedition? Destination: the lost monastery. Fortunately, he had an old Moskvich, good as any jeep—the most suitable type of transportation for terrain like this. The three of us jumped in, Tommy sat behind the wheel, and we drove straight to the foothills of Liubash. As we came out of the shadow of the peak, we turned right and proceeded at a snail pace along an overgrown, grassy road by a cavernous precipice to the left, circling the mountain to the right. We drove along the bumpy furrowed tracks until all discernible patterns suggesting the existence of a road ended—obliterated by wind-withered grass covering the rocky earth. There we left the car and continued on foot.

Soon we entered a forest of beech trees. There was no clear path to follow, only a shallow brook, its overflowing waters running fast, probably coming from a spring close to the top of the mountain. We kept walking along the marshy ground overgrown with wild vegetation, getting deeper and deeper into the woods, seduced by the intoxicating fragrance of flowers and greenery, by the sheaves of light streaming through the foliage of the trees that have transformed the forest into a magical place. We were in an enchanted kingdom!

The monastery, or what was left of it, was on a higher level at the other side of the brook, hidden by trees and vegetation. We must have passed it inadvertently for when we saw it, it was already behind us. To get there we had to turn back and climb a short steep path.

The ruins of a church dominated the grounds. Nearby were a couple of dilapidated nondescript structures, their original purpose hard to determine.

Judging by its remnants, the chapel must have been small and solidly built. Now, its roof had all but disappeared, as well as about a third of the walls—their debris strewn all over the floor. However, the portion of the remaining edifice, on the eastside, stood sound and thick—the frescoes on the inside still clear and surprisingly intact. With some difficulty we entered the ruins at the west side and, gingerly walking over the layers of fallen bricks, roof tiles and stones, crossed the length of the building to get close to the frescoes. The smell of rot and damp permeated the air, sharpening even further the eerie sensation of a mysterious presence.

We kept wondering who had built the place, when, and why.

After spending some time exploring the grounds, we headed back, retracing our steps through the forest, out of the enthralling world we had found.

In the village everybody was up, sitting on the verandah, sipping coffee. The three of us jumped from the car and rushed to join them. We had a story to tell…

In the first four years, until the place was ready for occupancy, we spent most of our summers in Sofia. And throughout this period, we observed a strange metamorphosis occurring. The former Communists—now calling themselves socialists—from being ardent internationalists, atheists and republicans, turned into fierce nationalists, faithful Christians, and even lukewarm monarchists. They flocked to the churches to christen their children, grandchildren, and themselves, though some in quite ripe old age, touchingly pious, accepting Christ and rejecting the devil, but in their hearts never rejecting the evil they had been serving up for the last forty-five years. And they hung crosses on their chests proclaiming their newfound faith. I had no choice but to take off the cross I was wearing and put it away.

The new flock of priests, taught and bred under the spiritual guidance of the Party-appointed Patriarch, rushed to take up a new position in the new Christian country, blessing the shops of the new shady businessmen, getting involved in all kinds of activities—rather peripheral to their responsibilities—reluctant to move to the small villages to take care of the needs of the people's souls. The spiritually hungry became an easy prey to all kinds of quasi-religious cults.

It was amazing how successful the relentless brainwashing had been. People had swallowed the propaganda painting the West as singularly materialistic, lacking in moral values. Accepting that these were the prerequisites for success, they began to emulate the worst of it, while remaining still distrustful of the system they had supposedly chosen and embraced to replace the discredited, oppressive totalitarian one. Freedom had lost its allure. Once gained, it was taken for granted. The concept of it misunderstood; at worst, it was equated with lawlessness.

In their confusion and gullible naiveté, they brought back the Communists to power. This time, it was the voice of the people. The new socialist government started a wholesale sabotage of the fragile democracy. A terror of crime rained: bandits vandalized cemeteries, robbed the old, and corrupted young vulnerable people. The homes in Sofia began to acquire the appearance of prisons—bars on the windows, heavy metal doors protecting the entrances. The situation was out of control. The government's message was, "It is all the fault of the changes."

It brought some old people to the state of insanity. Aunt Tina, Father's youngest sister and most devoted to him, was petrified of everything. She advised us not to go out in the dark, not to wear jewelry, not to let anybody into the apartment. She instructed us that if the bell rings, just go to the entrance and tell whoever is behind the wall "nobody is home," and do not open the door! On one occasion, the once-robust, energetic, immaculate housewife was reduced by fear to a panic-stricken, irrational woman who had to be taken away from the balcony of her apartment in a straight jacket while screaming for help from an imaginary gun-brandishing bandit running after her, intent on killing her.

Three years later, after mass protests, the socialist government fell. But great damage had been done. Hope and patience were wearing pretty thin. A new generation was lost; the enthusiastic young people we met on our visit seven years ago had lost their zest for change. Time was not on their side: they were beginning to sound like the parents they challenged in a moment of exhilaration and excitement.

And then there was the war...Bosnia...Kosovo...

We have seen the mass graves and the refugees on our television screen, and we have been moved to tears by their plight. We were outraged by the power-hungry, demented ruler of Yugoslavia, a pathetic remnant of the Communist era. We also felt hurt when the world bunched together all of the people of this land, the Balkans, and presented them as uncivilized, barbarian rabble who had been fighting among themselves for ages. Did it not know that for centuries these people had been living under foreign rule—their identity, their past, their differences and their old disputes forgotten, oblivious of everything but their struggle to survive? And they survived, and they fought and died for their freedom. The world saw their suffering, the atrocities they were subjected to, and their perseverance. Some admired them for that, some pitied them. But when they were finally free, the Great Powers came and cut them apart, put them together, arranged and rearranged their countries without asking them—guided only by their own interests. And the world did not want to talk about it. The new generations in the West did not want to take responsibility for, or at least acknowledge, the mess their forefathers had created. The deep hatred, intolerance, preoccupation with history, the volatility of the place—as though these were unique to this region—were referred to as the roots of this appalling war, but were never examined as consequences of gross injustices in the not-too-distant past.

The villa was ready. It was the second summer we were spending there. The house was comfortable and pretty and we loved it.

We had also reclaimed our place here, and that gave us a certain feeling of accomplishment. But there should be more…

At spirited discussions, or in simple conversations about everyday issues, we found ourselves more often than not on the side of the minority, or even alone. The pent-up disappointments and frustrations were disheartening. It was getting harder to keep the faith in the promise that we thought we saw looming so brightly ten years before…

Oh, why don't we just give up!

◆   ◆   ◆

The day is sunny and warm. Late in the afternoon the intensity of the heat subsides, and we decide to go for a walk. We have a collection of wooden staffs, all made by Andrei—his hobby is carpentry. The bunch stands by the door, handy to pick up on the way out. Each grabs a favorite, and we are on our way. As we pass by the house where the low road meets the upper road, the neighbor living there inquires as to our destination. We say, "Liubash."

She takes a long look at us and says, "There is always a cool wind up there. You might be cold." We are not convinced and press forward, carefully choosing which path to take. I avoid some of the locals, tired of their questions and comments, of their whisperings behind our backs. A bridge runs over the river where the road bends at almost 180 degrees in the opposite direction and proceeds to climb gently, hugging the base of Liubash. During this time of the year, the river is reduced to no more than a brook that passes at the bottom of our property. We stop at the bridge, lean against the rusty railings, and look down at the overgrown greenery that covers the riverbank. Here and there we glimpse the crystal-clear, fast-running water coming straight from the mountain. We try to avoid looking at the rubbish strewn about. Then we move on.

At one point we decide to leave the road and climb up the hillside. The wild grass is high and thick; it brushes against our legs. Among it, wild, delicate flowers tremble in the breeze. And, yes, there is a cool, brusque wind. We are trekking across the meadow, going up toward an area of large, protruding jagged rocks next to a deep green, ominous-looking pine forest. Suddenly a flock of sheep announces its presence by the melodious, soft chime of bells, and presently the whole flock emerges. The shepherdess follows and the dogs run in all directions, rounding up the animals. We stop for a chat. Every morning the sheep and goats from the village are gathered in the village square. From there, the flock is steered up to the mountains, every day to a different location. Every morning we run to the windows to see them go and wait to see and hear them in the evening when they are brought back for the milking and the nightly rest. This is one of the highlights of our days here.

While talking to us, the shepherdess keeps looking at the panorama that spreads below.

We continue, finally reaching the rocks. Each picks a spot and sits, leaning forward, resting on and supported by the wooden staff. The forest is to our right. Strange, spooky noises drift from its direction. We wonder: is that a bird or an animal? The wind pinches my cheeks. Ahead of us, the meadow stretches all the way down to the road on the outskirts of the village. For a moment I see in my mind Julie Andrews in the middle of it, her arms outstretched and her legs half hidden in the carpet of grass and flowers. The melody of "The Sound of Music" is buzzing in my head. Then, she disappears.

And there is more; the inexplicable, yet comforting sensation of an evanescent presence, from a world once mourned as lost forever. I can feel the protective shadow of Mother nearby…

It is peaceful. The air is crystal clear. We gaze to the left where a wall of summits stands, obscuring the view to the west. Then the eyes move to the panorama in front, the village: snuggled among the tall ash, walnut, and pine trees, white houses under bright red roofs—ours in the forefront, clearly visible, and behind it the twin houses of Aunt Nina's sons; to the right, more undulations, hills and peaks with a bluish hue. Behind one of them lies Zavala. And I am thinking, "Oh my God! How beautiful it is!"

The heaviness has lifted from my chest. I feel only tranquility and contentment. I am smiling. Next year we will be back.

August 1999

Foot notes:

*Page 95: Cherny Vrah = Black Peak
*Page 128, 147: "Bie" (colloquial) appellation, loosely translated as "uncle," form of respect in addressing, referring to, older men.

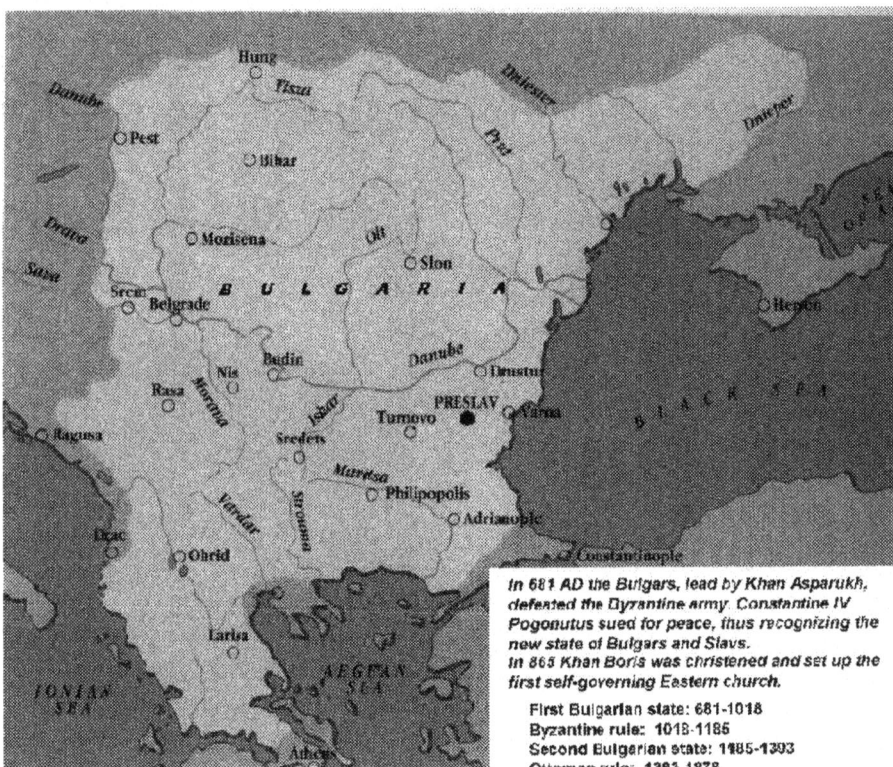

In 681 AD the Bulgars, lead by Khan Asparukh, defeated the Byzantine army. Constantine IV Pogonutus sued for peace, thus recognizing the new state of Bulgars and Slavs.
In 865 Khan Boris was christened and set up the first self-governing Eastern church.

First Bulgarian state: 681-1018
Byzantine rule: 1018-1185
Second Bulgarian state: 1185-1393
Ottoman rule: 1393-1878
Third Bulgarian state: 1878-present

Bulgaria under Tsar Simeon the Great
893-927

Bulgaria today

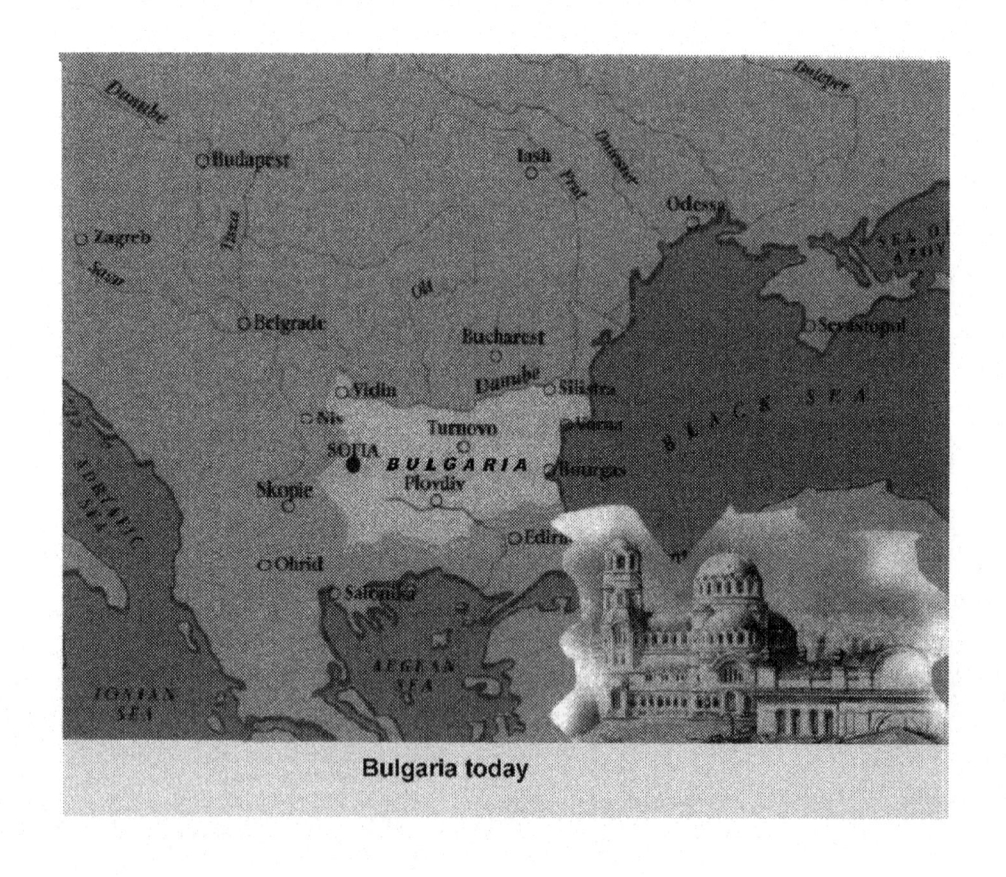

978-0-595-39071-7
0-595-39071-4